United States
Department of
Agriculture

Forest Service

Pacific Southwest
Research Station

General Technical Report
PSW-GTR-234

September 2010

Sudden Oak Death and *Phytophthora ramorum*: A Summary of the Literature

2010 Edition

John T. Kliejunas

Author

John T. Kliejunas, retired; former regional forest pathologist, U.S. Department of Agriculture, Forest Service, Pacific Southwest Region, Vallejo, CA.

Pesticide Precautionary Statement

This publication reports research involving pesticides. It does not contain recommendations for their use, nor does it imply that the uses discussed here have been registered. All uses of pesticides must be registered by appropriate state or federal agencies, or both, before they can be recommended.

CAUTION: Pesticides can be injurious to humans, domestic animals, desirable plants, and fish or other wildlife if they are not applied properly. Use all pesticides selectively and carefully. Follow recommended practices for the disposal of surplus pesticides and pesticide containers.

Cover photo: Photo by Stephen Joseph Photography, Pleasant Hill, California.

Abstract

Kliejunas, John T. 2010. Sudden oak death and *Phytophthora ramorum*: a summary of the literature. 2010 edition. Gen. Tech. Rep. PSW-GTR-234. Albany, CA:. U.S. Department of Agriculture, Forest Service, Pacific Southwest Research Station. 181 pages.

Sudden oak death and *Phytophthora ramorum*, both first recognized about a decade ago, have been the subject of hundreds of scientific and popular press articles. This document presents a comprehensive, concise summary of sudden oak death and *P. ramorum* research findings and management activities. Topics covered include introduction and background, identification and distribution, the disease cycle, epidemiology and modeling, management and control, and economic and environmental impacts.

Keywords: Sudden oak death, *Phytophthora ramorum*, invasive species, tanoak, coast live oak, mixed-evergreen forests.

Contents

Chapter 1: Introduction and Background

First Reports

An unusual die-off of tanoaks (*Lithocarpus densiflorus* (Hook. & Arn.) Rehd.) in the Mill Valley/Mount Tamalpais area of Marin County, California, was first documented in April 1995 (Svihra 1999b, 1999c, 2001), when homeowners reported scattered patches of dying tanoaks—with entire crowns dead and with bleeding basal cankers—to Pavel Svihra, University of California (UC) Cooperative Extension. The symptoms were also being reported by arborists and others on nearby tanoaks, including those at Muir Woods National Monument, and farther south in coastal Santa Cruz County and around Big Sur (Monterey County) in the same year. Heavy ambrosia beetle attacks and black fruiting bodies of a *Hypoxylon* fungus, later identified as *Hypoxylon* [*Annulohypoxylon*] *thouarsianum* (Swiecki 2001), were associated with the dying trees.

Undetermined Cause

Attempts by arborists, pathologists, and horticulturists to determine the cause of the die-off yielded only several saprophytic micro-organisms (including *Armillaria* sp., *Hypoxylon* [*Annulohypoxylon*] sp., *Pseudomonas tolaasii* and *Diplodia quercina*) (Svihra 1999a), and identification of two ambrosia beetles (*Monarthrum scutellare* and *M. dentiger*) and one bark beetle (the western oak bark beetle, *Pseudopityophthorus pubipennis*) from affected tanoaks. The micro-organisms identified and the beetles are considered secondary or opportunistic, attacking only stressed trees. It was postulated by some that several years of drought from 1990 to 1992 followed by excessively wet years (El Niño) in 1993 and 1994 resulted in tree stress, allowing the secondary fungi and beetles to attack the weakened trees, with bark beetle and ambrosia beetle populations subsequently building up to unprecedented levels (Hagen 1999; Svihra 1999a, 2001). Other stress factors—including overstocking, fire exclusion, construction, incompatible landscaping, and others—were also suggested as contributing to the die-off (Hagen 1999).

Epidemic Spread

By May 1997, not only tanoaks, but also coast live oaks (*Quercus agrifolia* Née) were dying in the Marin Municipal Water District lands and in China Camp State Park on San Francisco Bay (Svihra 2001). The symptoms on coast live oaks (seeping or bleeding areas on the trunk followed by fading of the foliage, beetle attack, and appearance of *Hypoxylon* fruiting bodies) were similar in appearance to those of dying tanoaks.

By spring 1998, beetle attacks on coast live oaks were resulting in a rapid increase of dying coast live oaks (Svihra 1999b, 1999c), and several California black oaks (*Q. kelloggii* Newb.) in the Novato area (Marin County) were reported with similar symptoms. Although the dominant thinking was that the primary cause of the widening mortality was bark and ambrosia beetles attacking stressed trees, some scientists noted that young tanoaks without oozing trunk cankers or beetle attacks were also dying, suggesting that an unknown pathogen was involved as the primary stress agent rather than drought followed by high rainfall.

Public Concern

The rapid spread of the disease in 1998, in an urban-wildland interface area inhabited by millions of people, heightened public concern. The highly visible disease was killing trees on public and private lands, threatening residential and forest land, parks, industries, water supply, soil retention, and wildlife. Weakened and dead trees were a hazard because they could fall, destroying life and property. They also posed a severe fire hazard. The unabated mortality, now being described as epidemic, increased through 1999 (McPherson and others 2000). Concerned homeowners pressed county supervisors, administrators, and politicians for investigation and treatment.

Because the causal agent was unknown at the time, the syndrome was commonly referred to after the most obvious symptoms—the trees dying in a somewhat sudden fashion. A University of California (UC) Cooperative Extension publication (Svihra 1999b) described the crown symptoms as appearing rather suddenly, resulting in rapid death. The mortality was referred to as "sudden oak death" in a second UC Cooperative Extension publication (Svihra 1999a) and the term was picked up by others, notably the press, to describe the phenomenon.

In 1999 a multidisciplinary research team of UC scientists was formed to address the cause and management options for control of sudden oak death. A 23-person team was formed, including forest pathologists, forest entomologists, ecologists, silviculturists, wildlife biologists, remote sensing/geographic information system experts, and urban forestry/arboriculture experts from UC Davis and UC Berkeley, and advisors from UC Cooperative Extension county offices. Funds were provided by both UC and the U.S. Department of Agriculture, Forest Service (USDA FS). The UC system provided $70,000 in emergency funding, and the USDA FS, Forest Health Protection provided $85,000 for research and monitoring. Susan Frankel, plant pathologist, then with the Pacific Southwest Region of the USDA FS, was instrumental in focusing and coordinating early efforts.

In June 2000, the Marin County Board of Supervisors passed a resolution declaring that sudden oak death had created a state of emergency. "We are in the midst of a catastrophe," Supervisor Cynthia Murray stated at the time (San Francisco Chronicle Nov. 5, 2000). Several months later, under the leadership of the California Forest Pest Council and the California Department of Forestry and Fire Protection, local, state, and federal agencies joined to form what would become, in August 2000, the statewide California Oak Mortality Task Force (COMTF). Involved early on were the California Department of Forestry and Fire Protection, the California Forest Pest Council, UC, and the USDA FS. The advisory group, chaired by Susan Frankel, undertook the challenge of establishing a cooperative, unified approach and offering guidance to funders, lawmakers, management agencies, research institutions, and others concerned with the disease. In November of that year, the state of California appropriated $100,000 for use by the newly formed COMTF, and federal officials announced that an additional $1 million would become available for research, monitoring, and outreach (San Francisco Chronicle Nov. 2, 2000). In Oregon, pathologists from the Oregon Departments of Agriculture and Forestry, Oregon State University (OSU), and the USDA FS formed a less formal coordinating group, and initiated sudden oak death (SOD) detection surveys in the southern part of the state.

From the beginning, political leaders and their constituents in the densely populated San Francisco Bay area of California were concerned. Efforts to obtain funding were fruitful largely because of the public outcry and media coverage that the new problem received and technical guidance of the COMTF. California's 2001–2002 state budget contained $3.6 million to address sudden oak death in the state, with the funds to be administered through the California Department of Forestry and Fire Protection, and the COMTF serving in an advisory capacity. At the federal level, $2.4 million ($1.4 million from a Federal Emergency Supplemental Appropriation, and $1 million from the USDA FS) was made available in 2002 for research, monitoring, and management projects.

Causal Agent Found

The availability of funding and similarity of the bleeding canker symptoms to those caused by species of *Phytophthora* elsewhere (Erwin and Ribeiro 1996) renewed efforts to find a causal agent (Garbelotto and Rizzo 2005). In June 2000, David Rizzo, UC Davis, consistently isolated a *Phytophthora* species from bleeding cankers on oaks and tanoaks at different locations. By early fall, Koch's postulates (criteria used to establish causal agent) had been completed on seedlings through artificial inoculations, and by late fall 2000, inoculation experiments on adult oaks and tanoaks were successfully completed (Garbelotto and others 2001, Rizzo and others 2002b). Inoculated trees developed large girdling stem cankers that started bleeding approximately a month after inoculation. *Hypoxylon* and beetles became visible on the trees only after the *Phytophthora*-caused lesions developed in the bark. Now that a cause was known, forces were focused on obtaining information on the causal organism.

In October 2000, British plant pathologist Clive Brasier, United Kingdom Forestry Commission, was visiting with Dr. Everett Hansen at OSU. At the conclusion of that visit, Dr. Brasier traveled to the San Francisco area to observe the impacted forests and the newly isolated *Phytophthora*. While there, he was shown laboratory cultures of the unidentified *Phytophthora* isolated from cankers. Several weeks after his return to the United Kingdom, Dr. Brasier heard a description of a new and unnamed *Phytophthora* species from rhododendron in Germany and the Netherlands isolated in 1993 (Werres and Marwitz 1997) and noted a striking similarity with the cultures he had been shown in California.

In Europe, the organism was at that time known only as a pathogen causing leaf blight and branch dieback of *Rhododendron* spp. and root collar cankers on *Viburnum* spp. This knowledge led California researchers to isolate a *Phytophthora* from rhododendron with leaf symptoms in a Santa Cruz container nursery surrounded by dying oak woodlands, in December 2000. The cultural morphology was identical to that of the sudden oak death *Phytophthora*, and by January 2001 Matteo Garbelotto, UC Berkeley, confirmed that the ITS (internal transcribed spacer) DNA sequence of isolates obtained from rhododendrons in that Santa Cruz County nursery was identical to that of isolates obtained from oaks (Garbelotto and Rizzo 2005). A later study (Mascheretti and others 2008), using microsatellite analysis techniques, determined that *P. ramorum* made its first appearance in California forests at two separate sites, one in Mount Tamalpais in Marin County and the second in Scotts Valley in Santa Cruz County. Forest strains of *P. ramorum* were identical to strains found in nurseries near the two sites about the same time, providing evidence that *P. ramorum* entered California via the nursery trade.

When researchers from California and Europe exchanged pathogen ITS sequences, a perfect match of the sequences from isolates collected in Germany and the Netherlands and from isolates collected in California was found (Garbelotto and Rizzo 2005). In April 2001, the pathogen was formally named *Phytophthora ramorum* Werres, de Cock, & In't Veld sp. nov. (Werres and others 2001).

Increased Spread and Public Concern

In North America

The discovery and naming of the pathogen was an essential step, but the problem in the United States continued to increase in intensity and concern. New hosts for *P. ramorum*—including California bay laurel (*Umbellularia californica* (Hook. & Arn.) Nutt.) and coastal redwood (*Sequoia sempervirens* (D. Don) Endl.)—were being reported with increasing frequency (the 2009 host list includes 109 plant species), and the pathogen was discovered in July of 2001 in a forest location in Curry County, Oregon. Attempts to eradicate that pathogen there on 2,400 acres of forest have cost $4.3 million through 2008 (Kanaskie and others 2010a). The extensive range of hosts and the spread of the pathogen will be covered in chapter 2.

In early 2001, the state of Oregon issued an emergency rule banning host plants and other plant products coming from California unless they had been treated. A few months later, the Oregon quarantine became permanent (March 27, 2001), and Canada issued a similar quarantine (March 9, 2001) prohibiting the import of nursery stock and unmanufactured nonpropagative material (such as logs and mulch) of all oaks (*Quercus*), tanoak, *Rhododendron* spp., and evergreen huckleberry (*Vaccinium ovatum* Pursh) and of soil from areas where sudden oak death occurs. At about the same time, the California Board of Forestry declared an official Zone of Infestation for the seven counties (Santa Clara, Marin, Sonoma, Napa, Santa Cruz, San Mateo, Monterey) known to be infested with *P. ramorum*. The creation of the zone allowed for use of California Department of Forestry and Fire Protection resources to combat the problem. On May 17, 2001, the California Department of Food and Agriculture issued emergency regulations that restricted the export of diseased oak products and rhododendrons from the seven infested counties. The USDA Animal and Plant Health Inspection Service followed by issuing an interim federal regulation (7 CFR Part 301) on February 14, 2002, for domestic interstate movement of *P. ramorum* host materials from the seven infested California counties. In 2004, an emergency order expanded the regulated area to include nurseries in all of California, Oregon, and Washington. Internationally, regulations prohibiting import of potentially infested material were issued by Canada, Mexico, the European Union, the United Kingdom, the Czech Republic, Australia, New Zealand, South Korea, and Taiwan. By 2009, more than 68 countries, including China, either included *P. ramorum* on their lists of regulated pests or mentioned the pathogen in their legislation (Sansford and others 2009).

Following the first nursery findings in California in 2001, the pathogen was subsequently found in 20 nurseries in Oregon, Washington, and British Columbia. Movement of the pathogen in the nursery trade in North America and in Europe became a major issue and concern. In 2004, *P. ramorum* was detected in two large southern California nurseries, and at one nursery in Oregon and one in Washington. It was subsequently determined by trace-back investigations that these nurseries had shipped potentially infected plants to over 1,200 nurseries in 39 states (Frankel 2008). By 2005, a federal order was put in place (USDA APHIS 2007a) requiring that all nurseries in California, Oregon, and Washington that shipped host plant nursery stock interstate, be inspected and certified free of evidence of *P. ramorum*. Microsatellite marker techniques found that a single NA1 genotype (see chapter 2 for discussion of *P. ramorum* genotypes) of the pathogen was shared among most states, and that isolates clustered into two genetic groups (one mainly containing isolates from Connecticut, Oregon, and Washington and the other group largely from California and the remaining states), suggesting two predominant eastward migration routes for NA1 individuals originating either in California or the Pacific Northwest (Goss and others 2010).

In Europe

Because *P. ramorum* was known to be present in Germany and the Netherlands, surveillance for the pathogen in England and Wales began in July 2001, and later in other European countries (Brasier and others 2006a). The first finding of *P. ramorum* in the United Kingdom was confirmed in a nursery in April 2002 on *Viburnum tinus* L. (Lane and others 2003). *Phytophthora ramorum* was subsequently found on southern red oak trees (*Quercus falcata* Michx.) in the United Kingdom, and on European beech (*Fagus sylvatica* L.) and American northern red oak (*Q. rubra* L.) in the Netherlands (Brasier and others 2004a). As in the United States, *P. ramorum* is known to have a wide and growing host range in Europe, affecting a large number of plant genera and species in the ornamental nursery trade, and in parks, gardens, and woodlands. Official controls currently include a ban on the import of susceptible host material from affected parts of the United States and plant passporting controls on the movement of *Rhododendron*, *Viburnum*, and *Camellia* within the European Union. Member States in the European Union are also required to conduct official surveys and to take action to prevent the spread of *P. ramorum* (Slawson and others 2006).

A complete chronology of important events in the *P. ramorum* story can be found on the COMTF Web site at http://nature.berkeley.edu/comtf/html/chronology.html. The European Union risk analysis for the pathogen (Sansford and others 2009) provides information and references on the history of *P. ramorum* in the European Union and other European countries.

The Genus *Phytophthora* as Forest Pathogens

Phytophthora ramorum was not the first member of this genus to be a concern in forest ecosystems. The closest related species genetically, the apparently introduced pathogen *P. lateralis*, has resulted in significant damage to native forest ecosystems containing Port-Orford-cedar (*Chamaecyparis lawsoniana* (A. Murray) Parl.) in California and Oregon (Zobel and others 1985). The pathogen is significant because infection results in mortality of a host with a relatively limited distribution. The introduction of *Phytophthora cinnamomi* to the Southeastern United States in the early 1800s resulted in mortality of the American chestnut (*Castanea dentata* (Marsh.) Borkh.) and related *Castanea* species (Crandall and others 1945, Mistretta 1984) as well as being associated with littleleaf disease of shortleaf pine (*Pinus echinata* Mill.). The introduction of *P. cinnamomi* to eucalypt forests of Australia (Shearer and Smith 2000) and to oak forests of several Mexican states (Alvarado-Rosales and others 2007, 2008; Tainter and others 2000) has resulted in similar drastic changes to forest ecosystems.

Brasier (2003a) noted that pathogens in the genus *Phytophthora* became a major threat to European forests during the 1990s. During that decade, 12 previously unknown *Phytophthora* species were discovered in European forests or nurseries (Brasier 2003a). The ecological roles or places of origin of the species were unknown (Brasier 2003a). One species, *P. alni*, is of significant concern in Europe as the cause of alder dieback (Brazier 1999, Brasier and others 2004c, Gibbs and others 2003). *Phytophthora alni* is a hybrid species of complex parentage (Brasier and others 2004c, Ioos and others 2006). Recent surveys of streams and soils associated with alder stands in Alaska have found *P. alni* ssp. *uniformis* (Adams and others 2008). In the United Kingdom, the exotic species *Phytophthora kernoviae* has caused damage to beech and a range of other trees (Brasier and others 2005). Subsequent studies have isolated *P. kernoviae* from soils in indigenous and exotic forests in several regions of the North Island, New Zealand, and historical data indicate that it was first recorded in New Zealand (as *Phytophthora* sp.) in the 1950s (Ramsfield and others 2009).

In addition to the above examples of the genus *Phytophthora* as an introduced pathogen, recent investigations have found numerous species of the genus in forests of California and Oregon (Hansen 2003, Hansen and others 2006c, Rizzo and Fichtner 2009), in Eastern and Central U.S. oak forests (Balci and others 2007, 2008), and in Europe (Brasier 1999, 2009; Brasier and others 1999). Hansen and others (2006c) discussed 15 distinct *Phytophthora* species from trees, soil, or streams in oak forests in Oregon and California. In California and Oregon, two species, *Phytophthora nemorosa* and *P. pseudosyringae*, overlap in their host and geographic ranges with *P. ramorum* (Linzer and others 2009, Martin and Tooley 2003), and symptoms on all hosts are indistinguishable from the symptoms caused by *P. ramorum* (Wickland and others 2008). The two species, along with 11 other species of *Phytophthora*, were found in a survey of ornamental nurseries in California (Yakabe and others 2009).

Brasier (2009) suggested that since the year 2000, 50 or more new species (species that have been morphologically and molecularly identified as unique although not yet necessarily formally described) of *Phytophthora* have been discovered. The ecological role and significance of these newly discovered species remains largely unknown.

Chapter 2: Causal Agent, Distribution, Hosts, Diagnosis

The Causal Agent

The pathogen *Phytophthora ramorum* Werres, de Cock & Man in't Veld was formally described in 2001 (Werres and others 2001). The previously undescribed species of *Phytophthora* had been observed since 1993 in Germany and the Netherlands associated with diseased rhododendron (*Rhododendron*), and since 1998 on diseased viburnum (*Viburnum* sp.). Pathogenicity to rhododendrons was demonstrated in 1997 (Werres and Marwitz 1997).

Classification

Phytophthora ramorum belongs to the Kingdom Stramenopila (formerly in the Kingdom Chromista), a major eukaryotic group that includes diatoms and brown algae, and is distinct from plants, fungi, and animals. In contrast to fungi, stramenopiles are more closely related to plants than to animals. The taxonomy of *P. ramorum* (Alexopoulos and others 1996) is as follows:

Domain:	Eukaryota
Kingdom:	Stramenopila (Chromista)
Phylum:	Heterokontophyta
Class:	Oomycetes
Order:	Peronosporales
Family:	Pythiaceae
Genus:	*Phytophthora*
Species	*Phytophthora ramorum*

The Oomycetes, the class to which the genus *Phytophthora* belongs, share some superficial morphological and biological characteristics of fungi. Previous taxonomic classifications often placed these two groups together. However, they have since been found to be genetically distinct. Like fungi, Oomycetes exhibit filamentous growth, produce sexual and asexual spores, and can feed on decaying matter or be obligate parasites of plants. However, the nuclei within the Oomycete filaments are diploid, with two sets of genetic information, not haploid or dikaryotic as in fungi. Another difference is that fungal cell walls are made primarily of chitin, whereas Oomycete cell walls are constructed mostly of cellulose and glucan. In addition, Oomycetes have motile zoospores with two types of flagella, whereas most fungal spores have no flagella (Rossman and Palm 2006).

Morphology

In culture, *P. ramorum* is characterized by the production of large, abundant chlamydospores and elongated, ellipsoidal, semi-papillate, deciduous sporangia. Hyaline chlamydospores (asexual survival structures) are produced on hyphal tips, becoming brown with age in culture and when produced on host tissue (Rizzo and others 2002b, Werres and others 2001). Chlamydospores are variously reported to range in size from 40 to 80 µm (Rizzo and others 2002b) and 20 to 91 µm (Werres and others 2001). The sporangia have a mean length of 43.6 µm (20 to 79 µm) and a mean width of 23.9 µm (12 to 40 µm) (Werres and Kaminski 2005). The heterothallic pathogen produces two mating types, A1 and A2. Oogonia with amphigynous antheridia are produced by pairings of opposite mating types (Brasier and Kirk 2004, Werres and Kaminski 2005, Werres and others 2001). Oospores are not readily produced in culture, and no evidence of oospore formation has been reported in nurseries where both mating types have been present (Grünwald and others 2008a) or elsewhere in nature.

Genetic Diversity

Molecular analyses using microsatellite marker techniques indicate that populations of *P. ramorum* are clonal, consisting of three lineages (Grünwald and others 2008a, Ivors and others 2006b, Martin 2008). Characteristics of the three lineages are presented in table 1. The EU1 lineage is the only lineage found to date in Europe, with a few reports in nurseries in California, northern Oregon, Washington, and British Columbia, Canada (Garbelotto and others 2006, Grünwald and others 2008a, Hansen and others 2003). There has been one report of the EU1 lineage in forests in North America. The EU1 isolates, along with NA1 isolates, have been found in a woodland, coastal stream about 2 km from an infested nursery containing EU1 isolates (but in a different watershed) in Humboldt County, California (COMTF 2007). The NA1 is associated with infestations in California and Oregon forests, and also with a few nursery infestations in North America. The NA2 has a very

Table 1—Nomenclature and characteristics of the known *Phytophthora ramorum* clonal lineages

Clonal lineage	Current distribution	Environment	Mating type	Colony type	Colony growth	Colony stability	Aggressiveness
EU1	Europe, North America	Gardens, woodlands, nurseries	A1	Aerial	Faster	Stable	Higher
NA1	North America	Forests, nurseries	A2	Appressed	Slower	Unstable	Lower
NA2	North America	Nurseries	A2	Aerial	Faster	Stable	Higher

Adapted from Grünwald and others 2008b, 2009; Sansford and others 2009.

limited distribution, being isolated to date from only a few nurseries in California and Washington State (Ivors and others 2006b). The NA2 lineage is distinctly different from EU1 and NA1; it behaves phenotypically like EU1 isolates but has a unique mitochondrial and microsatellite genotype. A Web site (http://people.oregonstate.edu/~grunwaln/index.htm) hosted by Oregon State University provides information on multilocus microsatellite genotypes of *P. ramorum* currently found in North America.

All three lineages have occurred in U.S. nurseries, emphasizing the role of commercial plant trade in the movement of *P. ramorum*. Although sexual reproduction in nature has not been observed, the presence of isolates of both mating types at a single site might lead to genetic recombination, which could lead to an increase in pathogen fitness and host range.

In addition to differing in mating type, the clonal lineages differ in growth rate and colony type (Brasier 2003b, Brasier and others 2006b, Werres and Kaminski 2005), aggressiveness (Brasier 2003b), nucleotide sequences in conserved genes (mitochondrial cytochrome c oxidase subunit 1) (Kroon and others 2004), and genetic diversity (Ivors and others 2004, 2006b). Isolates from the EU1 lineage are, on average, significantly more aggressive than isolates of the NA1 lineage isolates on *Quercus rubra* L. (Brasier 2003b, Brasier and others 2006b). EU1 isolates were more pathogenic than NA1 isolates on rhododendron (Pogoda and Werres 2002). Manter and others (2010) demonstrated that isolates belonging to clonal lineages EU1 and NA2 are generally more virulent, produce more sporangia, and produce more Ram-2 elicitin in vitro than do isolates belonging to lineage NA1.

Based on mitochondrial sequence analysis, Martin (2008) considered the EU1 lineage to be basal to the NA1 lineage, and the NA2 lineage to be ancestral to both. Using DNA sequence variation analysis, Goss and others (2009a) did not observe DNA sequence variation differences among isolates within each lineage, suggesting that the genetic divergence among lineages preceded introduction. Analysis with coalescent-based methods revealed that the lineages have been diverged for an evolutionarily significant period of time, roughly 165,000 to 500,000 years. Genes contained signatures of historical recombination between the NA1 and EU1 lineages, indicating that ancestors of the *P. ramorum* lineages reproduced sexually (Goss and others 2009a).

Distribution

The native distribution or range of *P. ramorum* is not known. Evidence indicates that the pathogen has been separately introduced into North America and Europe from a third area, or areas, which are as yet undiscovered (Brasier 2003b, Ivors and others 2004, Rizzo and others 2005). The divergence of the three clonal lineages of *P. ramorum* found by Goss and others (2009a) suggested to the authors that the three lineages originated from different geographic locations sufficiently isolated from each other to allow independent evolution prior to introduction to North America and Europe, and that the emergence of *P. ramorum* in North America and Europe was the result of three independent introductions.

The distribution of *P. ramorum* as an introduced nonnative species is now known to include the United States (specific nurseries in several states, and residential planting of infected stock from those nurseries in some cases; in wildlands only in Oregon and California) and Canada (nurseries only; under eradication) in North America, and several European countries (nurseries and limited outbreaks in parks and gardens/woodlands). See details provided below.

United States, in Forests

Since the disease was first noted in 1995, the pathogen has been confirmed in natural settings, primarily redwood/tanoak and coastal evergreen forests, on various native hosts in 14 coastal California counties (Marin, Santa Cruz, Sonoma, Napa, San Mateo, Monterey, Santa Clara, Mendocino, Solano, Alameda, Contra Costa, San Francisco, Lake, and Humboldt), and in Curry County, Oregon. The infested California counties are contiguous and in central coastal California. Humboldt County is also coastal, and north of and contiguous with Mendocino County, but the known infestation in Humboldt is approximately 177 km north of any other California infestations, so it is relatively isolated. About 209 km separates the known locations in Humboldt County and Curry County in southern Oregon. See http://nature.berkeley.edu/comtf/html/maps.html for current distribution maps of the pathogen.

The pathogen was detected in 2001 via aerial survey in Curry County near Brookings, Oregon, just north of the California border where it was killing tanoak (*Lithocarpus densiflorus* (Hook. & Arn. (Rehd.) and infecting Pacific rhododendron (*Rhododendron macrophyllum* D. Don ex G. Don) and evergreen huckleberry (*Vaccinium ovatum* Pursh) (Goheen and others 2002a). At that time, nine infested forest sites totaling 16 ha were identified, and a 23-km^2 quarantine area was established around the area of infestation. Eradication treatments (cutting and burning all infected and nearby host plants as soon as possible after detection) from 2001 through 2008 were completed on approximately 971 ha of forest at a cost of $4.3 million (Kanaskie and others 2010a).

United States, in Nurseries

Phytophthora ramorum was first recovered from a nursery setting in the United States in 2001, when it was isolated from rhododendron container plants in a Santa Cruz nursery. In 2003, 20 additional nurseries were reported infested. In March 2004, infestations of *P. ramorum* were detected in two large southern California nurseries. Those nurseries had shipped potentially infected plants to several thousand nurseries throughout most of the United States. Subsequently, 21 state and 176 nursery-related detections were made (Garbelotto and Rizzo 2005). The large increase in number of positive nurseries in 2004 was due to the interstate shipments out of California and Oregon from infested nurseries and to a Federal Order requiring inspection for the first time of approximately 1,400 nurseries that ship host plants or associated plants in California, Oregon, and Washington (Jones 2006).

For January through September 2009, the U.S. Department of Agriculture, Animal and Plant Health Inspection Service (USDA APHIS) reported detection of *P. ramorum* in 11 states (California, Oregon, Washington, Alabama, Georgia, Maryland, Mississippi, New Jersey, North Carolina, Pennsylvania, South Carolina) at 30 sites: 24 nurseries and 6 in the landscape (Washington, Maryland, Pennsylvania, South Carolina) (http://www.aphis.usda.gov/plant_health/plant_pest_info/pram/downloads/pdf_files/programupdate-2009-qtr3.pdf). All known infestations are apparently contained and under eradication (table 2).

Particularly noteworthy is the 2009 detection of *P. ramorum* on salal (*Gaultheria shallon* Pursh) in Pierce County, Washington. Water from a nearby infested nursery drains into the native forest containing salal. This is the first documented incident of the pathogen escaping from a nursery via runoff to infect native forest plants (COMTF 2009).

Table 2—Detection of *Phytophthora ramorum* in U.S. nurseries by year

Year	Number of positive nurseries	Number of states	
2000 (and prior)	0	0	
2001	1	1	(California)
2002	0	0	
2003	20	3	(California, Oregon, Washington)
2004	176	21	
2005	99	7	
2006	62	11	
2007	23	6	
2008	28	8	
2009 (through (September)	24	9	(plus landscape detections in four states)

Canada

Phytophthora ramorum was first reported in Canada in June 2003, when infected potted rhododendrons were found in a British Columbia nursery (Sabaratnam and Woodske 2006). Additional detections occurred in 2004 and 2005 at a few nurseries and garden centers in British Columbia. Immediate regulatory action by the Canadian Food Inspection Agency (CFIA) has apparently successfully eradicated these occurrences. One nursery in Pitt River underwent a controlled burn followed by disinfection of soil and production areas in an attempt to eradicate the pathogen (Sabaratnam and Woodske 2006). In 2006, *P. ramorum* was detected at three retail garden centers that had been positive in 2004 (but negative in 2005), and eradication efforts continued at one wholesale nursery where *P. ramorum* was detected in late 2005 (NAPPO 2006). In 2007, the Canadian national survey for *P. ramorum* found 10 positive nurseries in British Columbia; all were subject to eradication (Sela 2008). See (http://www.inspection.gc.ca/english/plaveg/pestrava/phyram/sodmsce.shtml) for survey results in Canada.

Europe

Since the first reports in Germany and the Netherlands (Werres and others 2001), *P. ramorum* has been discovered in additional European countries. In the European Union, *P. ramorum* has been recorded as present in Belgium, Czech Republic (eradicated nursery finding), Denmark, Estonia, Finland, France, Germany, Ireland, Italy, Latvia, Lithuania, Luxembourg, the Netherlands, Poland, Portugal, Slovenia, Spain (including Mallorca), Sweden, and all the United Kingdom (U.K.) countries, including the Channel Islands. Additional European countries where *P. ramorum* has been recorded include Norway and Switzerland (Delatour and others 2002, De Merlier and others 2003, Heiniger and others 2004, Herrero and others 2006, Lane and others 2003a, Lilja 2007, Moralejo and Werres 2002, Orlikowski and Szkuta 2002, Orlikowski and others 2004) and Serbia (Bulajić and others 2009). The pathogen was found in the Czech Republic on imported *Viburnum* plants in 2003, but this outbreak was considered eradicated as further surveys in 2004 and 2005 did not detect the pathogen (Běhalová 2006) (http://www.forestry.gov.uk/pramorum). In these European countries, the pathogen is mainly present on nontree hosts grown in containers at nurseries and retail garden centers. However, in Belgium, Denmark, France, Germany, Ireland, Luxembourg, the Netherlands, Slovenia, Spain, the United Kingdom, as well as the non-EU countries of Norway, Switzerland, and Serbia, some infected plants have been found outside nursery situations in managed parks and gardens and in woodland situations (Bulajić and others 2009, Sansford and others 2009).

In Europe, infected trees with *P. ramorum* bole cankers have only been found in the United Kingdom and the Netherlands (Brasier and others 2004b, Denman and others 2005a, Gewasbescherming 2004, Mycological Research News 2004, Sansford and others 2009). In November 2003, the first *P. ramorum*-infected tree outside the United States was confirmed on a mature (100-year-old) southern red oak (*Quercus falcata* Michx.) tree in Sussex, United Kingdom. Infection of several *Quercus rubra* trees in the Netherlands was confirmed about the same time. By 2007, a range of tree species in Cornwall, United Kingdom—especially beech (*Fagus sylvatica* L.) but also including turkey oak (*Q. cerris* L.), sessile oak (*Q. petraea* (Matt.) Liebl.), *Q. falcata*, evergreen oak (*Q. acuta* Thunb.), horse chestnut (*Aesculus hippocastanum* L.), sweet chestnut (*Castanea sativa* Mill.), roble beech (*Nothofagus obliqua* (Birb.) Blume), sycamore (*Acer pseudoplatanus* L.), and a species of *Schima*—had been found with bleeding bark cankers. Other trees have been found with only foliar or dieback symptoms, for example holm oak (*Quercus ilex* L.), castanopsis (*Castanopsis* sp.), camphor tree (*Cinnamomum camphora* (L.) J. Presl), ash (*Fraxinus excelsior* L.), *Michelia doltsopa* Buch.-Ham. ex DC., winter's bark (*Drimys winteri* Forsr.), evergreen maple (*Acer laevigatum* Wallich), *Cornus kousa* Hance x *capitata* Wall. ex Roxb., an unconfirmed species of *Eucalyptus*, Delavay osmanthus (*Osmanthus delavayi* Franch.) and Chinese guger tree (*Schima wallichii* (DC.) Korth.) as well as several species of *Magnolia* L. (Sansford and Woodhall 2007). Some tree hosts in Europe can exhibit both foliar and bole infections, e.g., turkey oak and sweet chestnut. Japanese larch (*Larix kaempferi* (Lam.) Carrière) was found as both a bole host and foliar (sporulating) host in Devon, Cornwall, and Somerset, southwest England, in 2009 (Forestry Commission 2009). Symptoms have also been found on western hemlock (*Tsuga heterophylla* (Raf.) Sarg.) and broadleaf species (beech [*Fagus* spp.], birch [*Betula* spp.], and some oaks) growing in the same area (Forestry Commission 2009). Infected rhododendrons (especially the invasive *R. ponticum* L.) have been in proximity to most bleeding canker infections on infected U.K. and Netherlands trees (Sansford and Woodhall 2007). Rhododendrons are not associated with many of the infected Japanese larch and western hemlock.

Hosts

Phytophthora ramorum is a generalist pathogen with a broad and diverse host range that continues to expand. The host list includes both hardwood and conifer trees, shrubs, herbaceous plants, and ferns. Some hosts are found in forest situations, whereas others are used widely as landscape and ornamental plants. In coastal California forests, *P. ramorum* infects many different plant species, and in some mixed-evergreen forests nearly all woody plants can serve as hosts for *P. ramorum* (Rizzo and others 2002a).

Plant species are designated as regulated hosts and as associated plants by the U.S. Department of Agriculture (USDA). The difference between hosts and associated plants is the demonstration of Koch's postulates (criteria designed to confirm that a micro-organism associated with symptoms of a disease is the cause of the disease). Proven or regulated hosts are hosts for which Koch's postulates have been completed, documented, reviewed, and accepted to confirm they are host plants of *P. ramorum*. All host parts, except the wood of non-bole hosts, are regulated (see *P. ramorum* quarantine and regulations at http://nature.berkeley.edu/comtf/pdf/APHIS-2005-0102-0001.pdf).

Associated plants are plants that have been found to be naturally infected with *P. ramorum*, and *P. ramorum* has been cultured and/or detected using polymerase chain reaction (PCR), but Koch's postulates have not been completed or documented and reviewed, and for which testing has not been completed. Taxa are moved from the Associated Plant List to the Regulated Host List when Koch's postulates are demonstrated and reviewed (Cave and others 2005). USDA APHIS-Plant Protection and Quarantine (PPQ) maintains an updated list of regulated and associated hosts at http://www.aphis.usda.gov/plant_health/plant_pest_info/pram/downloads/pdf_files/usdaprlist.pdf.

As of May 2008, the list contained 45 regulated hosts and 72 associated plants that are regulated as nursery stock. A list of natural hosts of *P. ramorum* in the United Kingdom, Europe, and North America is available in the 2009 European pest risk analysis for *P. ramorum* (Sansford and others 2009). The list includes the location of the finding (the United Kingdom, other European countries, Canada, the United States), symptoms, and literature reference.

A third category, experimental hosts, also exists. Experimental hosts, in contrast to the above two previously described groups where the pathogen is found on naturally infected plants, are those for which pathogenicity was determined by inoculating various plants to predict potential hosts. If the plant becomes infected, it is not added to the hosts or associated plants lists unless found naturally infected. More than an additional 40 plant genera have been susceptible to this pathogen in inoculation trials. Some of the literature that screened for potential hosts includes Brasier and others (2002), Chastagner and others (2006b), Denman and others (2005b), Hansen and others (2005), Parke and others (2002a), Rizzo and others (2002a), Tooley and Kyde (2003, 2007), and Tooley and others (2004). The European risk analysis (Sansford and others 2009) contains a table of the experimental host range (susceptible species determined experimentally) and references.

The California Oak Mortality Task Force (COMTF) Web site (www.suddenoakdeath.org) contains the most up-to-date information available on regulated hosts, associated plants, and experimental hosts. See http://nature.berkeley.edu/comtf/html/host_plant_lists.html#AssociatedHosts for lists of regulated and associated hosts. Also see the host lists maintained by RAPRA (risk analysis for *Phytophthora ramorum*) at http://rapra.csl.gov.uk/. Because the lists are being constantly updated, the Web sites and others should be checked for the latest information on hosts.

Symptoms

Three different diseases—stem or bole canker, twig blight (dieback) and leaf blight—are attributed to *P. ramorum* (Hansen and others 2002): "sudden oak death" in the United States, also known in Europe as "ramorum bleeding canker," characterized by bleeding bark cankers on the bole, which can be lethal; "ramorum shoot dieback," resulting from foliar infection or infection of stems; and "ramorum leaf blight," resulting from foliar infection. Thus, the symptoms produced by *P. ramorum* are diverse and range from trunk and branch cankers to foliar symptoms including leaf spots, leaf lesions, leaf/twig/stem blights, depending on the host plant and the part of the host affected. Individual plant species can display more than one disease type (for example, leaf blight, shoot dieback, and bleeding cankers on tanoak). A comparison of symptoms of sudden oak death and ramorum blight (a combination of shoot dieback and leaf blight) is presented in table 3.

The COMTF Web site (http://nature.berkeley.edu/comtf/html/plant_symptoms.html) contains descriptions and images of symptoms. Several diagnostic guides are available at that site with descriptions and pictures of symptoms on many host plants (Davidson and others 2003b, Storer and others 2002).

Table 3—Comparison of sudden oak death and ramorum blight caused by *Phytophthora ramorum*

Disease	Symptoms	Host categories	Typical hosts	Geography/ environment
Sudden oak death	Stem cankers; bleeding cankers	Forest and garden trees	Coast live oak, tanoak, European beech, others	North American forests, European gardens
Ramorum blight	Foliar and twig blight; tip and shoot dieback; leaf blight	Ornamental trees and woody shrubs; understory plants	California bay laurel, rhododendron, *Viburnum*, *Pieris*, coast redwood, tanoak, others	North American nurseries and forests, European nurseries and gardens

Modified from Grünwald and others 2008b.

Disease symptoms are reviewed and well-illustrated in many other publications including Garbelotto and others 2002a; McPherson and others 2002a; Parke and others 2003, 2004; Storer and others 2002; and Tjosvold and others 2005. McPherson and others (2002a) included descriptions of symptoms by host family. The RAPRA Web site (http://rapra.csl.gov.uk/background/hosts.cfm) contains links to images of symptoms on various hosts.

Phytophthora ramorum has been isolated from asymptomatic host tissue, including asymptomatic root tissue of infected tanoak seedlings (Parke and others 2006b); asymptomatic stems and roots of *Rhododendron* spp. (Bienapfl and others 2005); and leaves of *Rhododendron* "Cunningham's White" and holm oak (*Quercus ilex*) being used as trap plants (Denman and others 2009).

Similar-Looking Diseases

Signs and symptoms produced by *P. ramorum* are variable, not unique, and often indistinguishable from those caused by other plant pathogens (including other *Phytophthora* species), insect problems, abiotic or physiological conditions, and injuries. The presence of the pathogen can only be confirmed through laboratory diagnosis using species-specific diagnostic methods (for example, by isolation of the pathogen onto agar media, or by molecular tests).

Look-alike diseases, insect damage, or other injuries or conditions are described and illustrated in numerous publications. Some of the most comprehensive for oaks and tanoak include descriptions on the COMTF Web site (http://nature.berkeley.edu/comtf/html/look-alikes_misdiagnosis.html), the Forest Service Western and Eastern Pest Alerts (Frankel 2002, O'Brien and others 2002), and the University of California Pest Alert Number 6 (Storer and others 2002).

Diagnostics

For reasons stated above, diagnosis of *P. ramorum* based on symptoms alone is unreliable. Methods for detecting plant pathogens in host tissue—plating on selective media (isolation and culture), and molecular techniques/assays based on either proteins (Enzyme-linked immunosorbent assay [ELISA]) or DNA (methods based on the polymerase chain reaction [PCR])—have been used for *P. ramorum*. Culturing or molecular diagnostics are necessary for confident identification of *P. ramorum*.

Plating on Selective Media (Isolation and Culture)

Traditional isolation techniques used for other *Phytophthora* species are successful for recovery of *P. ramorum* from tissue of many host species. Plating host material taken from the leading edge of a canker or lesion onto semiselective media for *Phytophthora*, such as pimaricin-ampicillin-rifampicin-pentachloronitrobenzene (PARP) (Erwin and Ribeiro 1996), incubating the plates in the dark at 20 to 22 °C, and examining within 2 to 5 days has been commonly used (Davidson and others 2003b). Once *P. ramorum* is growing in culture, its identity is confirmed by microscopic examination for its unique morphological characteristics or by species-specific molecular tests (see below). The USDA APHIS-PPQ protocol for cultural isolation is found at http://www.aphis.usda.gov/plant_health/plant_pest_info/pram/downloads/pdf_files/cultureprotocol6-07.pdf . A diagnostic protocol developed by the European and Mediterranean Plant Protection Organization (EPPO) is available at http://www.furs.si/law/eppo/zvr/ENG/EPPO2004/diag_protokoli_PM7/pm7-66.pdf.

Although traditional isolation-based diagnostics are successful, there are several associated issues. Culturing of the pathogen from symptomatic plant material is time consuming, and under some circumstances, its success may be dependent on the species of the host or the environmental conditions from which the sample was taken (Martin and others 2004). Isolation success is extremely variable based on plant substrate and time of year (Davidson and others 2005b, Garbelotto 2003b). The fungicides and antibiotics in the selective media may sometimes suppress the development of hyphae from plant tissue or the development of *Phytophthora* propagules (Davidson and others 2003b). Furthermore, despite *P. ramorum*'s distinctive morphological characteristics, closely related *Phytophthora* species can have overlapping morphology characters, and the identification of an unknown culture solely on the basis of morphology requires training and experience. Because of these limitations, molecular diagnostic approaches have been developed and are used to augment detection and identification of the pathogen.

Serological Methods

The ELISA technique (Gaastra 1984) is a serological test used to detect the presence or absence of specific antigenic proteins produced by all *Phytophthora* species. If a large number of samples are to be processed for *P. ramorum*, ELISA is used as a low-cost, prescreen to reduce the number of samples that will need to be processed for subsequent tests. An ELISA test that is specific to *P. ramorum* is not yet available.

ELISA tests are available in packaged kit form. Single-test, self-contained ELISA kits are commercially available for laboratory use; the one produced by Agdia Inc. (Elkhart, Indiana) is approved by APHIS. Another kit, developed in the United Kingdom and marketed as a "lateral flow device" (LFD), principally for in-field use, by Forsite Diagnostics Ltd., York, for *Phytophthora* species, was evaluated by Lane and others (2007). Although false positives were common, their assay was simple to use, and provided results comparable to laboratory methods (isolation and real-time PCR) in a few minutes. Results suggested that the use of LFD at the time of inspection may be a useful primary screen for selecting samples for subsequent laboratory testing to determine species. Avila and others (2010) reported development of antibodies that, when used in ELISA, recognized *P. ramorum* and *P. kernoviae*, detected a smaller spectrum of other *Phytophthora* species, and did not cross react with *Pythium* species.

For making regulatory determinations, USDA APHIS-PPQ encourages the use of a procedure that incorporates Agdia's ELISA test for screening of all samples (http://www.aphis.usda.gov/plant_health/plant_pest_info/pram/downloads/pdf_files/ELISA.pdf). The procedures used by the USDA to determine the presence or absence of *P. ramorum* in plant samples, summarized by Berger (Berger 2006), is based on a combination of tests. The Agdia-based ELISA is encouraged so that further screening on *Phytophthora*-negative samples is avoided. ELISA negative samples are considered negative for *P. ramorum* by the USDA. Samples that are positive on the basis of ELISA are then subjected to further testing using DNA-based techniques. Laboratories have the option, either before or after ELISA testing, to try to culture the organism. Presumptive positive cultures are then sent to the National Mycologist in Beltsville, Maryland, for confirmation. If cultural isolation is confirmed, the sample is considered positive, even in rare cases where PCR (if done) is negative. For samples that are ELISA positive, but from which *P. ramorum* was not isolated, or that are ELISA positive and no culture was attempted, DNA is extracted and the DNA sent to the National Identification Service (NIS) (Beltsville, Maryland), for PCR analysis.

The complete and rather involved details of the APHIS-PPQ system for sample submission from provisionally approved laboratories, referred to as the "Potentially Actionable Suspect System" (PASS), are available at http://www.aphis.usda.gov/plant_health/plant_pest_info/pram/downloads/pdf_files/passpolicy_mar08.pdf.

DNA-based Techniques/Assays

Several DNA-based molecular techniques (among others, PCR of the ITS region or other regions of the genome, real-time PCR, amplified fragment length polymorphism (AFLP), inter simple sequence repeat (ISSR), microsatellites, sequence analysis of several genes and PCR-restriction fragment length polymorphism [RFLP]) have been developed for detection and characterization of *P. ramorum* (Bonants and others 2006, Kox and others 2007).

PCR—

Amplifying unique DNA sequences, such as the internal transcribed spacer (ITS) region, by using species-specific primers, has been used as a method for screening of other *Phytophthora* spp. (Bonants and others 1997, Cooke and others 2000b, Kong and others 2003b). Because the ITS region is conserved across *Phytophthora* spp. but differs among species within the genus, and the ITS sequence in that region is known for most *Phytophthora* spp. (Cooke and others 2000a, 2000b; Lee and Taylor 1992), ITS PCR has been used successfully for detection of specific *Phytophthora* species.

Based upon ITS sequence analysis, a species-specific PCR detection method for *P. ramorum* was developed and validated using stem and leaf material from plants infected with *P. ramorum* (Garbelotto and others 2002b, Kox and others 2002). The primers developed may show cross reaction with *P. lateralis* (Kox and others 2002) and with *P. cambivora* at high concentrations (Davidson and others 2003b). Primers developed by K. Hughes (Lane and others 2003a) are specific to *P. ramorum*. A PCR-based molecular diagnostic assay initially developed for *P. lateralis* (Winton and Hansen 2001) is also effective for *P. ramorum*, and remains the primary molecular diagnostic test used in Oregon for diagnosis of *P. ramorum* from the forest.

Nested PCR may be required to detect low levels of infection when small amounts of the pathogen are present (Bonants and others 1997, Gunderson and others 1996, Hayden and others 2004, Martin and others 2004). Nested PCR is basically the same as regular ITS PCR using species-specific primers, but the PCR reaction is run twice, with different combinations of primers. The test is thus able to detect much smaller amounts of DNA in a sample. However, nested PCR is much more prone to false positives resulting from laboratory contamination and other factors, including the presence of inhibitors. To be used with confidence, it requires dedicated laboratories with strict procedures and numerous internal controls. In a comparison between successful diagnoses in California forests using a nested PCR approach and traditional isolation techniques, nested PCR showed the greater sensitivity (Hayden and others 2004). However, PCR was not always successful in detecting the pathogen and was highly dependent on which plant part (for example, wood vs. leaves) or plant species was tested (Hayden and others 2004). The most promising results in forest surveys were obtained from traditional isolation combined with ITS PCR-based assays (Hayden and others 2004).

Real-time PCR assays, especially those based on TaqMan chemistry (Holland and others 1991), are increasingly preferred to gel-based PCR. They are quicker, less labor-intensive, and are less prone to post-PCR contamination because subsequent manipulation of amplified DNA is avoided (Schaad and Frederick 2002).

A nested real-time PCR assay, based on SYBR®-Green technology, was developed by Hayden and others (2004). These authors (Hayden and others 2004) developed and tested a real-time, nested PCR assay that was sensitive and host-specific for *P. ramorum*. The technique allowed the confirmation of *P. ramorum* in symptomatic plants and facilitated the expansion of the host range by 10 hosts and four California counties far sooner than if identification had been based on pathogen isolation alone.

A real-time quantitative PCR method that measures PCR product accumulation through a dual-labeled fluorogenic probe (TaqMan® probe) was developed in 1996 (Heid and others 1996). Real-time PCR methods based on TaqMan chemistry do not require certain pre-amplification steps and therefore reduce the risk of cross-contamination. A TaqMan probe has been developed for *P. ramorum* based upon the ITS sequence (Ivors and Garbelotto 2002).

Hayden and others (2006) developed and tested a nested TaqMan assay that included a first-round amplification step. The assay was as sensitive as the real-time PCR assay developed by Hayden and others (2004) that used SYBR-Green for detection. The nested TaqMan method successfully detected *P. ramorum* in field-collected samples (Hayden and others 2006). Sensitivity of the assay was markedly increased with the nested protocol vs. single-round, with detection rates more than doubled (Hayden and others 2006). Their technique provided for both detection and quantification of *P. ramorum* in plant material, even in the presence of inhibitors and low concentrations of *P. ramorum* DNA. However, because the assay requires two reactions and the moving of the product to a new tube, it has a risk of contamination.

When comparing isolation of *P. ramorum* using PARPH medium (cultural isolation using a variation of the PARP medium previously described) with a real-time PCR TaqMan assay developed by the Central Science Laboratory (York, United Kingdom), the two techniques were equally reliable and robust for diagnosis of *P. ramorum* from the U.K. plant material tested (Hughes and others 2006a). A single-round, real-time TaqMan PCR assay for the detection of *P. ramorum*, involving no post-amplification steps or nested PCR, has been developed (Hughes and others 2006c). The single-step protocol eliminates possible contamination introduced between the first and second round of PCR when using nested PCR. The assay detected *P. ramorum* in plant material containing as little as 1 percent infected material by weight. The real-time protocol gave results comparable with a traditional isolation technique for diagnosis of *P. ramorum* in plant material from common U.K. hosts (Hughes and others 2006c). This assay is routinely used at the Central Science Laboratory in the United Kingdom, in conjunction with isolation techniques, for the detection of *P. ramorum* in symptomatic plant material in the laboratory.

Amplification of more than one region of DNA simultaneously (multiplex PCR) was first used as a diagnostic test for *Phytophthora* by Winton and Hansen (2001). Their technique amplifies a very highly conserved region of DNA as well as the piece of ITS DNA specific to *Phytophthora lateralis* and *P. ramorum*, resulting in a built-in check on the reaction (if the conserved region, found in all living organisms, does not amplify, then something is wrong with the test). Multiplex PCR, which can be used for simultaneous (multiplex) detection of more than one pathogen species in a sample of plant tissue and is a next step from single-species detection, provides benefits to programs such as national surveys where large numbers of samples are involved. In addition, multiplex PCR can be used to incorporate a variety of control reactions to measure the quantity and integrity of the DNA tested. Various modifications of existing TaqMan assays and other new approaches are being developed for parallel testing. For example, Tooley and others (2006) used a real-time PCR method based on TaqMan in a three-multiplex format to simultaneously detect *P. ramorum*, *P. pseudosyringae,* and plant DNA in a single tube. Schena and others (2006) developed a real-time multiplex PCR assay based on TaqMan PCR to simultaneously identify and detect *P. ramorum*, *P. kernoviae*, *P. quercina*, and *P. citricola* within the same plant extract.

Bilodeau and others (2009) developed two multiplex real-time PCR assays using TaqMan probes with different reporter dyes targeting *P. ramorum* (ITS), *Phytophthora* genus (β-tubulin), oomycetes (ribosomal 5.8S subunit), and host plants (RuBisCO). This allowed simultaneous detection of *P. ramorum* while verifying DNA extraction and the presence of other oomycetes in the DNA sample. The multiplex assays detected *P. ramorum* accurately while decreasing the cost and increasing throughput. The advantage of the multiplex assays is that the presence of an internal control should reduce the rates of false negatives by identifying reactions that failed owing to poor DNA extraction or to the presence of inhibitors (Bilodeau and others 2009).

Fingerprinting or barcoding methods—

Single-strand conformation polymorphism (SSCP) analysis is an effective molecular fingerprinting technique for species differentiation in the genus *Phytophthora*, and *P. ramorum* shows a unique pattern of ribosomal DNA ITS 1 when analyzed (Kong and others 2003b, 2003c, 2004). The SCCP procedure separates species based on the PCR-amplified ITS DNA sequence, but indirectly. Differences in sequence between species cause the strands of DNA to assume different shapes (conformations) and thus to move at different speeds through an electrophoresis gel. The SSCP analysis reported by Kong and others (2004) was rapid and efficient, and SSCP profiles easily distinguished *P. ramorum* from other described *Phytophthora* species. The authors suggested that SSCP analysis may be a superior technique to other existing molecular fingerprinting methods such as restriction fragment length polymorphism (RFLP). However, because each *Phytophthora* species is identified by a profile of three bands, presence of multiple species in the same sample may be confusing; in addition, SSCP from environmental rather than cultural samples may result in spurious bands (Garbelotto 2003b). A modification of the technique using fluorescent-labeling chemistry and an additional marker locus was successfully used to allow quantitative matching of *Phytophthora* isolates from streams, soil, and plants with reference species (Hansen and others 2006a). Kong and others (2006) reported a modification of their 2003 (Kong and others 2003c) technique that provided reliable diagnoses of *P. ramorum*, whether it is a single infection or dual infection (a second *Phytophthora* species involved). The technique also provided accurate diagnoses of diseases caused by 12 other species of *Phytophthora* without additional work.

Microsatellite techniques and amplified fragment length polymorphism (AFLP) have been successfully used to differentiate between the North American and European lineages of *P. ramorum* (Hansen and others 2003). An AFLP DNA fingerprinting showed significant differences between EU and U.S. populations (Bonants and others 2002, Ivors and others 2002). Using sequence differences between EU and U.S. isolates of *P. ramorum* in the mitochondrial cytochrome c oxidase subunit 1 (cox1) gene, Kroon and others (2004) developed a single-nucleotide polymorphism (SNP) protocol to distinguish between isolates of *P. ramorum* originating in Europe and those originating in the United States. All isolates could be consistently and correctly allocated to either the European or the U.S. populations using the SNP protocol. Whereas European isolates of *P. ramorum* shared a unique RFLP profile, U.S. isolates had a different RFLP profile similar to that of *P. brassicae*. However, *P. brassicae* showed additional fragments and was distinguishable from *P. ramorum* isolates (Kroon and others 2004). Elliott and others (2009) developed techniques to identify *P. ramorum* isolates according to each of the three lineages using PCR-RFLP of the cox1 gene.

Microsatellite analysis of *P. ramorum* was first developed in the Hansen lab at Oregon State University. Large numbers of *P. ramorum* isolates have been analyzed with AFLP (Ivors and others 2004). Results show two clusters, with EU isolates and U.S. isolates grouping separately. Using the recently assembled whole-genome sequence of *P. ramorum*, simple sequence repeat (SSR) techniques were used to fingerprint large numbers of *P. ramorum* isolates originating from different host species within Europe and the United States (Ivors and others 2006a). Many loci showed variation between the EU and U.S. populations. Minor variation was found within the EU populations and even less variation within the U.S. population.

Onsite real-time PCR techniques—

Tests that can be reliably used immediately at the point of sampling rather than requiring one to send samples to a central laboratory for testing and to wait for results would be useful in certain instances. For example, availability of onsite testing techniques would permit the targeted testing of known *P. ramorum* hosts, such as imported nursery stock, at points of entry with minimal disruption to trade. In addition, onsite testing would reduce the need to hold suspect material while waiting for a laboratory test result. If an onsite test is suitably sensitive, samples that test positive in the field can then be sent to a diagnostic laboratory for confirmation. Because the current methods for the molecular detection of fungal pathogens in plant material require the extraction of DNA (Schaad and Frederick 2002), onsite molecular testing requires a portable real-time PCR platform and a suitable assay, as well as a simple and robust method for extracting DNA in the field.

Tomlinson and others (2005) developed a rapid and simple method for DNA extraction from symptomatic foliage and stems in the field, followed by a real-time PCR (TaqMan) assay using a portable real-time PCR platform (Cepheid SmartCycler II) for accurate onsite detection of *P. ramorum* within 2 hours. The combination of an extraction method, real-time PCR assay, and lyophilized, field-stable reagents, all optimized for use in the field, allowed the detection of *P. ramorum* in naturally infected material at the point of sampling, with results comparable to those of real-time PCR testing in the laboratory. A variation of that method was successfully evaluated under U.S. conditions using leaf and stem samples from 20 plant species collected from five sites around San Francisco, California (Hughes and others 2006b).

Tomlinson and others (2007) developed a number of assays based on their earlier method (Tomlinson and others 2005) that had various advantages for use in the field. A variation of a real-time PCR assay called "scorpion runs," was twice as fast as TaqMan, and allowed the detection of *P. ramorum* in less than 30 minutes. They also designed a loop-mediated isothermal amplification (LAMP) assay, which allowed sensitive and specific detection of *P. ramorum* (as indicated by a color change visible to the naked eye) in 45 minutes using only a heated block to maintain a single constant temperature.

Riedel and others (2010) are developing a stationary PCR chip with integrated microstructured heaters and temperature sensors for the amplification of specific *Phytophthora* DNA fragments. A microfluidic system connects the PCR chip with a microarray where the labelled DNA fragments are detected. The miniaturization of the chip-formatted PCR and array system enables high portability, low input of energy, smaller amounts of expensive analytic chemicals, and very fast reaction times owing to low reaction volumes.

APHIS PPQ Protocol

The current (as of June 5, 2007) diagnostic protocol used by APHIS PPQ (USDA APHIS 2007b) for samples that have regulatory significance states that all samples that are ELISA positive and/or culture negative must be assayed using the validated nested PCR method by USDA or at authorized USDA laboratories. The DNA is extracted from ELISA positive samples (see http://www.aphis.usda.gov/plant_health/plant_pest_info/pram/downloads/pdf_files/pcrprotocol4.pdf), and these DNA extracts are forwarded to the National Identification Services (NIS) Molecular Diagnostic Lab (which at present is the only authorized laboratory) as described in the protocol. If the diagnostic laboratory has not performed the ELISA test, then culture negative samples need to have DNA extracted and these extracts sent to the NIS Molecular Diagnostic Lab for analysis. Several labs outside of USDA authorized labs have been provisionally approved to process diagnostic samples using the USDA validated protocols. For the majority of regulatory samples, these labs provide final determinations. Only potentially actionable suspect samples need to be forwarded for USDA confirmation. This laboratory approval program has several quality assurance measures in place to ensure participating laboratory capabilities and proficiency.

The APHIS PPQ protocol utilizes two PCR tests for *P. ramorum* determination (Berger 2006). The first is the multiplex PCR developed by Oregon State University (OSU) (Winton and Hansen 2001). Although it is not as sensitive as the main diagnostic test and can produce false positive results with a few other closely related *Phytophthora* species, the OSU test is used as a quality assurance procedure to ensure that DNA received by PPQ is of sufficient quantity and quality to be amplifiable in the nested PCR test. Any DNA samples that do not meet these criteria are not tested further, and a new sample is requested. The second assay, assuming that amplifiable DNA is present in the sample, is a validated nested PCR test, modified slightly from the technique developed at the University of California at Berkeley, and described in http://www.aphis.usda.gov/plant_health/plant_pest_info/pram/downloads/pdf_files/pcrprotocol4.pdf. Any sample DNA that passed amplification quality control, and that reacted to produce either a nested PCR or a *Phytophthora*-specific multiplex PCR product, or both PCR products, is retested using both conventional PCR assays, and is tested in the real-time PCR assay. Results of different replications of assays on individual samples are compared to confirm that the results were both repeatable, and robust. If the results of different replications of the assays for any sample are not all conclusive and compatible, DNA sequences are obtained for conventional PCR products, and these sequences are compared to those of reference sequences contained in public and local databases to aid in completing a diagnosis. Although a rare occurrence, if a diagnosis cannot then be obtained, a new sample is requested (Berger 2008).

APHIS also has validated an additional real-time PCR assay for *P. ramorum*. This test is based on the test currently used in the United Kingdom and developed by the Central Science Laboratory (York, United Kingdom). It is robust and sensitive, incorporates DNA quality controls into the single reaction, and has higher throughput than current APHIS methods. Comparative analysis with the primary PCR diagnostic demonstrated that this real-time PCR protocol is less sensitive than the original test, so some samples that cannot be confirmed with this test because of low concentration of *P. ramorum* need additional testing for confirmation. Recent research has provided a comparative analysis to determine the correlation among ELISA, culture, real-time, and conventional PCR detection and is described below (Bulluck and others 2006). In addition, collaborative work involving several U.S., Canadian, and U.K. laboratories has occurred to help identify the most promising tests for entrance into the validation process.

EPPO Protocol

The European and Mediterranean Plant Protection Organization (EPPO) publishes standards on diagnostic protocols for regulated pests of the EPPO region, including the European Union. The provisional diagnostics protocol for *P. ramorum*, approved September 2005, was published as PM (phytosanitary measures) 7/66(1) in 2006 (OEPP/EPPO 2006). The publication contains a summary of sampling procedures for plants, water, and soil; methods for isolation from plants, water, and soil; and a section on identification of the pathogen, including growth and morphology in culture, biochemical methods, and molecular methods. Web link (via EPPO Web site): http://www3.interscience.wiley.com/cgi-bin/fulltext/118562438/PDFSTART.

Relative Sensitivity and Specificity of Diagnostic Techniques

In addition to those already mentioned, several research efforts designed to obtain information on the relative sensitivity and specificity of the diagnostic tests used for

P. ramorum identification—including culturing, ELISA, nested PCR, and real-time PCR—have been conducted or are underway.

In a comparison of diagnostic techniques within a nursery setting (Bulluck and others 2006), a block of 300 camellia (*Camellia* spp.) plants within a California nursery known to be infested with *P. ramorum* was simultaneously assayed for visual symptoms, growth medium pH, and moss presence. Host plant leaf tissue or leaf bait from the growth medium extracts were either plated on PARP-V8, tested using ELISA, or subjected to either nested-PCR or single-round real-time PCR analysis. Diagnostic sensitivity and specificity of the assays were determined to compare the performance of each method for diagnosis of *Phytophthora* spp. or *P. ramorum* in camellia tissues and associated potting medium. All diagnostic assays were highly correlated with one another and disease symptoms, with nested PCR having the best correlation with symptoms, followed by real-time PCR, ELISA, and then culture. A second research effort underway at UC Berkeley is designed to obtain similar data, but also investigate the influence of different hosts, environmental conditions, and other factors on the ability to accurately detect and identify the pathogen.

Using three regions of the nuclear genome of *P. ramorum* (ITS, ß-tubulin, and elicitin gene regions) to construct species-specific markers, Bilodeau and others (2006, 2007) evaluated three real-time PCR technologies (molecular beacons, TaqMan probes, and SYBR-Green assays) for sensitivity and specificity. The best performing system (TaqMan probes) was also used to compare the three DNA regions. Overall, TaqMan assays with ITS or elicitin had the best combination of sensitivity and specificity.

Kox and others (2007) compared six methods for the detection of *P. ramorum* in plants using naturally infested rhododendron plant material: isolation followed by morphological identification; two immunological methods, ELISA (Agdia) and lateral flow immunochromatgraphy (LFD, Pocket Diagnostic); and three molecular tests based on PCR using TaqMan chemistry, including two assays designed for specific detection of *P. ramorum* and one designed for genus-level detection of *Phytophthora*. The *Phytophthora* spp. TaqMan PCR, ELISA, and LFD had higher sensitivities than the *P. ramorum*-specific methods, which make them useful as prescreening methods, where positive results must be confirmed by PCR or isolation. The authors suggested that in critical situations (for example, in the case of a first finding on a new host or site), it is advisable to use both a *P. ramorum* TaqMan assay and culture. For routine testing, in most cases, it will be sufficient to rely on the TaqMan results.

A PCR-based mitochondrial DNA detection system for determining if a *Phytophthora* species was present in symptomatic plant tissue and clarifying if it was *P. ramorum*, *P. nemorosa*, or *P. pseudosyringae* was developed by Martin and others (2004). Results obtained with their system correlated well with the results obtained at the California Department of Food and Agriculture (CDFA) diagnostics laboratory for pathogen recovery from symptomatic tissue, and with PCR amplification for *P. ramorum*, using the rDNA ITS *P. ramorum*-specific primers of Garbelotto and others (2002b). For *P. ramorum*, no differences in results were obtained; all samples that scored positive for *P. ramorum* in the CDFA laboratory also were positive with the mitochondrial markers. The results for four of these samples were validated by sequence analysis of the *Phytophthora* genus-specific amplicon and comparison with data from purified cultures of this pathogen. The mitochondrial marker system also identified 16 additional samples infected with other *Phytophthora* spp. that could not be identified with the ITS marker system (Martin and others 2004).

Chapter 3: The Disease Cycle

Background

The effective management of any plant disease is based on an understanding of the disease cycle, including the pathogen's modes of survival and dissemination, and the role of environmental factors in disease development. The disease cycle, or disease process, consists of several stages, including production of inoculum, dispersal of inoculum, establishment of infection (entry into the host), colonization (invasion), symptom development (interaction of the pathogen with the host), and survival. Those stages—except for symptoms, which were discussed in chapter 2—are discussed below for *Phytophthora ramorum* Werres, de Cock, and Man in't Veld.

A diagrammatic disease cycle for *P. ramorum* (Courtesy N. Ochiai; reproduced with permission from Parke and Lucas 2008) is presented in figure 1. Although at first glance the *P. ramorum* disease cycle appears complex because of the different habitats and range of hosts involved, it follows the basic steps of any plant disease cycle. In general, *Phytophthora* species that infect aerial parts of plants spread through production of asexual sporangia and zoospores. Survival structures such as chlamydospores, or sometimes sexually produced oospores, may also have a role in dissemination and spread in those species that produce one or both of these structures. Disseminated spores can then initiate infections of host tissue. The new infections can serve as another source of spores to begin the cycle again. Appropriate environmental conditions (temperature and relative humidity), as well as a means of pathogen survival (either as spores or mycelia), are necessary for each step of the cycle. Transport of infected host tissue or contaminated growing media or soil containing the pathogen can introduce the disease to new areas where the pathogen may establish if it can complete the cycle described above (Davidson and Shaw 2003).

Inoculum Production

This is the stage of the disease cycle where the pathogen produces a structure or structures to initiate infection.

Types of Inoculum

Like most *Phytophthora* spp., *P. ramorum* produces asexual sporangia, zoospores, and chlamydospores in culture and in nature (Parke and others 2002a; Rizzo and others 2002a, 2005; Werres and others 2001). Sexual structures—oogonia, antheridia, and oospores—have not yet been found in nature (see for example: Ivors and

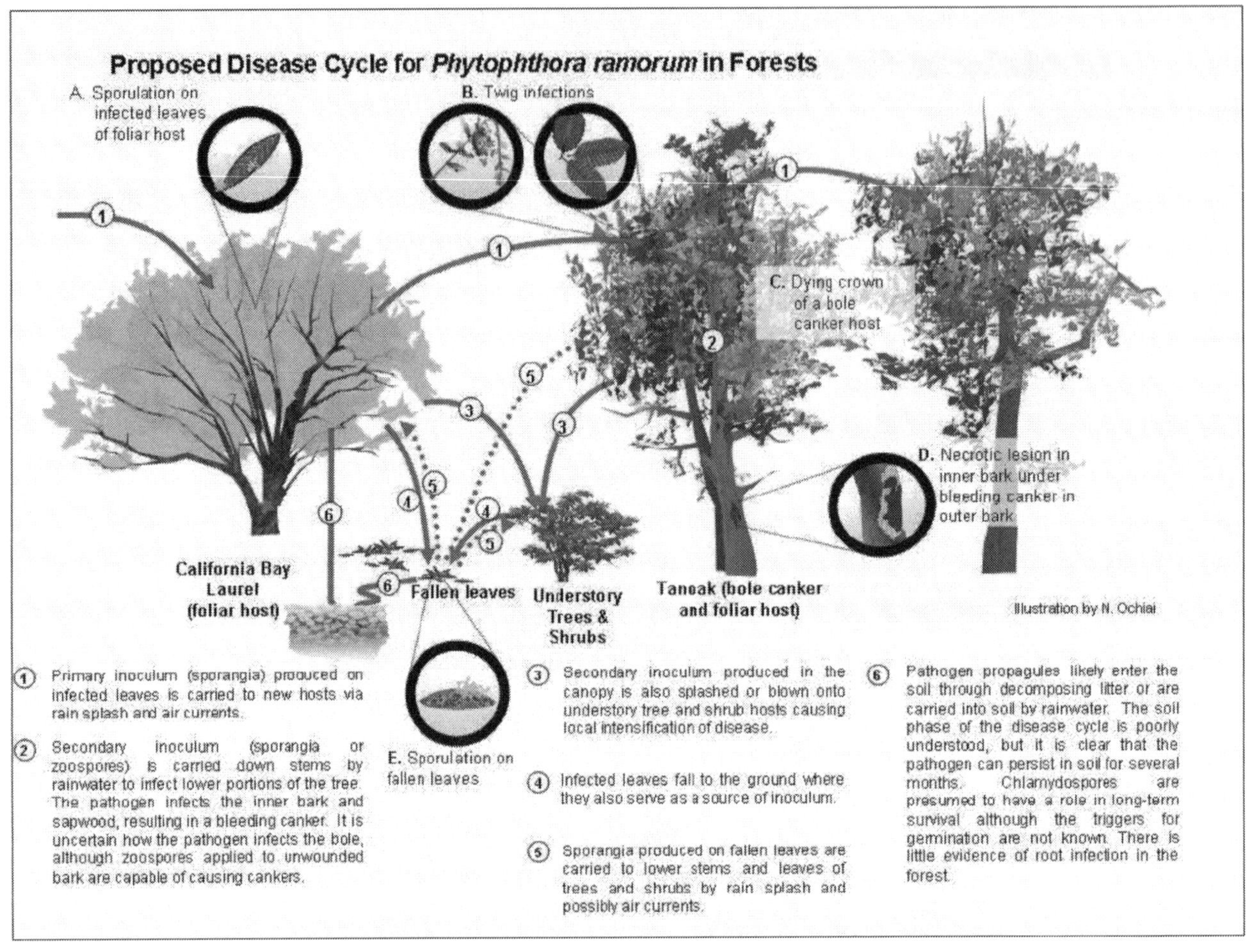

Figure 1—Proposed disease cycle for *Phytophthora ramorum* in forests. Source: Parke and Lucas 2008.

others 2006b, Prospero and others 2007). The production of sexual oospores has only been observed in the laboratory. The pathogen is heterothallic and pairing of opposite mating types is needed for sexual reproduction. In artificial pairings, oospores have been observed in plants and on agar medium (Boutet and Chandelier 2009, Brasier and Kirk 2004, Werres and Zielke 2003), but the mating system may not be fully functional (Boutet and Chandelier 2009, Brasier and others 2007).

Additional multihyphal reproductive structures, similar to sporodochia of mitosporic fungi, were produced by *P. ramorum* on fruits and adaxial leaf surfaces following inoculation (isolates or isolate source not stated) of some woody Mediterranean shrubs (strawberry tree [*Arbutus unedo* L.], carob bean [*Ceratonia siliqua* L.], bay laurel [*Laurus nobilis* L.], mastic [*Pistacia lentiscus* L.], Italian buckthorn [*Rhamnus alaternus* L.] and *Viburnum* tinus L.) (Moralejo and Descals 2006, Moralejo and others 2006). Occasionally sporangia and chlamydosori (packed clusters of chlamydospores) were formed on the stromata after emergence through the adaxial leaf surface. Although these structures have not been observed in nature, Moralejo and others (2006) suggested that the subepidermal position of the stroma initials may protect the pathogen from a dry atmosphere or solar radiation, or that they serve as over-summering survival structures.

Host Impacts on Sporulation

Sporulation can be affected by a variety of biotic and abiotic factors, including host and factors of the environment such as rainfall, temperature, light, and humidity.

Host and production of sporangia and chlamydospores—
The production of sporangia and chlamydospores differs with the foliar host; some hosts support rapid and prolific reproduction, whereas other hosts do not (table 4). Davidson and others (2002b, 2005b) found abundant sporangial formation on moistened leaves of infected California bay laurel (*Umbellularia californica* (Hook. & Arn.) Nutt.) and *Rhododendron* spp. within 72 hours in the laboratory. Chlamydospores were also observed on the surface of moistened bay leaves. Under natural conditions, chlamydospores are produced within host tissues and do not appear to be adapted for dispersal.

Parke and others (2002a) reported that the production of sporangia, zoospores, and chlamydospores of *P. ramorum* (source of isolates not mentioned) on inoculated leaf disks was greatest and most rapid on California bay laurel compared to other hosts tested (tanoak [*Lithocarpus densiflorus*], madrone [*Arbutus menziesii*] Pacific rhododendron [*Rhododendron macrophyllum*], evergreen huckleberry [*Vaccinium ovatum*]), and at the time nonhosts (vine maple [*Acer circinatum*], salal [*Gaultheria shallon*], red alder [*Alnus rubra*], Oregon white oak [*Quercus garryana*]); abundant sporangia and active zoospores were released within 24 hours, and zoospores continued to be released for several days (table 4). The authors found that tanoak also supported production of numerous sporangia and zoospores soon after infection, usually within 24 hours. On madrone leaf disks, only chlamydospores were produced. Sporangial production on other species tested ranged from a few to many over the course of several days, with chlamydospore production following. Of the nonhost species tested, inoculum production was most abundant on vine maple and salal (Parke and others 2002a). These two species have since been reported as occasional hosts in nature.

Detached-leaf assay tests in the United Kingdom (U.K.) (Turner and others 2005), using two EU1 European isolates (BBA 16/99 and 1604) and two (NA1) North American isolates (0-217 and 1004.1) of *P. ramorum* on ornamental and understory hosts, also found that sporulation potential differs with host species

Table 4—Host leaves supporting sporulation of *Phytophthora ramorum*

Host	Propagule type		Reference
	Sporangia	Chlamydospores	
California/Oregon hosts			Parke and others 2002a; Davidson and others 2002b, 2005b
California bay laurel (*Umbellularia californica* (Hook. & Arn.) Nutt.)	+	+	
Tanoak (*Lithocarpus densiflorus* (Hook. & Arn.) Rehder)	+	+	
Ornamental rhododendron (*Rhododendron* sp.)	+	-	
Pacific rhododendron (*Rhododendron macrophyllum* D. Don ex G. Don)	+	+	
Evergreen huckleberry (*Vaccinium ovatum* Pursh)	+	+	
Vine maple (*Acer circinatum* Pursh)	+	+	
Salal (*Gaultheria shallon* Pursh)	+	+	
Red alder (*Alnus rubra* Bong.)	+	+	
Oregon white oak (*Quercus garryanna* Dougl. ex Hook.)	+	+	
Madrone (*Arbutus menziesii* Pursh)	-	+	
Coast redwood (*Sequoia sempervirens* (Lamb. ex D. Don) Endl.)	+	+	Maloney and others 2005, 2007
Coast live oak (*Quercus agrifolia* Née)	+	+	Vettraino and others 2008
Europe, ornamental and understory hosts			DEFRA 2006, Turner and others 2005
Lilac (*Syringa vulgaris* L.)	+	+	
Pieris (*Pieris japonica* (Thunb.) D. Don ex G. Don)	+	-	
Mountain laurel (*Kalmia latifolia* L.)	+	-	
Camellia (*Camellia japonica* L.)	+	-	
California bay laurel (*Umbellularia californica* (Hook. & Arn.) Nutt.)	+	+	
Ponticum rhododendron (*Rhododendron ponticum* L.)	+	+	
Dog rose (*Rosa canina* L.)	+	+	
Black elderberry (*Sambucus nigra* L.)	+	-	
European ash (*Fraxinus excelsior* L.)	+	+	
Honeysuckle (*Lonicera periclymenum* L.)	+	-	
Sycamore maple (*Acer pseudoplatanus* L.)	+	-	
Wych elm (*Ulmus glabra* Huds.)	+	+	
Crabapple (*Malus sylvestris* (L.) Mill.)	+	-	
English yew (*Taxus baccata* L.)	+	+	
Bramble blackberry (*Rubus fruticosus* L.)	+	-	
English ivy (*Hedera helix* L.)	+	-	
European cranberrybush (*Viburnum opulus* L.)	+	+	
Lingonberry (*Vaccinium vitis-idaea* L.)			
Bearberry (*Arctostaphylos uva-ursi* (L.) Spreng.)			

Table 4—Host leaves supporting sporulation of *Phytophthora ramorum* (continued)

Host	Propagule type		Reference
	Sporangia	Chlamydospores	
European tree species			Denman and others 2006
Horse chestnut (*Aesculus hippocastanum* L.)	+		
Sweet chestnut (*Castanea sativa* Mill.)	+		
European ash (*Fraxinus excelsior* L.)	+		
Turkey oak (*Quercus cerris* L.)	+		
Holm oak (*Quercus ilex* L.)	+		
Sessile oak (*Quercus petraea* (Matt.) Liebl.)	+		
English oak (*Quercus robur* L.)	+		
Common lilac (*Syringa vulgaris* L.)	+		
English elm (*Ulmus procera* Salisb.)	+		
Catawba rhododendron (*Rhododendron catawbiense* Michx.)	+		
Woody Mediterranean species			Moralejo and Hernández 2002
Holm oak (*Quercus ilex* L.)	+	+	
Italian buckthorn (*Rhamnus alaternus* L.)	+	-	
Strawberry tree (*Arbutus unedo* L.)	+	+	
Laurustinus viburnum (*Viburnum tinus* L.)	+	+	
Mastic tree (*Pistacia lentiscus* L.)	+	+	

(table 4). The two NA1 isolates were generally less vigorous in sporulation than the two EU1 isolates. Chlamydospore production was generally less abundant than sporangial production (Turner and others 2005).

In detached-leaf assays to determine sporulation on the leaves of European tree species (Denman and others 2006), European ash (*Fraxinus excelsior*) supported consistently high sporulation, whereas significantly fewer sporangia were observed on horse chestnut (*Aesculus hippocastanum*) and sessile oak (*Quercus petraea*) (table 4). In tests on English oak (*Q. robur*), holm oak (*Q. ilex*), catawba rhododendron (*R. catawbiense*) and turkey oak (*Q. cerris*), holm oak and catawba rhododendron supported more sporangia than English oak and turkey oak. Differences among the EU1 and NA1 isolates were not mentioned.

The results of detached-leaf assays using plants of Mediterranean evergreen oak forest and maquis-type vegetation (Moralejo and Hernández 2002) are presented in table 4.

Mycelial colonization and chlamydospore formation in xylem tissue beneath infected bark has been observed in some hosts (Brown and Brasier 2007, Parke and others 2008). Sporangial production on attached, infected bark of tree hosts probably does not occur, or occurs rarely and is insignificant (Davidson and others 2005b, 2008; Garbelotto and others 2003a; Tjosvold and others 2002c). However, sporulation has been observed on detached bark from tanoak and coast live oak (*Q. agrifolia*) cankers floated on water (Davidson and Shaw 2003).

Epidemiologically important hosts—
Phytophthora ramorum apparently does not sporulate on bleeding bole cankers of bark hosts. (Davidson and others 2002b; DEFRA 2005a, 2006; Garbelotto and others 2003a). Sporangia occasionally observed in ooze from bleeding trunk cankers are considered external contaminants. In a study of infected coast live oaks and tanoaks in California (Tjosvold and others 2002c), less than 2 percent of the isolations attempted from the ooze were positive, and no spores were observed in the ooze. All tests for inoculum production on coast live oak cankers (incubation of cankers in growth chambers; pieces of cankered bark in moist chambers), were negative for spore production (Davidson and others 2005b), and *P. ramorum* was not found on the surfaces and exudates of cankers of infected coast live oak bark. Because sporulation on oak wood is apparently rare, true oak species have been regarded as noncontagious dead ends in the life cycle of the pathogen (Davidson and others 2005b, Garbelotto and Rizzo 2005). Tree hosts that are susceptible to trunk infections producing bleeding cankers, but not susceptible to foliar infections, do not provide their own inoculum, and are therefore referred to as terminal tree hosts.

Several tree canker hosts are also foliar hosts. Tanoak is a canker and foliar host that produces inoculum on leaves. Vettraino and others (2008) have reported *P. ramorum* infecting leaves of several coast live oak saplings in the forest, and the potential of coast live oak foliage to produce sporangia and chlamydospores after inoculation in vitro (table 4). The epidemiological role of those leaf infections in the field is not known.

In California mixed-evergreen forests where coast live oak and California bay laurel are the dominant species, infections on California bay laurel are the main producer of *P. ramorum* inoculum (sporangia) (Davidson and others 2005b, 2008). Sporangia are also produced on infected shoots and leaves of tanoak and coast redwood (*Sequoia sempervirens*) in coastal redwood forests (dominated by coast redwood, tanoak, and California bay laurel), but the sporulation rate in California bay laurel is significantly higher than for tanoak (Davidson and others 2008).

In California forests, sporangia produced on tanoak are a significant source of inoculum in some situations (Davidson and others 2005b, Maloney and others 2005). In plots with few California bay laurel stems, high disease levels were associated with the presence of understory tanoaks (Maloney and others 2005). The pathogen has been confirmed on tanoak in a Bishop pine (*Pinus muricata* D. Don)-tanoak forest at a campground within a state park just north of Fort Bragg in coastal northern California. California bay laurel is not found within or adjacent to the campground area (COMTF 2009). Pacific rhododendron is also considered a significant spore-producing host, but it produces lower numbers of sporangia than California bay laurel or tanoak shoots and leaves (Davidson and others 2002b). The pathogen sporulates on new infections on coast redwood needles and shoots (Maloney and others 2007) (table 4), but at significantly lower levels than on California bay laurel leaves and tanoak leaves and shoots (Garbelotto 2004, Garbelotto and Rizzo 2005).

Studies in California have shown a clear association between the presence of the foliar host California bay laurel and *P. ramorum* infection on true oak species (Kelly and Meentemeyer 2002, Swiecki and Bernhardt 2001), indicating the importance of California bay laurel in the disease cycle of the pathogen in California forests. The presence and abundance of California bay laurel within plots was identified as a significant plot-level predictor of disease risk (Swiecki and Bernhardt 2001). Several related variables, including counts and percentage canopy cover of California bay laurel trees within the study plot, were significant predictors of *P. ramorum* risk (Swiecki and Bernhardt 2004), showing that disease risk increases with increasing California bay laurel density and cover within 8 m of a coast live oak. Disease risk and severity were greatest at California bay laurel foliage-coast live oak trunk distances of 1.5 m or less, and were minimal at a distance of 10 m or more (Swiecki and Bernhardt 2008). Bay laurel cover within 2.5 m of the trunk was the best single predictor of disease risk and severity. The results suggest that removing California bay laurel from within 2.5 m of the trunk of a susceptible oak will greatly reduce, but not eliminate, the risk of disease.

In addition to the association between the presence of California bay laurel and the risk of *P. ramorum* infection, higher abundance of California bay laurel is associated with greater levels of infection (Condeso and Meentemeyer 2007, Maloney and others 2005, Meentemeyer and others 2008b).

In general, coast live oak and California black oak (*Quercus kelloggii* Newb.) mortality increases with increasing amounts of inoculum on leaves of California bay laurel (Rank and others 2010). Although genetic variation in susceptibility to *P. ramorum* occurs in California bay laurel, local environmental factors (especially temperature and moisture) rather than genetics mediates expression of susceptibility in nature (Anacker and others 2008).

Although not a common occurrence in California forests, establishment of *P. ramorum* in tanoak forests without California bay laurel appears to be the typical situation in forests in southwestern Oregon (Rizzo and others 2005). Initial infection and inoculum production in Oregon tanoak stands apparently occurs on leaves and twigs in the upper crowns of tanoak trees. Examination of tanoak trees with green foliage but with bole cankers and adjacent green trees without bole cankers, found *P. ramorum* leaf and twig lesions in upper crowns of 11 of 15 tanoak trees with bole cankers, and from 3 of 12 nearby canker-free trees. Infected rhododendron and huckleberry in the understory were found only in the immediate vicinity of cankered trees (Hansen and others 2006b).

In Europe, a parallel situation exists, with *Rhododendron ponticum* serving as the key sporulating host from which inoculum can spread to susceptible tree hosts. Most tree stem infections in the United Kingdom (principally on European beech [*Fagus sylvatica* L.]) and individuals of several oak species) and The Netherlands (European beech and American northern red oak, *Quercus rubra* L.) have been associated with direct proximity to infected *R. ponticum* plants in the understory (Brasier and Jung 2006, Brasier and others 2006a, Brown and others 2006, Sansford and Woodall 2007). In addition to *R. ponticum*, other hosts (holm oak, sweet chestnut, bilberry [*Vaccinium myrtillus* L.]) have been suggested as being potentially significant sources of inoculum for tree infection in northern Europe (Inman and others 2005, Sansford and others 2009). In southern Europe, foliar hosts including holm oak, Italian buckthorn, and mastic tree produce significant inoculum (Moralejo and others 2007) and may contribute to increased disease levels in Mediterranean forests and in maquis shrubland (Sansford and others 2009).

Environmental Factors Affecting Sporulation and Germination

Laboratory studies—

Phytophthora ramorum produces spores under a broad range of temperature and light conditions. In a laboratory study of four U.S. isolates (NA1) and three European isolates (EU1) of *P. ramorum*, chlamydospores were produced by U.S. isolates at 10 to 28 °C (optimum of 14 to 24 °C, depending on isolate), and by EU isolates at 10 to 26 °C (optimum of 22 to 26 °C), with one isolate producing chlamydospores at 6 °C (Englander and others 2006). Sporangia were produced at all temperatures tested: 10 to 30 °C (optimum of 16 to 22 °C, depending on isolate) for U.S. isolates, and 6 to 26 °C (optimum of 22 °C) for EU isolates. The U.S. isolates grew less and produced fewer sporangia and chlamydospores when exposed to increasing doses of near-UV radiation and visible radiation. The EU isolates were exposed to near-UV only, which significantly reduced growth of one of three isolates, but had no significant effect on spore production (Englander and others 2006).

Differences in humidity had the greatest effect on sporangial production and zoospore germination in vitro, whereas sporangial germination was less sensitive (Turner and Jennings 2006, 2008). Maximum levels of sporangial production and zoospore germination occurred at 100 percent humidity.

In laboratory trials, zoospore production on California bay laurel leaves was influenced by temperature (Davidson and others 2005b). Zoospores were produced at 5, 10, 15, 20, and 25 °C, but not at 30 °C, with the highest numbers released at 15 to 20 °C. Turner and Jennings (2006) reported that optimum temperature for sporulation and zoospore germination ranged from 20 to 30 °C depending upon experimental conditions.

On agar media (V8, cornmeal with antibiotics [CAR], and water agar plates), chlamydospore germination rate (0.5 to 10.7 percent) (isolate source not stated) after 24 hours was low and variable compared with published chlamydospore germination rates of other *Phytophthora* species (Smith and Hansen 2008).

Forests/woodlands—

In California mixed-evergreen forests, sporulation and production of inoculum are seasonal, largely dependent on rainfall events and temperature. In California, *P. ramorum* is commonly recovered from rain traps from December into the spring months, peaking during warm rains in May (Davidson and others 2005b). At one study site in a mixed-evergreen forest, sporulation of *P. ramorum* was correlated with rain events and air temperature (Davidson and others 2005b). Detectable levels of *P. ramorum* inoculum were present largely during the period of winter rains, and were absent during the hot, dry summer (Davidson and others 2005b). The authors observed a lag period between the start of the rains and the onset of detectable inoculum production at the site, with the highest levels of spore production occurring at the end of the rainy season. Possible explanations include the need for some time for inoculum to build up as California bay laurel leaves become infected, or the occurrence of lower air temperatures during the beginning of the rainy season, which would inhibit sporangial production (Davidson and others 2005b, Fichtner and others 2006).

Recovery of *P. ramorum* from rain traps at five plots in a redwood/tanoak forest type did not show a lag period, with sporangial production beginning soon after the start of the rainy season (Maloney and others 2002, Rizzo and others 2005). Explanations for the sporangial production in redwood/tanoak woodlands being earlier than in mixed-evergreen forests include less shedding of California bay laurel leaves and more active lesions on California bay laurel leaves after the hot summer period because of the wetter, cooler conditions in the redwood/tanoak forest type (Davidson and others 2005a).

In contrast, *P. ramorum* inoculum (most likely dehiscent sporangia) in infested forests of southwest Oregon can be produced throughout the year whenever there is water available (Hansen and others 2008). The authors found inoculum on infected tanoak leaves and twigs during periods of leaf wetness, even in extended periods without rain but only fog, any time during the year.

Spore production varies yearly as well as seasonally. In California forests, relatively high levels of winter/spring rainfall extending into early summer are often followed by high levels of disease (Davidson and others 2005b, Rizzo and others 2005). Epidemic mortality of coast live oak occurred 1 to 2 years after increased spring rainfall in 1998 and again in 2005 (El Niño years) (Davidson and others 2005b, Rizzo and others 2005). In Oregon, Kanaskie and others (2008a) attributed an unexpected and large amount of disease expansion from eradication sites to two consecutive years of unusually wet spring and early summer weather. Hansen and others (2008) reported that late May rains following a dry April triggered an infection event at two sites, resulting in dieback and new growth of tanoak and rhododendron, and numerous new *P. ramorum* bole infections. These data point to the importance of changes in climate in the establishment and spread of a largely aerial pathogen such as *P. ramorum* (Rizzo and others 2005).

Inoculum Dispersal

Phytophthora ramorum inoculum produced on host tissue may be spread or dispersed by various means. Local dispersal is by rain splash or wind-driven rain, intermediate dispersal is thought to occur by turbulent air, and long-distance dispersal occurs primarily through the movement of infected plant material moved in trade; movement of contaminated soil or spread in watercourses can also result in long-distance dispersal. Other undetermined mechanisms are also likely.

Local Dispersal

Local dispersal occurs primarily through rain splash of sporangia (Davidson and others 2002b). Rain splash from leaves and soil is the primary means by which inoculum is dispersed from infected leaves in the shrub canopy to tree stems or from leaves in the overstory to hosts below. Infested soil may serve as primary inoculum for foliar infection of California bay laurel and tanoak by splash dispersal during rain events (Fichtner and others 2009a). Infection of conifer seedlings and rhododendron placed under infected California bay laurel occurred only during periods of precipitation and only when the plants were within 4.4 m of the infested overstory (Chastagner and others 2008d).

Wind Dispersal

In California, inoculum has been shown to be dispersed up to 15 m during wind-driven events (Davidson and others 2005b). High winds associated with storm events may blow raindrops with spores even farther, thus serving as a means of longer distance dispersal (Davidson and others 2005b). In the United Kingdom, *P. ramorum* has been detected in spore traps at least 50 m from the nearest source of inoculum (Turner 2007b, Turner and others 2008a).

In southwest Oregon, most new infections occur within 300 m of infected trees, but rare events lead to dispersal up to 4 km (Hansen 2008a). Hansen (2008a, 2008b) has suggested that the observed dispersal over hundreds of meters in Oregon forests could be explained by turbulent dry air dispersal. Hansen hypothesized that clearing weather following spring rains results in overnight dew and fog, with the lifting of fog as day progresses resulting in lofting of sporangia; the sporangia are carried by prevailing winds and settle on fog-moistened host leaves in the evening to initiate infection.

Long-Distance Dispersal

Movement of host material—

Movement of infected plant material (for example, wood, green material products, and especially nursery stock) is a primary means of long-distance spread of many pathogens, including *P. ramorum*. International trade in ornamental plants is postulated as a main driver for the initial emergence of *P. ramorum* (Davidson and Shaw 2003). Local, national, and international trade in plants and plant products is a major pathway by which *P. ramorum* arrives in new areas and spreads once it reaches them. It is the main pathway for long-distance spread of the pathogen, which is carried on foliage and stems and also in the associated growing medium (see for example, Prospero and others 2009). In the United States, the dispersal of the pathogen nationwide from one nursery has been documented (Frankel 2008, Garbelotto and Rizzo 2005, Stokstad 2004), and is discussed in chapter 2. All three identified lineages of this pathogen have been detected in some U.S. nurseries (Ivors and others 2006b), indicating that the commercial nursery trade is unknowingly aiding the movement, and probably the introduction, of *P. ramorum* into North America (Garbelotto 2004, Goss and others 2009b, Mascheretti and others 2008, Prospero and others 2009). In Europe, *P. ramorum* was introduced to Majorca, Spain, via a shipment of infected rhododendrons, and many of the infections found in nurseries in the United Kingdom can be traced to plant transport from other nurseries (Davidson and Shaw 2003). *Phytophthora ramorum* has continued to be found on material having a plant passport (see chapter 5) in England and Wales (Slawson and others 2008), supporting the view that the pathogen is continuing to move in trade.

Watercourses—

Propagules of *P. ramorum* are dispersed readily in stream water. Contaminated watercourses represent a potential pathway for pathogen spread, especially if water is used for the irrigation of susceptible plants. Davidson and others (2005b) detected inoculum by baiting stream water 4 to 6 km from an inoculum source in a coast live oak-bay laurel forest. The pathogen is regularly recovered from streams draining infested sites in Oregon, even 5 years after eradication treatment (Goheen and others 2008). The U.S. Department of Agriculture, Forest Service (USDA FS) has developed a national *P. ramorum* stream monitoring program for the early detection of *P. ramorum* infestation in the United States (Oak and others 2006, 2008). As a result of these activities, 12 first detections of *P. ramorum* have been made in seven states from 2006 through 2008 (Oak and others 2010). In the United Kingdom, *P. ramorum* can be found in watercourses at outbreak sites (Turner 2007b). At an infested site in West Sussex, *P. ramorum* was recovered from the river catchment area originating from the site, but inoculum disappeared within a few kilometers downstream of the outbreak source (Turner 2007b).

Monitoring of inoculum levels in water has shown seasonal patterns in amounts of inoculum in California and the United Kingdom. In California, the pathogen has been detected in water samples taken from streams during the winter/spring rainy season, but only at reduced levels in the summer months (Davidson and others 2005b). Tjosvold and others (2002b) recovered *P. ramorum* very rarely (on one occasion in September from one river following a short rain in the river's drainage) during the dry summer months. In a study using rhododendron leaf baits placed in California streams within a redwood/tanoak forest (Maloney and others 2002), detection was reported in both spring and summer months, regardless of any rain event. At U.K. study sites, the highest levels of inoculum, as detected by rhododendron leaf baits, generally occurred in winter and spring and the lowest levels in summer (DEFRA 2007, Turner 2007b, Turner and others 2008a). In another U.K. study, baiting of watercourses within a garden infested with *P. ramorum* generally showed low levels of *P. ramorum* in the summer and winter, but samples taken in the spring, and to a lesser extent in the autumn, were frequently positive for *P. ramorum* (Lockley and others 2008). In contrast, no seasonal effect on recovery from streams has been found in Oregon (Sutton and others 2009).

Soil—

Human movement of soil infested with *P. ramorum* is a means of local as well as longer distance dispersal. Although there is no direct evidence of new *P. ramorum* infections occurring in forest situations as a result of human movement of infested soil, soil attached to hikers' boots and vehicles has been shown to contain the pathogen. In studies conducted in Sonoma County California, symptom levels and spread of the pathogen were greater in areas with high human activity (Cooper and Cushman 2006; Cushman and Meentemeyer 2006a, 2006b). In the spring rainy periods, baiting for *P. ramorum* yielded a 40 to 60 percent recovery rate for trail soil and 40 to 95 percent recovery rate for soil removed from hikers' shoes; the pathogen was not recovered from trail soil or shoe soil in the dry summer period (Tjosvold and others 2002a). Davidson and others (2005b) also demonstrated human spread of infested soil during the rainy season. When they baited soil taken from hikers' shoes after they walked a preserve trail in Sonoma County California, the pathogen was recovered from 7 of 15 samples in one trial and from 5 of 15 samples in a second trial. Hikers dispersed *P. ramorum* in soil on their shoes a distance of at least 60 to 100 m into areas of a nature reserve in California that lacked local inoculum sources (Cushman and others 2008). If the soil was kept moist, *P. ramorum* could be isolated from the soil up to 72 hours after the infested soil was picked up by hikers (Cushman and others 2008).

In U.K. studies, *Phytophthora* spp. were present in about 30 percent of samples collected from boots prior to disinfection upon leaving woodland outbreak sites. The most commonly occurring species was *P. citricola*, but 10 to 15 percent of the samples contained *P. ramorum* or *P. kernoviae* (Webber and Rose 2008).

Other agents—

Although it has been suggested that insects may vector spores or sporangia of the pathogen (McPherson and others 2002b), no evidence of insect transmission has been found (DEFRA 2005a, Kanaskie and others 2002, McPherson and others 2002b). Birds have also been suggested as vectors, but as with insects, no evidence of birds serving as vectors of *P. ramorum* has been demonstrated. In laboratory studies (Parke and others 2008), feces from gray garden slugs (*Deroceras reticulatum*) that were fed cultures of *P. ramorum* or allowed to graze on infested leaves contained viable chlamydospores, sporangia, and hyphae of the pathogen. Under controlled conditions, *P. ramorum* was transmitted by slugs or their feces to rhododendron leaves and to tanoak leaves and logs (Parke and others 2008).

Dispersal in nurseries—

Local dispersal of *P. ramorum* in nurseries and garden centers occurs by many of the same means as in the forest. The pathogen may be transmitted through plant-to-plant contact, rain or overhead irrigation splash dispersal, irrigation and the movement of infested debris, growing media, and freestanding water or surface water runoff. In experiments designed to compare relatively long-distance (1 to 4 m) and short-distance (pot-to-pot) dispersal among rhododendrons in simulated nursery conditions, new infections were only detected on plants within a short distance (adjacent and up to 30 cm away) of a centrally located artificially infected plant (Tjosvold and others 2006b). No infection was detected in the long-distance experiments and no inoculum was detected in rain traps located 1 to 4 m away from the infected plant during rain events. Note, however, that sporangia have been detected up to 5 m from infested forest canopy (Davidson and others 2002b), demonstrating that height of release influences distance of splash. Werres and others (2007) demonstrated survival of *P. ramorum* in nursery water reservoirs containing contaminated irrigation water during all seasons. Disease symptoms on rhododendron were observed in as little as 7 days after irrigation with contaminated water.

Infection

In the infection stage of the disease cycle, the pathogen germinates, penetrates the host, and establishes a parasitic relationship with the host plant.

Environment

Phytophthora ramorum is considered a cool-temperature organism, with optimal growth between 18 and 22 °C (Werres and others 2001). Germination of *P. ramorum* sporangia may be direct, by emergence of hyphae through the sporangial wall, or indirect, by formation and release of motile zoospores. With many species of *Phytophthora*, indirect germination predominates at temperatures below about 12 °C, and direct germination occurs at higher temperatures (Ribeiro 1983). The presence of free water or high humidity favors zoospore germination and infection. Maximum levels of zoospore germination occurred at 100 percent humidity or water potentials of 1; a broad range of temperatures (10 to 30 °C depending on the water potential) supported zoospore germination (Kessel and others 2007, Turner and Jennings 2008). The infection rate for California bay laurel leaves averaged 92 percent at 18 °C, but only 50 percent at 12 °C and 37 percent at 30 °C (Garbelotto and others 2003a).

Free water enhances infection. A minimum of 6 to 12 consecutive hours of free water is a prerequisite for the infection of California bay laurel leaves (Garbelotto and others 2003a). Infection by zoospores tends to occur on susceptible plant parts where water accumulates, such as at leaf tips.

Infection Courts

Openings in host tissue—either natural openings such as stomata or lenticels, or wounds—are entry courts for hyphae originating from germinated spores (Florance 2002, 2006; Inman and others 2005). The likely sites of initial infection on *Camellia* leaves were stomata on adaxial surfaces, as well as subepidermal oil glands (Geltz and others 2006).

Studies by Lewis and Parke (2006) suggested that wounded tissue of *Rhododendron* leaves was more susceptible to infection than nonwounded. Using scanning electron microscopy, they observed that germinating cysts were more abundant at wound sites than at stomatal openings. A study in the United Kingdom (DEFRA 2005a) found that infection occurred when lower leaf surfaces, where stomata occur, were inoculated, but did not occur when unwounded upper leaf surfaces with no stomata were inoculated. A separate experiment (DEFRA 2005a) found that some hosts (*Camellia japonica*) required leaf wounding for infection to occur, whereas others (*R. ponticum*, *R. catawbiense*, *Fraxinus excelsior*) did not. Hansen and others (2005) reported many species developed substantial leaf necrosis in leaf dip inoculation, but few or no leaf symptoms from plant dip inoculation, the difference possibly being—in addition to a higher effective inoculum dose as well as more favorable incubation conditions—the wounds provided on detached leaves.

Phytophthora ramorum zoospores are capable of directly penetrating bark of mature trees. Brown and others (2006) reported that *P. ramorum* zoospores were able to penetrate intact European beech bark. Wounding of mature European beech (*Fagus sylvatica* L.) logs, American red oak (*Quercus rubra* L.), sweet chestnut, English oak, Sitka spruce (*Picea sitchensis* (Bong.) Carrière) and Douglas-fir (*Pseudotsuga menziesii* (Mirb.) Franco) was not necessary for the infection of logs from mature trees by zoospores (Webber 2004). Inoculations resulted in infection and phloem necrosis development 2 weeks after inoculation of intact bark in the absence of any wound. Infection occurred most frequently in the thin-barked species (American red oak, sweet chestnut, European beech).

Bark of saplings of some tree hosts is less susceptible to direct bark infection than bark of mature trees (DEFRA 2005a). Three-year-old saplings of various species (Douglas-fir, sweet chestnut, American red oak, English oak, Sitka spruce, wild cherry (*Prunus avium* (L.) L.), European beech, horse chestnut, small-leaved linden (*Tilia cordata* Mill.), European ash, sycamore maple, and hornbeam (*Carpinus betulus* L.) were only infected when wounded, and trees were more susceptible in the summer than in the winter, with Sitka spruce, horse chestnut, and hornbeam not developing symptoms following winter inoculations (DEFRA 2005a).

Swiecki and Bernhardt (2006) reported that bark thickness and unweathered brown tissue within bark fissures of coast live oak were positively correlated with *P. ramorum* disease risk. The authors suggested that those areas of bark expansion tissue may represent relatively rapidly expanding regions of the outer bark in fast-growing trees that may be more easily breached by *P. ramorum* zoospores. Alternative suggestions include that the outer periderm in these areas may be so thin that plant substances can diffuse from them when the bark surface is wet, which may attract *P. ramorum* zoospores, increasing the chance of infection, or that the bark fissures may be wetter longer than other areas of the bark, which would also favor infection.

Although *P. ramorum* has not been reported to cause root infection on mature trees, several reports of root infection by the pathogen occur in the literature. Root infection of tanoak seedlings in the forest has been reported (Parke and others 2006c). Lewis and others (2004) and Parke and Lewis (2007) reported root infection of 3-year-old rhododendron following replanting of the cuttings into potting soil containing inoculum of *P. ramorum*, indicating transmission of *P. ramorum* from infested potting media to stems via infected, symptomless root tissue. Isolation of *P. ramorum* from healthy-appearing rhododendron roots 4 weeks after inoculation of soils with chlamydospores was reported by Colburn and others (2005). Bienapfl and others (2005) isolated *P. ramorum* (NA2 lineage) from asymptomatic roots of commercially grown rhododendron obtained from a California commercial nursery. The pathogen has been isolated from asymptomatic roots in laboratory-inoculated host plants (Shishkoff 2007). Artificial inoculation of *Viburnum tinus* led to the formation of chlamydospores in root tissue (Shishkoff 2008), and *P. ramorum* has been reported (Fichtner and others 2008a, 2009b) from roots of naturally infected *R. ponticum* shrubs in U.K. woodlands.

Host Etiology

Host leaf age—

Host leaf age affects susceptibility (De Dobbelaere and others 2008, Hansen and others 2005). In detached-leaf dip assays, young leaves of tanoak and California bay laurel (known as myrtlewood in Oregon) were more susceptible than mature leaves (Hansen and others 2005). In a test of 80 different *Rhododendron* species and cultivars, De Dobbelaere and others (2008) found that leaf age affected susceptibility to *P. ramorum*. When using wounded leaves, young leaves of all cultivars tested showed a higher level of susceptibility than mature leaves. However, when nonwounded leaves were used, young leaves of some cultivars were less susceptible than older leaves. This effect was correlated with the presence of hairs on the young leaves of those cultivars, which probably form a barrier to the zoospores and prevent tissue penetration.

Temperature exposure—
Exposing *Rhododendron* plants to high temperatures for several hours before collection of the leaves decreased susceptibility in most experiments (De Dobbelaere and others 2008). The authors suggest that the increase in temperature may have resulted in stomatal closure, which may have reduced penetration capacity.

Seasonal Variation of Log Susceptibility

Hansen and others (2005) reported smaller lesions following *P. ramorum* inoculation on tanoak logs harvested in January than on tanoak logs harvested in March, September, or November, whereas lesions on Douglas-fir inoculated in January were larger than at other times of the year. Brasier and Kirk (2001) observed similar seasonal variation in susceptibility of various trees to log inoculations with other *Phytophthora* spp. They concluded that trees in the United Kingdom were most susceptible in late summer and fall, and essentially immune in April.

Inoculum Pressure

The amount of inoculum (inoculum pressure) affects infection potential. Differences in susceptibility with different levels of *P. ramorum* inoculum have been reported (DEFRA 2005a, Hansen and others 2005). For example, at low inoculum levels (1.3×10^3 zoospores/ml), common elderberry (*Sambucus nigra*), lilac (*Syringa vulgaris*), California bay laurel and honeysuckle (*Lonicera periclymenum* L.) were not infected in detached leaf assays with unwounded leaves. However, when the amount of inoculum level was increased (2.3×10^5 zoospores/ml), 67 to 100 percent of the leaves inoculated became infected (DEFRA 2005a). The same study (DEFRA 2005a) found that unwounded leaves of *C. japonica* remained uninfected at both low and high inoculum pressures, but 33 percent of wounded leaves were infected at the low inoculum pressure and 100 percent at the high inoculum pressure. Hansen and others (2005) reported that inoculum dose affected susceptibility in detached-leaf assays, with higher zoospore concentrations generally resulting in more symptoms.

Colonization (Invasion)

The invasion stage of the disease cycle occurs when the pathogen grows on or in the host and obtains nutrients from it.

Following entry through the bark of woody hosts, hyphae of *P. ramorum* grow within the phloem and cambial tissues, and then into xylem tissues (Brown and

Brasier 2007, Parke and others 2007, Rizzo and others 2002a). Xylem colonization is the norm. Rizzo and others (2002) noted that infection on *Quercus* spp. and tanoak appeared to begin in the outer bark, progress to the cambium, and eventually reach the xylem. Discoloration was generally more extensive in the cambium and secondary phloem tissues than in the xylem; typically black discoloration extended less than 1 mm into xylem tissues, but was occasionally observed up to 3 cm into the xylem. Brown and Brasier (2007) found that *P. ramorum* commonly occupies xylem beneath phloem lesions, that the pathogen can penetrate xylem tissue, and that it spreads in xylem tissue ahead of phloem lesions. Parke and others (2007) demonstrated that the pathogen colonized tanoak sapwood, and then spread through xylem vessels. Hyphae were abundant in the xylem vessels, ray parenchyma, and fiber tracheids; chlamydospores were observed in the vessels. The authors found reduced sap flux and specific conductivity in infected tissues compared to noninfected, and suggested that the reduction may result from increased embolism caused by *P. ramorum* infection, the presence of fungal structures, and the increased abundance of tyloses present in the vessels. They further suggested that the reduced stem water transport may contribute to crown mortality associated with *P. ramorum* infection. Further studies (Collins and others 2009) found that infection by *P. ramorum* induces tyloses in the xylem vessels of tanoak stems and demonstrated that tylosis formation is associated with reduced hydraulic conductivity of the sapwood.

Several studies have examined *P. ramorum* colonization of *Rhododendron*. Pogoda and Werres (2004) found that *P. ramorum* colonized the cortex, phloem, xylem, and pith of the necrotic zone. The authors also found hyphae in the cortex and pith of healthy-looking material about 1 cm below visible discoloration; chlamydospores were only observed in the necrotic zone where they developed mainly in the cortical parenchyma. This study also showed that *P. ramorum* can grow both intra- and intercellularly, but chlamydospores were only observed in the intercellular spaces.

Using epifluorescence microscopy, Riedel and others (2008) found *P. ramorum* hyphae in the cortex and pith of infected *Rhododendron* plants when discoloration was present. In healthy-looking stem and root segments located adjacent to the discolored areas, hyphae were found most often in the secondary xylem. With one exception, chlamydospores were only located in discolored parts of infected *Rhododendron* plants, being present in the cortex (stem) and palisade mesophyll (leaf). Less frequently, chlamydospores were observed in the pith of necrotic stem segments. Using the same epifluorescence microscopy technique, Parke and Lewis

(2007) observed attraction of zoospores to wounds and root primordia of *Rhododendron* tissue culture plantlets in vitro, and colonization of the cortex and vascular tissues of roots and stems, including the xylem.

Survival

The disease potential for a pathogen, including *P. ramorum*, is partially dependent on its ability to survive during conditions unfavorable for growth and reproduction. Like most species of *Phytophthora*, *P. ramorum* survives during conditions unfavorable for growth—such as hot, dry summer months in California—in host tissues or in various nonhost substrates (such as organic matter, soil, and potting media) as hyphae or as asexual structures. For most species of *Phytophthora*, chlamydospores are the typical survival structures in the disease cycle.

Survival in Vitro

In moist conditions, zoospores and chlamydospores of *P. ramorum* remain viable for at least 1 month, with chlamydospores probably able to survive much longer (Davidson and others 2002b). Zoospores and chlamydospores did not germinate on a selective medium after 30 minutes on dry filter paper. After 30 minutes on moist filter paper, 41 percent of chlamydospores and 20 percent of zoospores germinated. In deionized water, 75 percent of chlamydospores and 20 percent of zoospores germinated on a selective medium after 30 days (Davidson and others 2002b). Laboratory studies (Fichtner and others 2007) demonstrated a decline in *P. ramorum* survival in soil with gradual drying.

A U.K. laboratory study (DEFRA 2005a) found that sporangia and chlamydospores germinated on agar after exposure to -2 °C for 24 hours. Chlamydospores were not capable of germinating after exposure to 55 °C for 1 hour. No chlamydospores germinated following exposure to 40 °C for 24 hours or -25 °C for just 4 hours. Sporangia did not germinate after a 2-hour exposure to these temperatures. Sporangia germinated after 6 hours, but not 24 hours, at room temperature in dry conditions. In a study to determine the effects of temperature and composting treatments on the viability of *P. ramorum* (Swain and others 2006), the pathogen was not recovered from compost by plating on selective medium or by baiting with pears following temperatures of 55 °C for 1 hour or 40 °C for 24 hours. The pathogen was also not detected using PCR, suggesting that *P. ramorum* was absent from the treated compost and not just suppressed or dormant. Similar results were reported by Turner and Jennings (2006); chlamydospores germinated after 2 months storage in vitro at 0, 5, 15 and 30 °C, but not at -25 °C or 40 °C.

Survival in Host Material

An important means of *P. ramorum* survival over the hot, dry summer months in California is in infected California bay laurel leaves (Davidson and others 2005b, Rizzo 2006). Survival in attached leaves was found to be higher than in abscised leaves (Davidson and others 2002a, 2003a). Survival (as assessed by cultural isolation) in attached bay laurel leaves declined from approximately 90 percent in June to 50 percent in August, but persisted throughout the summer. Survival in abscised leaves collected from leaf litter in June, July, and August was nearly zero. The same study determined that infected bay leaves were significantly more likely to abscise in drier mixed-evergreen forest as opposed to tanoak-redwood forest. The authors surmised that, given that survival of *P. ramorum* occurs in attached rather than abscised leaves, the observed differences in abscission rates of *P. ramorum*-infected bay leaves in coast live oak versus tanoak-redwood forests may be one factor contributing to differences in the onset of detectable inoculum production in these two forest types during the winter rainy season.

Fichtner and others (2008b) compared summer survival of *P. ramorum* associated with California bay laurel leaves in redwood-tanoak and mixed-evergreen forests. Pathogen isolation from attached leaves ranged from 40 to 100 percent at each site in May and declined to a range of 0 to 40 percent in August, with higher isolation recovery observed in redwood-tanoak forests than in mixed-evergreen forests.

In leaf-debris survival experiments in Oregon (McLaughlin and others 2006), *Rhododendron* and tanoak leaves inoculated with *P. ramorum* were placed in the field; the leaves were shaded or unshaded, and placed above ground or buried. Pathogen survival was higher (89 percent) in buried leaves after 8 weeks than in those on the soil surface in shade (66 percent recovery) or on the soil surface exposed to the sun (26 percent recovery).

Shishkoff and Tooley (2004) reported survival of *P. ramorum* in infected *Rhododendron* leaf tissue containing chlamydospores buried in mesh bags in potted nursery stock for up to 155 days after burial. In additional experiments, Shishkoff (2007) recovered *P. ramorum* from moist potting mix or sand for many months, whether buried as infected plant leaf tissue or as mycelia bearing chlamydospores. The author found no significant difference in recovery over time among treatments (sand or potting mix; infected plant tissue or mycelia); after approximately a year, colonies could be recovered at 0.8 to 14.3 percent.

The pathogen can survive in artificially infected leaf debris buried in soil for at least two U.K. winters (Turner and others 2005). Chlamydospores of *P. ramorum* in lilac (*S. vulgaris*) and rhododendron leaves, either as surface leaf litter or buried

5 cm deep in soil, survived the winter season in experiments conducted in northern England and Scotland (Turner and others 2005). Pathogen survival gradually decreased over time, but *P. ramorum* was recovered from at least 50 percent of leaves in all treatments. Survival was slightly higher on the host (rhododendron) that had thicker and more durable leaves compared to the host (lilac) that had more fragile and less durable leaves. Survival was highest on rhododendron leaves that had been buried 5 cm below the soil surface, with over 80 percent of leaves still yielding the pathogen after 4 months. Tests carried out in Scotland in a parallel experiment showed similar survival under ambient conditions over the same period. In an experiment in the Netherlands to monitor the persistence of *P. ramorum* after infected rhododendrons were cut down and chipped, the pathogen was detected up to 2 years later in the chips left in situ (Steeghs 2008).

The pathogen has been recovered from host tissues at eradication sites. At Oregon eradication sites, *P. ramorum* was recovered from tanoak sprouts around 88 percent of the tanoak stumps sampled (Hansen and Sutton 2006). Initial sprouts were destroyed, and subsequent exams found no infection on later establishing sprouts or seedlings (Hansen 2007). At one eradication site in the United Kingdom, the pathogen was observed on new shoots emerging from cut rhododendron stumps (DEFRA 2007).

Phytophthora ramorum also survives, probably as chlamydospores, in wood. Shelly and others (2006) isolated *P. ramorum* from 1 of 30 specimens of tanoak and coast live oak logs that had air-dried for 6 months, demonstrating that *P. ramorum* could survive on log for at least 6 months. Brown and Brasier (2007) reported survival of the pathogen in exposed wood of trees for up to 2 years.

Survival in Soil and Potting Media

In California, *P. ramorum* is rarely isolated from mixed-evergreen forest soils during the hot, dry summer period (Davidson and others 2002b and 2005b), although the pathogen survives in infected leaves in the soil or litter over the summer period, especially in redwood-tanoak forests (Fichtner and others 2006, 2007). Davidson and others (2002b, 2005b) did not recover *P. ramorum* from soil and litter surrounding infected oaks within a coast live oak woodland in the summer months. The failure to detect the pathogen in soil during the summer coincided with a drop in mean soil water content to less than 15 percent, indicating that seasonal drying is sufficient to reduce viability of spores in these substrates. Maloney and others (2002) also found that recovery of *P. ramorum* from soils dropped to zero during the summer months, with frequency of recovery from soil during the rainy season approximately 20 percent, but summer soil collections showing no *P. ramorum* recovery.

In contrast, Fichtner and others (2006, 2007) demonstrated that *P. ramorum* survives and produces chlamydospores in forest soils over summer, providing a possible inoculum reservoir at the onset of the fall disease cycle. Although Davidson and others (2002a, 2005b) could not detect *P. ramorum* in soils associated with oaks within approximately 1 month of the last spring rain event, Fichtner and others (2006, 2007) recovered the pathogen from soils up to 3 months after the last rain event. Fichtner and others (2007) reported that recovery frequency of *P. ramorum* was highest under California bay laurel and intermediate under tanoak, with only occasional recovery under redwood. Fichtner and others (2009a) reported suppression of chlamydospore production in moist, redwood-associated soils. Recovery of the pathogen from infected rhododendron leaf discs after 8 weeks was highest in the soil (80 percent), intermediate in the litter/soil interface (60 percent) and poor (1 percent) on the leaf litter surface. The differences between the two studies may be explained by the fact that Davidson and others (2002a, 2005b) monitored soil inoculum in a mixed-evergreen forest using pear baits, whereas Fichtner and others (2006, 2007) monitored soils in a redwood/tanoak forest using rhododendron leaf baits.

Lockley and others (2008) reported variable results with survival of *P. ramorum* at a site in the United Kingdom. At one site, where the infected host (*Rhododendron*) was removed and composted mulch applied to the soil surface, the pathogen could not be detected in soil samples. At a second site, where host removal was impractical and the only treatment was removal of lower branches of the rhododendrons, detection of *P. ramorum* in soil samples gradually declined. In The Netherlands, Aveskamp and others (2006) found that the pathogen remained viable for at least 1 year in sandy soil. The authors reported that the pathogen was more abundant at a depth of 20 cm than at the soil surface.

Phytophthora ramorum has also been found at depths of up to 15 cm in soil in areas of severe plant infection (Turner and others 2008a). Monitoring at sites where eradication attempts were made early in the disease epidemic has shown that, in the absence of inoculum sources, residual contamination in soil declined slowly over time and in some cases declined to below thresholds of detection (Turner 2007a). At five eradication sites in Oregon, *P. ramorum* was recovered over a 4-year period from soil at the base of selected stumps at three sites, only in the initial sample at one site, and never recovered from soil at one site (Goheen and others 2008).

Phytophthora ramorum has a high potential for infesting and remaining viable in potting media. Linderman and Davis (2006b, 2006c) reported survival of *P. ramorum* in potting media or soil for up to 6 months when the pathogen was introduced to the media as sporangia, and 12 months when introduced as chlamydospores. Potted *Rhododendron* became infected following inoculation of potting mix with *P. ramorum* (Grünwald and others 2008c). Colburn and others (2005) found no decline in chlamydospore populations after 4 months in sand, potting soil mix, or forest soil held at 4 °C, but the population declined in forest soil at 22 °C. Jeffers (2005) reported recovery of *P. ramorum* from a composite sample container mix (containing plants shipped from California to South Carolina retail nurseries) after storage for 6, 8, and 12 weeks at 4 °C, but not from another sample stored for 10 weeks at room temperature.

In a study designed to help define treatments capable of inactivating chlamydospores in soil substrates, Tooley and others (2008) investigated germination potential over a 7-day temperature treatment by incubating chlamydospores in sand at low (0, -10, -20 °C) and high (30, 35, 40 °C) temperature treatments. Near 100 percent germination was observed at temperatures of 0 °C for up to 7 days in the low temperature treatments, but almost no germination occurred at -10 or -20 °C over the 7-day period. For the high-temperature treatments, high levels of chlamydospore germination were observed over the 7-day period at 30 °C, whereas no growth was observed at 40 °C. At 35 °C, high levels of chlamydospore germination were observed at day 1, but recovery (growth on selective agar medium) declined steadily and was zero by 7 days.

The role of *P. ramorum* oospores as survival structures is unknown, as they have not been observed in the field. In other species of *Phytophthora*, the thick-walled oospores typically serve as survival structures.

Summary

For any pathogen to successfully complete its disease cycle, a suitable environment and the presence of a susceptible host that will support sporulation are key factors. The exotic, introduced organism *P. ramorum* has found a favorable environment and suitable hosts in the mixed-evergreen, redwood/tanoak, bishop pine, and tanoak forests of coastal California and southwest Oregon; in gardens, woodlands, plantations, and parks in the United Kingdom (DEFRA 2004); and in nurseries.

The life cycle of *P. ramorum* is similar to that of other *Phytophthora* species. The pathogen produces sporangia on the surfaces of infected leaves and twigs of foliar hosts that can be splash-dispersed to neighboring hosts or driven longer distances by wind and rain. *Phytophthora ramorum* is also spread downstream of infested areas in rivers and streams, and can be carried in infested soil. Upon contact with a suitable host and environment, the sporangia germinate to produce zoospores that encyst, penetrate the host, and initiate a new infection. Chlamydospores are readily produced in infected plant material and serve as resting structures in soil, allowing the pathogen to survive adverse conditions. Moisture is essential for survival and sporulation, and the duration, frequency, and timing of rain events during the winter months plays a key role in inoculum production.

Knowledge of the disease cycle and the environmental requirements of *P. ramorum* to complete each stage of the cycle are needed to effectively manage the diseases the pathogen causes. Some examples of potential management actions based on the disease cycle of *P. ramorum* are summarized in Rizzo and others (2005). For instance, the findings that *P. ramorum* inoculum survives in soil has led to recommendations to avoid movement of soil from infested to uninfested areas.

Chapter 4: Modeling Disease Distribution and Spatial-Temporal Patterns of Mortality

Introduction

This chapter discusses the development and use of models to predict areas at risk for *Phytophthora ramorum* occurrence, and summarizes the literature on modeling of the spatial-temporal aspects of the disease.

Risk Models

Disease models are used to predict and describe the interaction between the environmental, host, and pathogen variables that result in disease. The variables used are based on laboratory and field data regarding the host and the pathogen, as well as on disease spatial and temporal variability (http://www.ipm.ucdavis.edu/DISEASE/DATABASE/diseasemodeldatabase.html). Using climate and *P. ramorum* host distribution data, computer models that predict areas at risk for pathogen occurrence have been developed. These risk models are valuable tools used by researchers, managers, and policymakers to assist in early detection, survey, prevention, and regulatory policy decisions.

Regional Risk Models

California—

Models predicting the potential distribution of *P. ramorum* in California have been developed. Meentemeyer and others (2004) developed an expert-knowledge-driven, rule-based geographic information system (GIS) infection risk model (a rule-based model uses research data and expert input, rather than statistical inference, to determine the importance of predictor variables), to predict the risk of spread and establishment of *P. ramorum* in California based on plant host susceptibility and weather variables (precipitation, relative humidity, maximum temperature, and minimum temperature). Host distribution and monthly weather conditions were analyzed in a GIS to generate risk rankings per variable and per month. Spread risk predictions were then generated by combining the variables over the 6-month pathogen reproductive period (December through May) and averaged to generate the risk map (fig. 2). The model characterized the climate of coastal California—from Del Norte County in the north to San Luis Obispo County in the south—and the western slopes of the northern Sierra Nevada in Butte and Yuba Counties, as

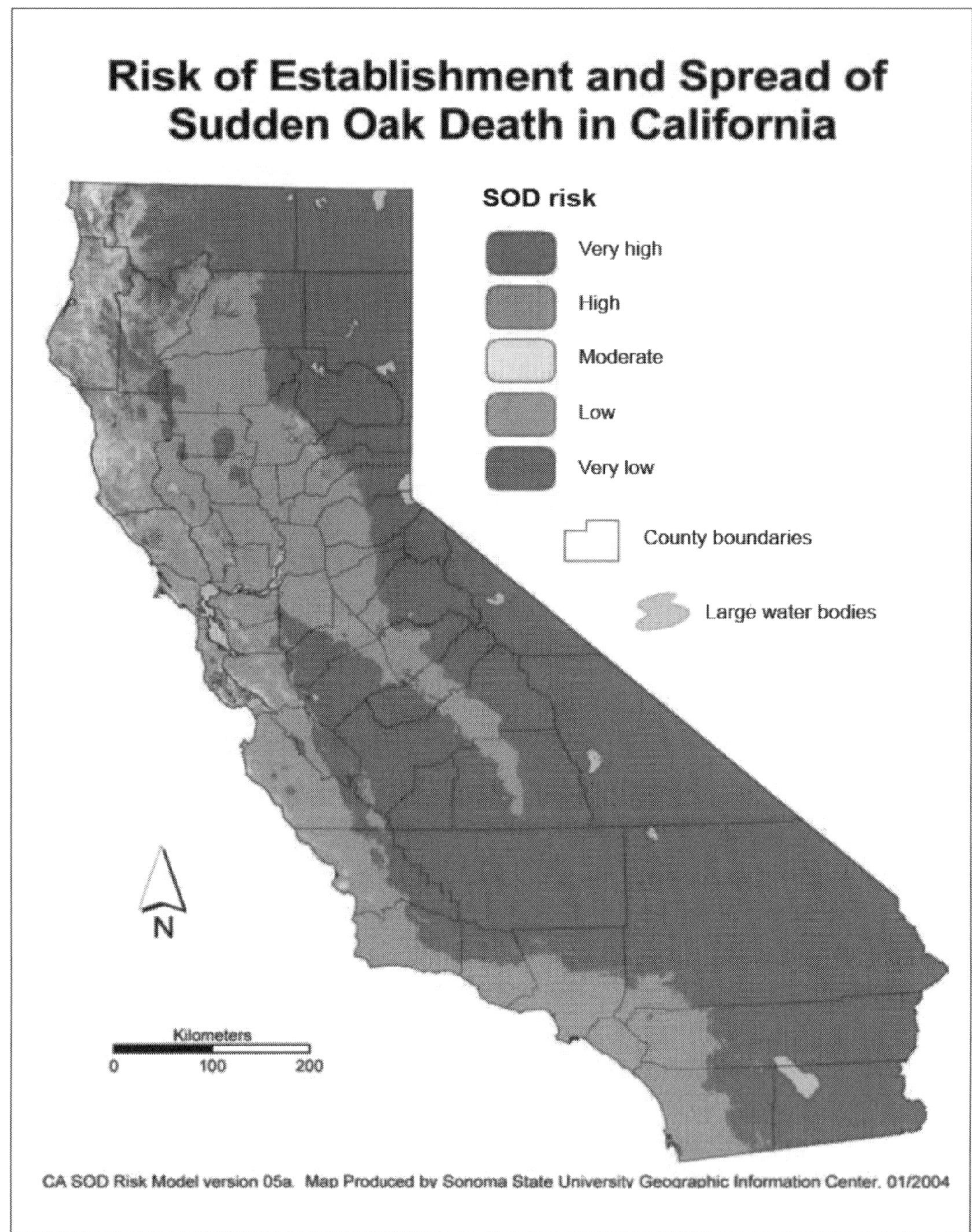

Figure 2—Six-month average (December–May) predicted spread risk map for *Phytophthora ramorum*, cause of sudden oak death (SOD), in California (Meentemeyer and others 2004).

moderately to highly suitable for establishment and spread of *P. ramorum* from December to May.

Guo and others (2005) used and compared one-class and two-class support vector machine (SVM) techniques[1] to predict the potential distribution of *P. ramorum* in California. Because the data often required by other methods to map the predicted spread of a disease may be unknown with a recently introduced pathogen such as *P. ramorum*, the authors compared one-class SVM models (using presence-only data) and two-class SVM models (using both presence and pseudo-absence data). Fourteen variables (seasonality of climatic variables such as temperature, precipitation, and solar radiation—which are considered key to limiting *P. ramorum*—as well as distance to main roads and distance to edges of patches of hosts) were used to predict the potential distribution of *P. ramorum* in California. The one-class SVM predicted a greater risk area (fig. 3), including much of the foothills of the central Sierra Nevada, and along the coast in Humboldt County to the north and Los Angeles County to the south. The authors suggested that one-class SVMs are computationally more efficient (no need to generate pseudo-absence data) than two-class models, and are more applicable in the case of a new invasive species where absence data are not available.

[1] Techniques for separating data points into classes. Support vector machines derive nonlinear boundaries to optimally separate clouds of points.

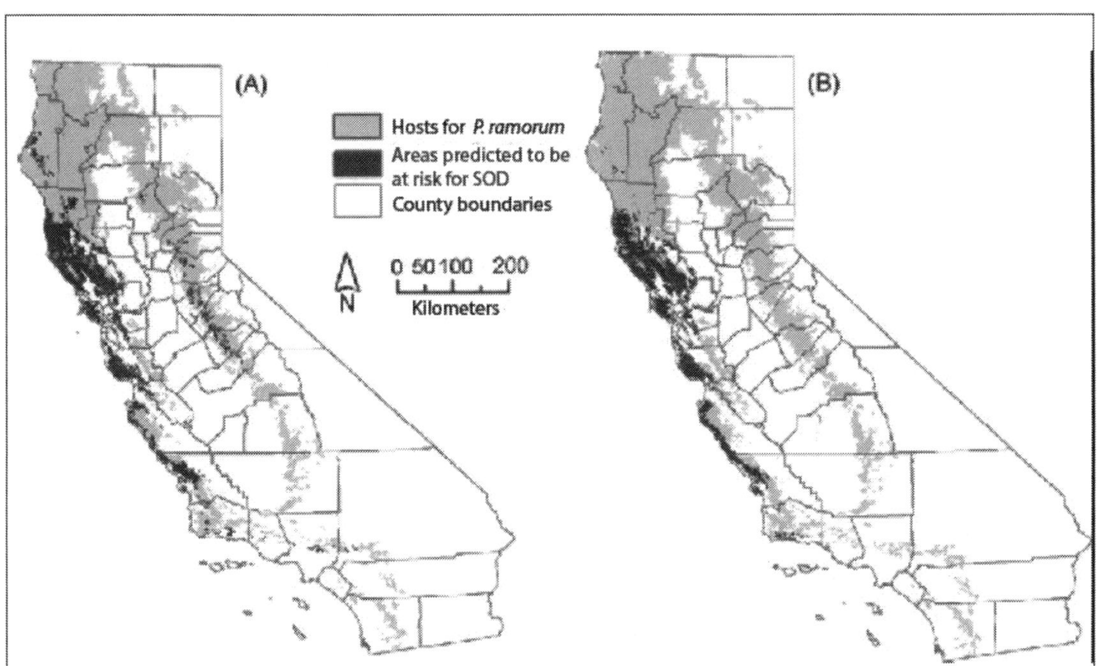

Figure 3—Predicted area of sudden oak death (SOD) risk in California. Mapped results from (A) one-class support vector machines (SVMs) and (B) two-class SVMs (Guo and others 2005).

Oregon—

For western Oregon, Václavík and others (2010) developed two GIS predictive models—based on weather and climate variability, host vegetation susceptibility and distribution, and dispersal—of *P. ramorum* establishment and spread risk for use in target monitoring and eradication activities. The first was a heuristic (rule-based) model, using a multicriteria evaluation (MCE) method, to identify the areas at potential risk of pathogen establishment and spread. The resulting risk map displayed a distinct geographical pattern of *P. ramorum* establishment and spread risk in western Oregon based on the influence of host species abundance and climate parameters (fig. 4). Although large areas had low to very low *P. ramorum* risk in the eastern part of the area (owing to low host availability and unfavorable climate conditions), vast areas of forest across the western region of the state appear to be susceptible. The forests at greatest risk of disease spread are concentrated in southwestern Oregon where the highest densities of susceptible host species exist, in particular tanoak (*Lithocarpus densiflorus* (Hook. & Arn.) Rehd.).

For the second model, the authors used maximum entropy (MAXENT) to predict the current distribution of *P. ramorum* infections within the 2008 quarantine area in Oregon. Probability of infection was calibrated based on the correlation

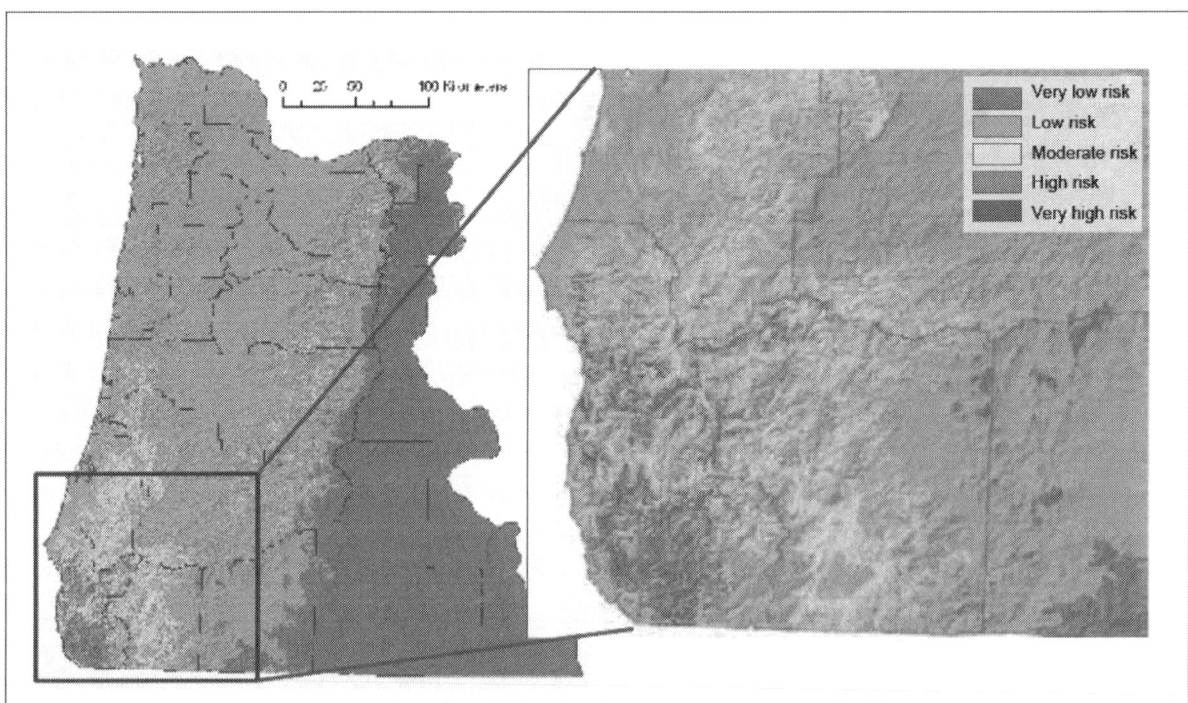

Figure 4—Predicted risk map of *Phytophthora ramorum* potential risk of establishment and spread in western Oregon (Václavík and others 2010).

between 500 field observations of disease occurrence and predictor variables including climate variability, host susceptibility and abundance, topographic variables, and a dispersal constraint. The model indicated that likelihood of the disease is positively associated with temperature and precipitation, and negatively associated with elevation and potential solar radiation. Tanoak abundance was strongly associated with disease presence.

National Risk Models

The U.S. Department of Agriculture, Forest Service (USDA FS) developed a national risk map for *P. ramorum* in 2002 as part of the sample design for a national SOD detection survey (Smith and others 2002, USDA FS 2004). Variables used included (1) distribution of hosts known or likely to be susceptible to the pathogen, (2) climatic conditions adequate for survival and propagation of the pathogen, and (3) pathways for introduction of the disease outside the currently infested region. The resulting map consisted of hexagons indicating three levels of risk (high, moderate, low; the larger the hexagon, the less the risk) covering the conterminous United States (fig. 5).

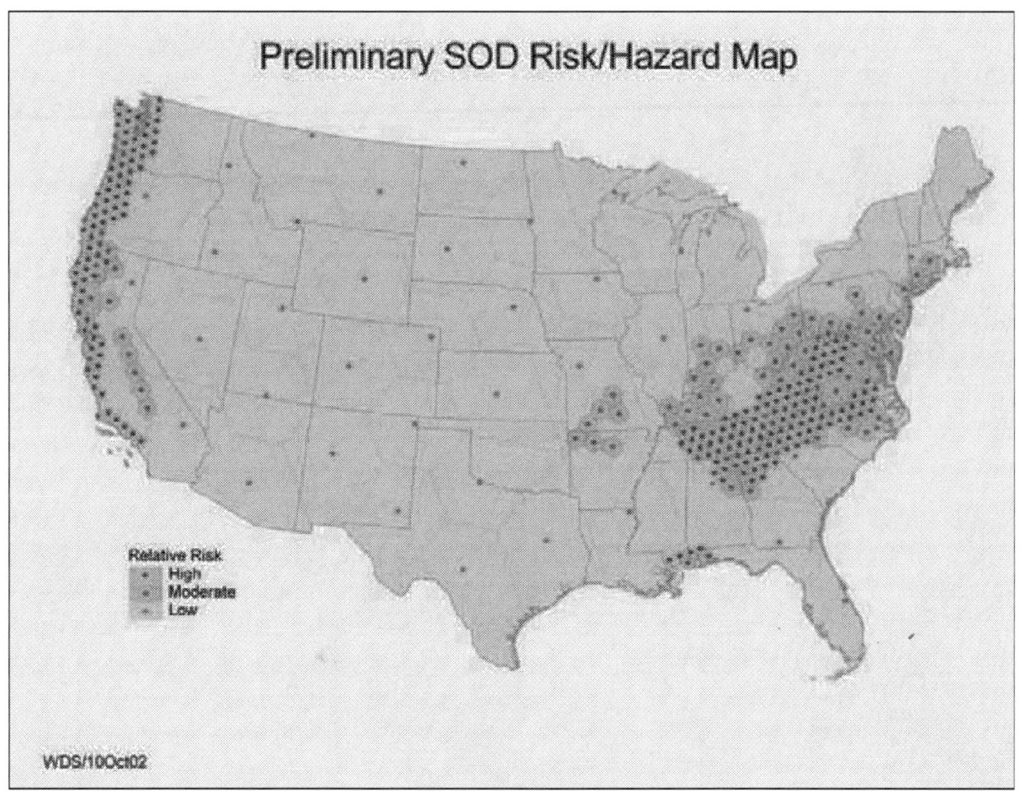

Figure 5—U.S. Department of Agriculture, Forest Service national sudden oak death (SOD) risk map, 2002 (Smith and others 2002).

An updated national risk map was created (Koch and Smith 2008) by incorporating current data and approaches (recent host information, daily rather than monthly weather data, exclusion of areas where the minimum temperature was below 0 °C for 150 or more days, and consideration that *P. ramorum* could escape from ornamental plantings in residential landscapes into natural forests) to better depict principal factors of *P. ramorum* risk. The resulting map (fig. 6) showed an expansion of risk areas in the Southeastern United States and a shifting of risk in portions of mid-Atlantic and south-Midwest States from moderate to low.

Magarey and others (2006) used the North Carolina State University/Animal and Plant Health Inspection Service (APHIS) Plant Pest Forecast System (NAPPFAST) (Borchert and Magarey 2004) to construct a climate and host risk map for *P. ramorum* (fig. 7). The map was based on an assumption that *P. ramorum* occurrence would be climatically limited by temperature and moisture requirements. They used 10-year historical climate data. Initially, the daily combination of minimum temperature, optimum temperature, maximum temperature, and total hours per day of leaf wetness was used to estimate the annual number of days suitable for infection. A second modeling effort examined the effects of soil temperatures less than -25 °C, which reduce survival of *P. ramorum* sporangia and chlamydospores in laboratory tests (DEFRA 2005b). The cold temperature exclusion reduced the

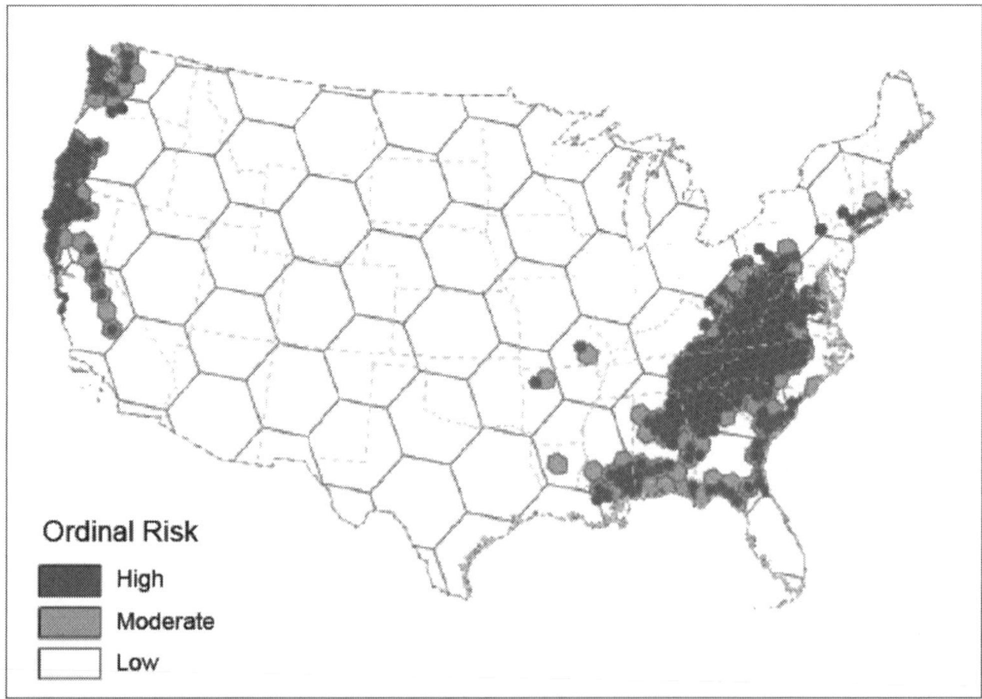

Figure 6—Revised U.S. Department of Agriculture, Forest Service national sudden oak death risk map, 2008 (Koch and Smith 2008).

northern extent of risk from the pathogen. Magarey and others (2008) then incorporated understory sporulator hosts (seven Ericaceae hosts of *P. ramorum*) into the model to further refine the at-risk infection areas (fig. 7).

Kelly and others (2007) compared and evaluated the performance of five spatial risk models (rule-based expert-driven GIS overlay, logistic regression [LR], classification and regression trees [CART], genetic algorithms [GA], and SVMs) generated from common input parameters to map risk from *P. ramorum* across the conterminous United States (fig. 8). All models were consistent in their prediction of some SOD risk in coastal California, Oregon, and Washington; in the northern foothills of the Sierra Nevada in California; in an east-west-oriented band including eastern Oklahoma, central Arkansas, Tennessee, Kentucky, northern Mississippi, Alabama, Georgia, and South Carolina, parts of central North Carolina, eastern Virginia, Delaware, and Maryland.

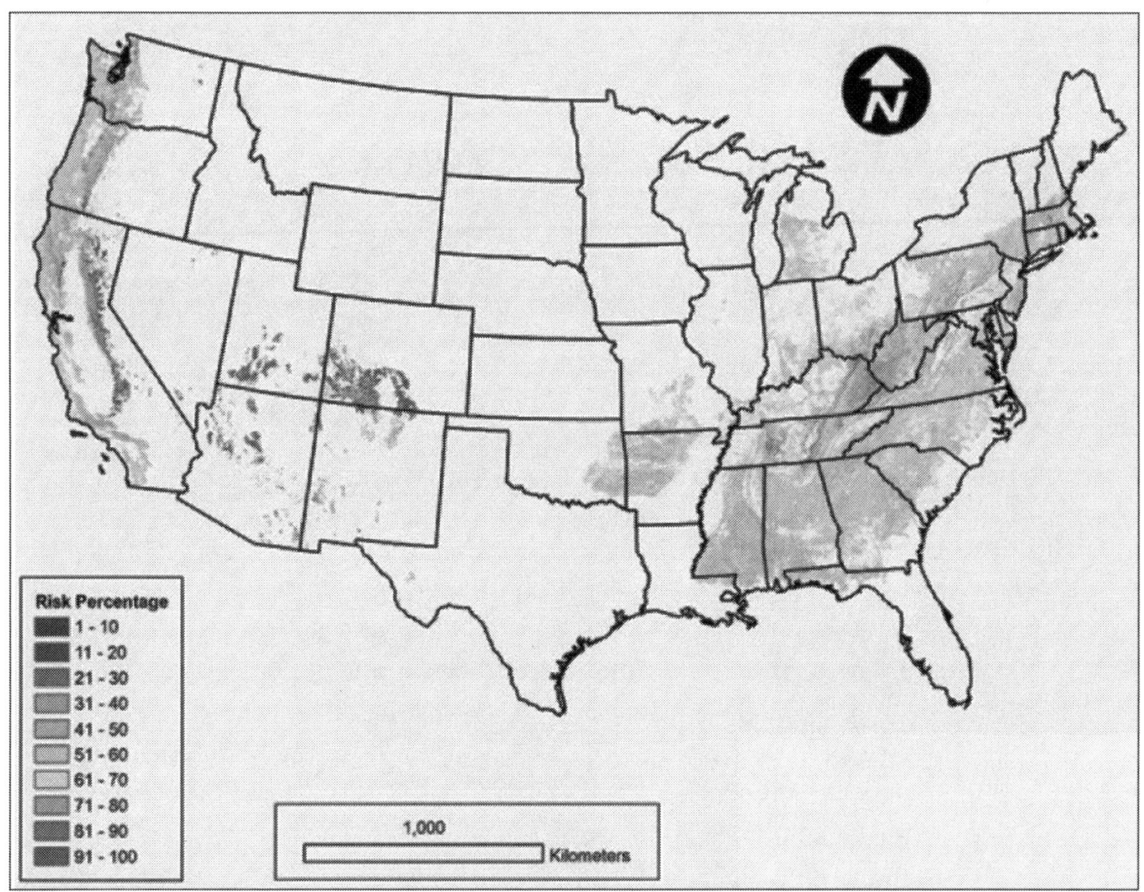

Figure 7—The chance of occurrence based upon at least 60 favorable days for infection by *Phytophthora ramorum*, hardwood hosts, understory sporulator hosts, and -25 °C lethal soil temperature exclusion (DEFRA 2005b; Fowler and others 2006; Margarey and others 2007, 2008).

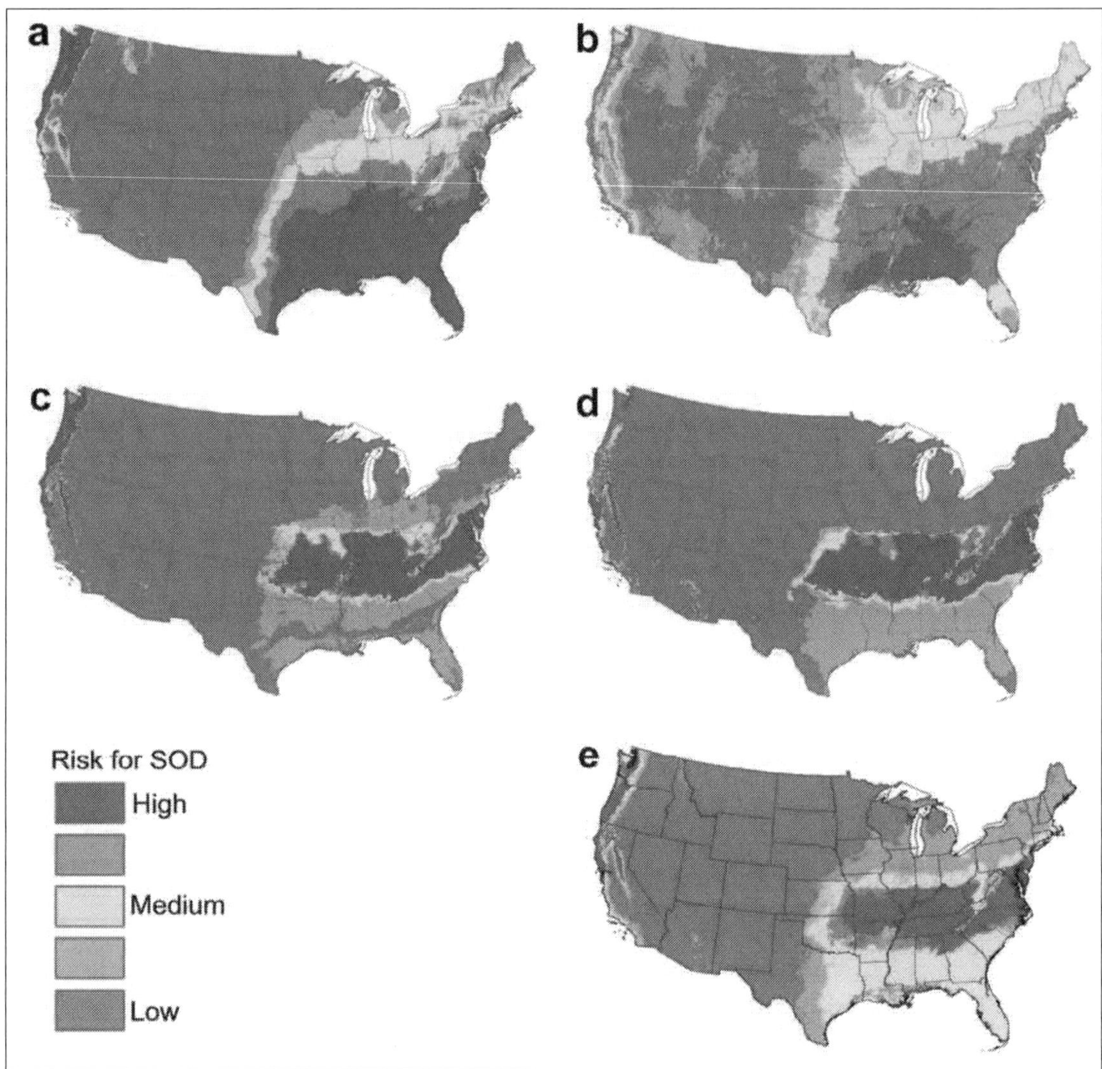

Figure 8—Risk for sudden oak death (SOD) in the conterminous United States from five spatially referenced models: (a) rule-based, (b) logistic regression, (c) classification tree, (d) genetic algorithm, and (e) support vector machine (Kelly and others 2006, 2007).

The results from the five models were combined together to create a final map based on model agreement (fig. 9) (Kelly and others 2007).

A national rule-based and expert knowledge model to characterize suitable habitat for *P. ramorum* across the United States was developed by Venette and Cohen (2006). With the assumption that adequate inoculum and susceptible hosts are uniformly present across the contiguous United States and the use of CLIMEX software, the model focused on climate as the limiting factor in establishment of the disease. Model outputs (fig. 10) identified many areas within the United States that do not have a climate suitable for the establishment of *P. ramorum*, including most

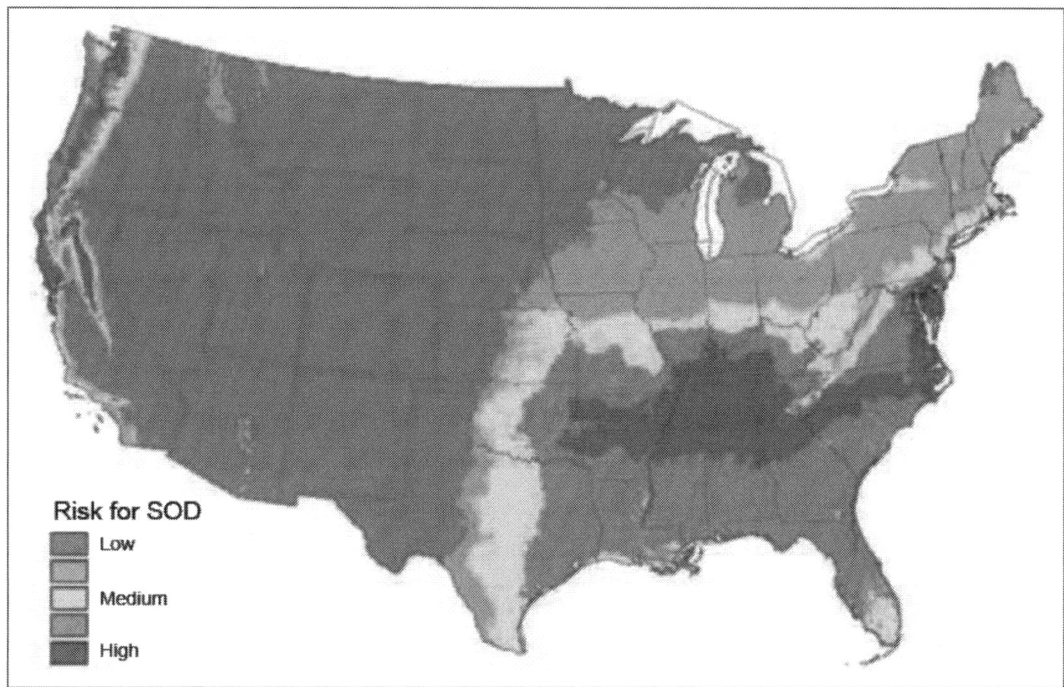

Figure 9—Risk for sudden oak death (SOD) in the conterminous United States based on agreement between five spatially referenced models (Kelly and others 2007).

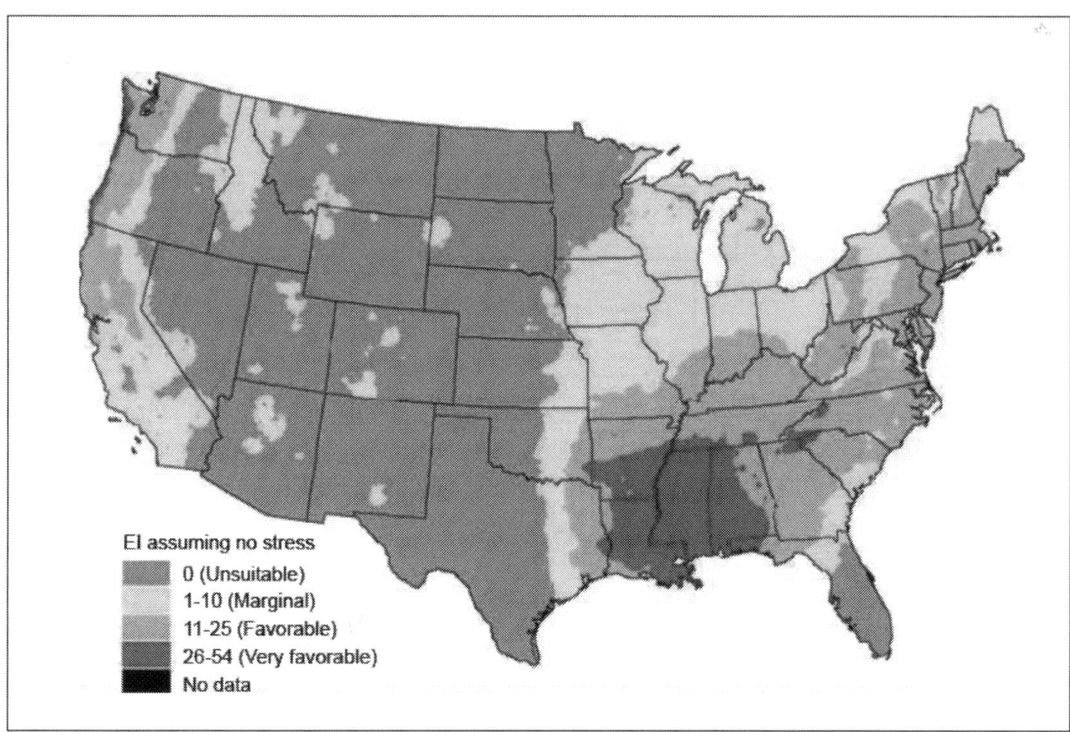

Figure 10—Predicted climatic suitability for establishment of *Phytophthora ramorum* in the contiguous United States based on the ecoclimatic index (EI) from CLIMEX excluding environmental stresses (Venette and Cohen 2006).

of the Great Lakes, Plains, or Intermountain States. In addition to the Pacific Coast, climate is relatively more suitable for establishment in Southeastern, Northeastern, and Mid-Atlantic States.

The risk map produced by Venette and Cohen (2006) was consistent and in general agreement with other national risk models for *P. ramorum*, providing a degree of confidence in the conclusions from the models.

In 2005, the USDA Animal and Plant Health Inspection Service (APHIS) compared eight national-scale risk models for *P. ramorum*. A summary of the comparisons is presented at http://nature.berkeley.edu/comtf/pdf/P%20ramorum%20v5%20BRS%20rev.pdf. The models were subdivided into two groups: those that use *P. ramorum* observations and those that do not. In general, models that use *P. ramorum* observations predicted a more restricted distribution than those that do not. The models were generally consistent in showing a national pattern of high risk in the coastal Northwest and the central Appalachian Mountains, and a low risk in the Great Plains. The models differed in predicting the degree of risk in the Northeast, coastal California, parts of the Southeast and the northern Midwest. The greatest uncertainties among the models were the extent of the northern boundary of risk east of the Rocky Mountains and the degree of risk in the Southeast. The review paper recommends comparing the output from several models rather than using a single model for decisionmaking.

North American Temperature Model

McKenney and others (n.d.) presented a map based on North American continent-wide extreme minimum temperature models (fig. 11). Based on a Department for Environment, Food and Rural Affairs (DEFRA) report that indicated all *P. ramorum* spores are killed after 4 hours exposure to -25 °C (DEFRA 2005b), the map may be useful in indicating climate limitations on potential distribution of the pathogen. Although useful in identifying possible environmental limits, a map based on minimum temperature only does not take into account other host-pathogen-environment interactions involved in disease introduction (McKenney and others 2003).

Europe

The European risk analysis for *P. ramorum* (Sansford and others 2009) presents various climatic models for predicting presence of the pathogen in Europe. A climate-based risk map for Europe, using the ranking system developed by Meentemeyer and others (2004) to predict potential *P. ramorum* distribution in California, is presented in fig. 12. The model uses climatic parameters that favor *P. ramorum*, with scores, ranks, and weights assigned to precipitation, maximum temperature,

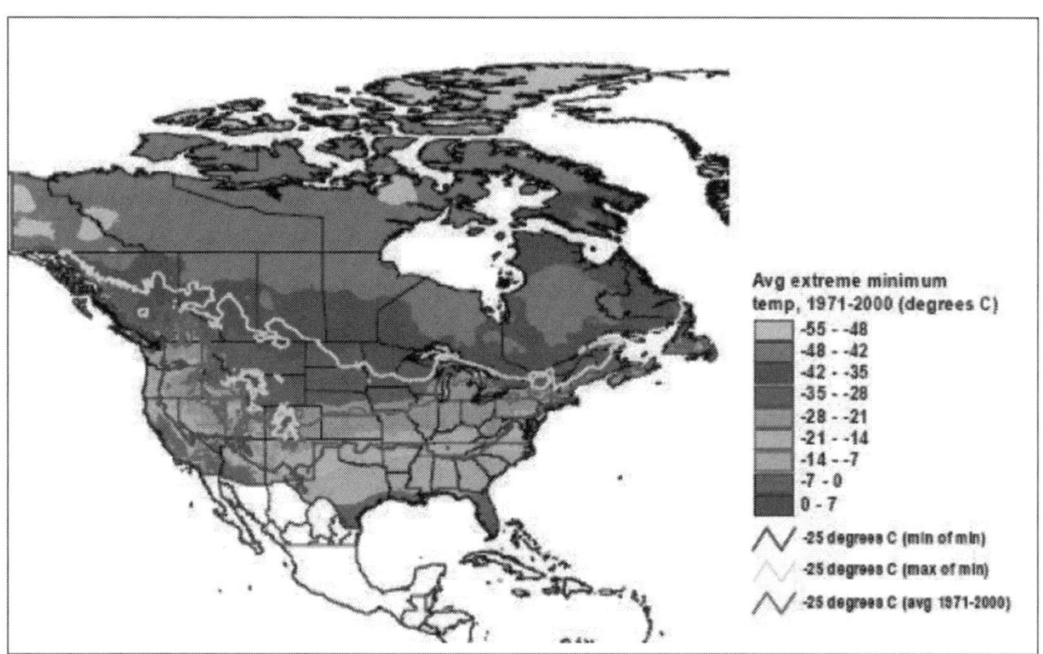

Figure 11—Extreme minimum temperature models for North America (McKenney and others, n.d.).

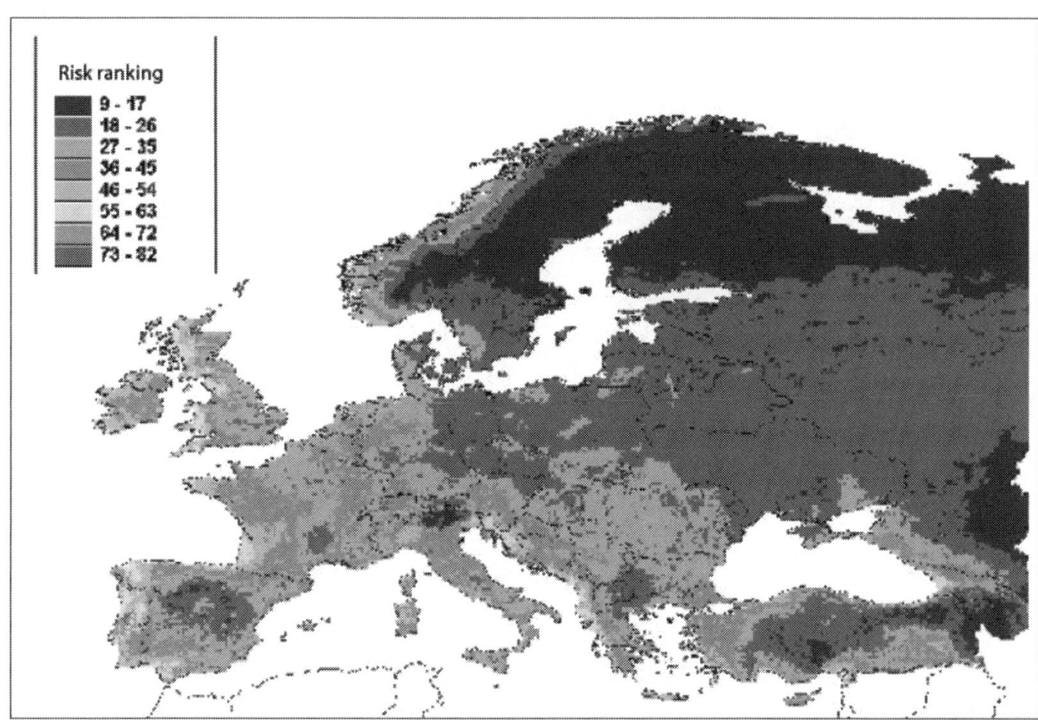

Figure 12—*Phytophthora ramorum* risk ranking model for Europe, based on Meentemeyer and others (2004).

relative humidity, and minimum temperature. However, because of a lack of high-resolution data for host distribution and host associations, it does not incorporate the host-species index of Meentemeyer and others (2004). The most suitable climatic locations for establishment are northern Portugal, northwestern Spain, the southern tip of Spain, the Adriatic coast of the Balkan peninsula, southwestern France, northwest France (Brittany), northern coastal Spain, southern Turkey, western United Kingdom and southwest Ireland. Note that those areas that are climatically favorable are only at risk where there are susceptible host plants that are capable of supporting *P. ramorum* sporulation.

International Risk Model

An international risk model for *P. ramorum* was created using NAPPFAST (Magarey and other 2006, 2008) (fig. 13), and the Intergovernmental Panel on Climate Change data set (historical climate data for the last 10 years). The data set contains variables describing average temperature, precipitation, humidity, and

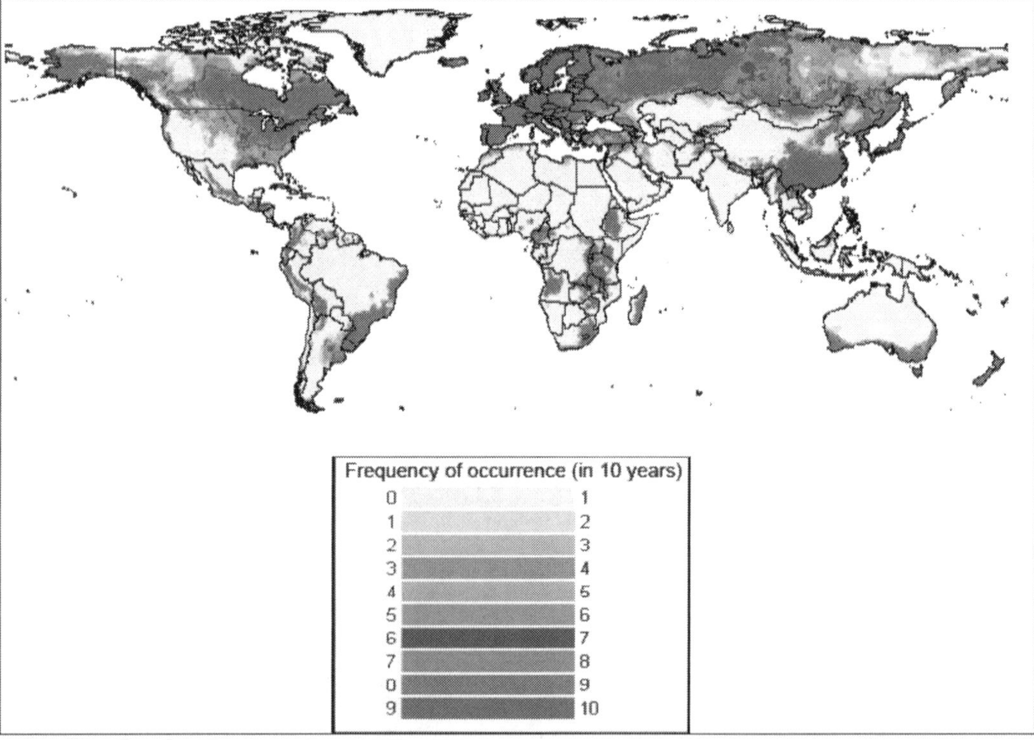

Figure 13—The North Carolina State University/APHIS Plant Pest Forecast System (NAPPFAST) Intergovernmental Panel on Climate Change (IPCC) model for *Phytophthora ramorum* assuming at least 2 favorable months (Magarey and others 2006).

cloud cover. The model was based on a favorable month requiring average maximum monthly temperature to be less than 28 °C, average minimum temperature to be greater than 3 °C and at least 10 days with precipitation. Although Margarey and others pointed out that the model overestimates potential areas of pathogen occurrence because minimum precipitation data are not included, they suggested that the model may be of use in searching for the origin of the pathogen.

Refinement of the regional, national, and international risk models developed for *P. ramorum* will occur as host range, environmental factors favoring spread and establishment, and the effects of spatial and temporal variables affecting the pathogen are better understood (Rizzo 2006). The differences that exist among the risk models point out uncertainties and the need for additional information on suitable environmental niches for the pathogen.

Modeling Spatial-Temporal Patterns of Disease Distribution and Spread

Kelly and Meentemeyer (2002) and Liu and others (2007) used remote sensing and spatial analysis to quantify the clustering of overstory mortality associated with SOD across large scales. High-resolution imagery in combination with GIS and spatial modeling was used by Kelly and Meentemeyer (2002) to determine the presence and scale of oak mortality clustering over a 2-year period (2000 and 2001) at a location in Marin County (China Camp State Park), California. They found clustering patterns between 100 and 300 m. They also developed a classification tree model to predict spatial patterns of risk for oak mortality based on landscape variables. Factors correlated with oak mortality included proximity to forest edge, topographic moisture index, proximity to trails, abundance of California bay laurel (*Umbellularia californica* (Hook. & Arn.) Nutt.), and potential summer solar radiation. Their results suggested that forest structure was an important risk factor in spatial pattern and spread of the disease.

Liu and others (2007) analyzed the spatial-temporal patterns of overstory oak tree mortality at the same Marin County location (China Camp State Park) over a 4-year period using point patterns mapped from high-spatial-resolution remotely sensed imagery. Univariate spatial-point pattern analyses showed that the point patterns of dead oak trees are significantly clustered at different scales and spatial extents through time; and that both the extent and the scale of the clustering patterns decrease with time. Multivariate spatial-point pattern analyses showed that newly dead oak trees tend to be located within 300 m of dead oak trees, and that a strong spatial association exists between oak tree mortality and California bay trees within 150 m.

Because remote sensing used by Kelly and Meentemeyer (2002) and Liu and others (2007) does not capture understory or tree-specific symptomology, Kelly and others (2008) used two-dimensional transect data to cover large areas and capture vegetation detail and spatial location. Kelly and others (2008) investigated the spatial-temporal patterns of symptoms associated with SOD across landscape scales (hundreds of meters) at China Camp State Park. Using two-dimensional spatial analysis tools with data gathered in point-centered-quarter format in 2001 and 2004 at the park, they quantified the clustering of dead trees across the landscape and then investigated the relationship between disease symptoms and dead trees through space and time. The work provided an estimate of the density of symptomatic trees at different levels of disease across a forest landscape affected by *P. ramorum*. Dead trees were strongly clustered at smaller scales (about 300 m) in 2001, but after 3 years (2004), the clustering was less pronounced despite an increase in dead crowns. These patterns supported those found using remotely sensed data across the park (Guo and others 2007, Kelly and Meentemeyer 2002, Kelly and others 2004, Liu and others 2006), where clusters of overstory tree mortality of 200 to 400 m across were found. Results showed that bleeding trees occur early in clusters and separate from existing dead trees, suggesting a new cohort of infected trees; that beetle-attacked trees exist throughout the forest and are not well correlated with overstory mortality; and that the saprophytic sap rotting fungus *Hypoxylon* [*Annulohypoxylon*] *thouarsianum* is strongly related to tree mortality through time (Kelly and others 2008).

In a study at Sonoma Mountain, Sonoma County, California, Condeso and Meentemeyer (2007) showed that disease severity (derived by counting the number of symptomatic leaves on each California bay laurel stem greater than 2 cm in diameter at 1.4 m for 90 seconds), was greater in forests with high connectivity and with high abundance of host species. More connected forests had more disease than smaller and more isolated forests, suggesting to the authors that forest fragmentation may keep inoculum levels low and reduce pathogen spread. They also demonstrated that, in the system they used, optimum microclimatic conditions for *P. ramorum* reproduction and growth are influenced more by elevation than by landscape pattern.

In a followup study, Meentemeyer and others (2008b) reported that altered forest structure and composition, probably largely owing to fire suppression, facilitated spread of *P. ramorum*. Using detailed aerial photography records between 1942 and 2000 within a 150-m radius around 102 plots within a 275-km^2 area of northern California, they found that oak woodlands increased in area by 25 percent over the 58-year period, while grasslands and chaparral (nonhost vegetation types) had both significantly decreased. Path analysis showed that the woodland expansion resulted in larger forests with higher densities of the primary host trees (*U. californica*, *Quercus agrifolia* Née, *Quercus kelloggii* Newb.) and cooler understory conditions. The authors concluded that enlargement of woodlands and closure of canopy gaps facilitated the establishment of *P. ramorum* by increasing contagion of hosts and enhancing forest microclimate conditions.

Although Meentemeyer and others (2004), Guo and others (2005), and Venette and Cohen (2006) mapped the potential spread risk of *P. ramorum*, Meentemeyer and others (2008a) provided a quantitative estimate of the pathogen's realized spatial distribution. Meentemeyer and others (2008a) used niche modeling and dispersal estimation to examine the degree to which local habitat conditions vs. force of infection predict invasion by *P. ramorum*. Linear modeling indicated that the probability of invasion is limited by both niche constraints and dispersal. Probability of invasion was positively related to precipitation and temperature in the wet season and the presence of the inoculum-producing foliar host *U. californica*, and decreased exponentially with distance to inoculum sources. Model predictions suggested that future early detection sampling should concentrate on distances within 33 km (the maximum distance an infection was detected) from a known source of inoculum.

In a preliminary abstract, Hunter and others (2008) described the development of a spatially explicit epidemic model that predicts susceptible-infectious (SI) transitions at discrete time steps using a geographic cellular automata approach. They developed a mathematical model that simulated spatial and temporal patterns of *P. ramorum* spread at large spatial scales. Using data (daily rainfall and temperature, host abundance and susceptibility, human population density, and pathogen dispersal characteristics) from field and laboratory studies, they parameterized the variables to develop a model that was implemented in GIS to simulate disease spread across California. The model predicted about 80 percent of the spatial variability in current patterns of spread of *P. ramorum* and identified numerous forest ecosystems at high risk of infestation.

Meentemeyer and others (2008c) quantified host mortality caused by P. *ramorum* across the Big Sur ecoregion using remote sensing (high-resolution aircraft imagery) in combination with regression models and field observations. Application of the regression models in a GIS estimated 235,678 standing dead trees in 2005 and 12 650 m^2 of tree basal area removed from the ecoregion (79 366-ha study area), with 64 percent of mortality occurring in redwood-tanoak forests and 37 percent in mixed-oak woodlands.

The spread of *P. ramorum* in the nursery trade has been modeled using the concept of networks (a set of nodes connected by links). Nodes are the nurseries trading susceptible species, and links are shipments of those plants between nurseries. If nodes are connected to other nodes randomly (with a certain probability p), then the network is random. Scale-free networks are characterized by the presence of hubs, or super-connected individuals. Modeling of *P. ramorum* spread through nursery networks in England and Wales has demonstrated pathogen movement on a scale-free (compared with random) network, indicating that action at places of production (critical nodes) will help limit future spread (Jeger and others 2007, Pautasso and others 2008).

A model framework useful to those concerned with the accidental introduction of *P. ramorum* into the Eastern United States from infected nursery plants was presented by McKelvey and others (2008). They are developing a spatial network model framework, using potential interstate nursery stock movements on a bipartite network. A Bayesian approach is used to model probabilities of transmission of *P. ramorum* from entry to destination nodes within the network. Probabilities of transmission of *P. ramorum* from source to destination nodes within the network are based on nursery stock flow volumes along the links connecting each origin/destination pair. The objective is to identify locations throughout the United States that are most likely to receive nursery stock infected with *P. ramorum*. Such information would increase the efficiency of ongoing national survey programs for the pathogen.

Chapter 5: Management and Control

Introduction

Although diseases caused by *Phytophthora ramorum* Werres, Cock, & Man in't Veld have been studied only since about the year 2000, the literature abounds with results of numerous research and administrative study efforts to manage and control the pathogen. The existing literature is found in a wide array of publications (journals, popular articles, research summaries) and formats (printed articles, Web-based articles, abstracts, posters). The objective here is to summarize the literature on management and control of *P. ramorum* so that it will be available to researchers, managers, and publics concerned with the pathogen and the diseases it causes. The hope is that the increased availability of the literature will improve treatments and thus forest health.

Disease Management Principles

Basically, disease management involves **prevention**—any action taken before the host is infected to protect it from disease, or **suppression**—an action taken against the pathogen after the host is infected. Several different systems have been used to group and discuss prevention and suppression strategies. Whetzel (1929) described four general disease control principles: exclusion, eradication, protection, and immunization (resistance). Although these principles have been expanded or altered to some extent over the years, they remain valid. Whetzel's (1929) breakdown is used here to structure the literature on management and control of *P. ramorum*. The first two principles, exclusion and eradication, involve pathogen control; the second two, protection and resistance, deal primarily with plant defenses. Some actions may fall into more than one of the categories.

The four disease control principles can be summarized as follows:

Exclusion: Any strategy that attempts to prevent the introduction of a pathogen into an area where it is not yet present. Exclusion is aimed at preventing the introduction of inoculum, or reducing the amount of initial inoculum introduced, from outside sources.

Eradication: The strategies are aimed at eliminating or reducing a pathogen after it is introduced into an area, but before it has become well established or widely spread. Eradication involves strategies that eliminate, destroy, or inactivate the inoculum through sanitation, removal of reservoirs of inoculum, removal of hosts or alternate hosts, and other methods.

Protection: Protection strategies assume that the pathogen is present and that infection will occur without the intervention of protective measures. Protection prevents or reduces infection by means of a toxicant or some other barrier to infection. It establishes a barrier between the pathogen and the host plant or the susceptible part of the host plant. It is usually thought of as a chemical barrier such as a fungicide, bactericide, or nematicide, but it can also be a physical, spatial, or temporal barrier.

Resistance: Resistance strategies use a host or hosts that are resistant to or tolerant of infection. Cultivars or varieties that reduce the rate of inoculum production, the rate of infection, or the rate of pathogen development are deployed. Use of disease-resistant plants can be an effective and environmentally sound method to manage plant diseases if plants of satisfactory quality and adapted to the growing region with adequate levels of durable resistance are available.

Early plant pathologists stated the principles of control in absolute terms, such as eliminate, exclude, and prevent. Today, we realize that absolute control to eliminate a pathogen is often not possible, but that management of the disease to acceptable levels is a more realistic goal.

Exclusion

Exclusion involves a combination of quarantines or regulations and best management practices (BMPs) designed to prevent pathogen introduction. *Phytophthora ramorum* can be moved with infected plants, in water, in infested soil, and via wood or potentially other infected plant products (see chapter 3, "Inoculum Dispersal" section). There is, therefore, the need for regulations and BMPs to prevent spread.

Regulations

To reduce or eliminate *P. ramorum* spread, regulatory actions are being implemented and enforced in countries worldwide. The U.S. Department of Agriculture, Animal and Plant Health Inspection Service (USDA APHIS) issued a national strategic plan (USDA APHIS 2005b) that addresses the control and management of *P. ramorum* in cultivated and natural environments. The strategy's first defense is exclusion, to prevent pathogen introduction and disease development in new areas. The primary objective of the national strategy is to "prohibit introduction, or significantly reduce the rate of introduction or reintroduction, of *P. ramorum*, into presently noninfested regions of the United States, and to manage presently infested nursery systems, forests, and urban landscapes to minimize and mitigate damage." Numerous countries have placed restrictions on the movement of affected plants and plant parts from the United States (Purdue University Center for Environmental and Regulatory Information Systems Export Certification Project 2007, Rizzo and Garbelotto 2003). Worldwide, the European Union pest risk analysis for *P. ramorum* (Sansford and others 2009) lists 68 countries for which *P. ramorum* is either on their lists of regulated pests or mentioned in their legislation.

Federal regulations in the United States and Canada—
In the United States, USDA APHIS is responsible for promulgating and enforcing interstate and international plant quarantine measures. In addition, state agencies regulate within-state quarantines. The first *P. ramorum* quarantine was issued in 2001 by the state of Oregon. It banned host plants and host plant products coming from California unless they had been treated (Frankel 2008). Canada issued a similar quarantine the same year, prohibiting the import of nursery stock and unmanufactured, nonpropagative host material (such as logs and mulch) from areas where *P. ramorum* had been found (Frankel 2008). Then, on 17 May 2001, the California Department of Food and Agriculture (CDFA) issued emergency regulations that restricted the export of diseased oak products and rhododendrons from each of the seven infested counties (Frankel 2008). The USDA APHIS followed by issuing an interim federal regulation (7 CFR Part 301) in February 2002 for domestic interstate movement of *P. ramorum* host material from the known infested California counties. The regulation 7 CFR Part 301 was amended in 2007 (USDA APHIS 2007a).

In January 2005, a new federal order (Emergency Federal Order Restricting Movement of Nursery Stock From California, Oregon, and Washington Nurseries December 21, 2004, USDA) was issued. The order (USDA APHIS 2005a) regulates interstate movement of nursery stock from uninfested areas in California, Oregon, and Washington. Under the federal order, all nurseries with host or associated host plants on site must be inspected and found free of *P. ramorum* before they can ship nursery stock interstate (Frankel 2008). If *P. ramorum* is detected at a nursery, the Confirmed Nursery Protocol (USDA APHIS 2004) requiring the destruction of the infested plants and all other host and associated host plants in the contiguous block as the infected plant is implemented. The block is considered contiguous until there is a 2-m break of either no plants or no hosts or associated host plants. The site is delimited, and all host plants are held and monitored for 90 days. The nursery will continue to be monitored for at least 2 years. The protocols, regulated articles and scope of the U.S. federal regulations may be found on the USDA APHIS *P. ramorum* Web site (http://www.aphis.usda.gov/plant_health/plant_pest_info/pram/). An examination of nursery survey data for the Western States from 2004 to 2006 found that the number of *P. ramorum*-infested nurseries dropped by more than 50 percent (from 110 nurseries to 50) (Suslow 2008a). See table 2 in chapter 2 for U.S. nursery detections by year. In addition to the effectiveness of the 2005 federal order, the drop was attributed to training of nursery growers and to implementation of nursery research findings (Suslow 2008a).

Regulations and quarantines are continuously updated to reflect new findings. Consult the USDA APHIS PPQ (Plant Pest and Quarantine) *P. ramorum* Web site (http://www.aphis.usda.gov/plant_health/plant_pest_info/pram/regulations.shtml) for up-to-date information, or see the www.suddenoakdeath.org Web site for regulations and regulatory updates in the United States.

A residential protocol is also provided by APHIS. The residential protocol (USDA APHIS 2009) specifies actions that are to be taken when a positive *P. ramorum* infection is confirmed in plantings in residential or commercial landscape settings. The objective is pathogen eradication from the site.

European Union/international regulations—
In November 2002, the European Union adopted emergency measures to prevent the introduction and movement of *P. ramorum* into and within the EU nations. Legislation (2002/757/EC) to control the introduction of susceptible hosts into the European Community, in particular, the import of susceptible plants and plant products from the United States, was enacted (OJEC 2002). For export of susceptible plants from the United States to member countries in the European Union, plants must originate from a *P. ramorum*-free area or from a place of production that has been inspected by U.S. authorities and found free from symptoms. The movement of *Rhododendron*, *Viburnum*, and *Camellia* (the main hosts of *P. ramorum* in Europe; *Camellia* was added in 2004) within the European Union are controlled via "plant passports," certificates verifying that the plants have had the required statutory inspections and have been found free from quarantine pests (including *P. ramorum*). The legislation also calls for all EU member states to undertake surveys for *P. ramorum* and disseminate the results. If *P. ramorum* is found, then all susceptible plants within 2 m are destroyed. Any additional susceptible plants within 10 m are held for a period of 3 months' active growth, with at least two additional inspections before being released. The rest of the facility is intensively reinspected before allowing plants to be moved. The legislation was amended in 2004 (Commission of European Communities 2004) to incorporate *Camellia* as a host requiring a plant passport, and in 2007 (http://www.eppo.org/ABOUT_EPPO/EPPO_MEMBERS/phytoreg/eu_texts/2007-201-EC-e.pdf) (OJEC 2007) to add measures relating to destruction of associated growing media and plant debris and other appropriate phytosanitary measures applied to the growing surface. An analysis of the effect of these measures on the prevalence of *P. ramorum* during the period 2004 to 2006 (Slawson and others 2008) showed a reduction in the percentage of inspections positive for *P. ramorum* and a reduction in the number of outbreaks at nurseries;

however, the continued pathogen findings indicated that the phytosanitary measures have not been completely effective.

Best Management Practices

Best management practices are methods, measures, practices, or procedures that have been determined to be effective means of preventing or reducing adverse effects. Through experience, research, and knowledge of the disease cycle of *P. ramorum*, BMPs to prevent or reduce pathogen spread have been compiled. Many of the practices are meant to exclude *P. ramorum* from noninfested areas by preventing or reducing the risk of spread. They are usually most effective when applied as a system rather than as individual practices.

BMPs in wildlands and urban-interface zones—

Numerous publications outline BMPs to prevent or reduce the spread of *P. ramorum*. These BMPs provide guidelines to prevent or minimize the introduction and subsequent spread of *P. ramorum* by limiting movement of host material or infested soil. The California Oak Mortality Task Force (COMTF) at www.suddenoakdeath.org has compiled BMPs for a number of activities and user groups on wildlands and in urban-interface zones. They include guidelines for forestry, recreational users, forest collectors, arborists, homeowners, firefighters, tribal plant gatherers, and Christmas tree growers (California Oak Mortality Task Force 2004a, 2004b, 2004c, 2004d, 2005, 2006a, 2006b, 2006c). In 2002, the Management Committee of the COMTF compiled BMPs for zone of infestation-regulated areas (California Oak Mortality Task Force 2002); measures to prevent spread of the pathogen during tree removal or pruning in regulated areas, and measures to minimize the movement of host material and soil from infested areas are presented.

In the United Kingdom, a best practice guide for woodlands, parks, and gardens (P. ramorum—*A Practical Guide for Established Parks & Gardens, Amenity Landscape and Woodland Areas*) is available from the Department for Environment, Food and Rural Affairs (DEFRA) Web site at: http://www.fera.defra.gov.uk/plants/publications/plantHealth/documents/pramparks.pdf.

BMPs in nurseries—

The management of *P. ramorum* in nurseries is based on minimizing the risk of introduction and preventing pathogen establishment. Numerous BMPs or guidelines on *P. ramorum* in nurseries are available. The guidelines are designed to encourage general cleanliness standards to minimize introduction and establishment of the pathogen. On December 21, 2004, the USDA APHIS adopted an Executive order that requires all nurseries in California, Oregon, and Washington that export nursery stock interstate to be surveyed for *P. ramorum*. The Oregon Department of

Agriculture adopted a similar regulation shortly thereafter (*Phytophthora ramorum* Regulated Area for Nursery Stock). Based on these regulations, guidelines were developed in cooperation with the California Association of Nurseries and Garden Centers, the Oregon Association of Nurseries, the Washington Nursery and Landscape Association, Oregon State University, the Oregon Department of Agriculture, and the Washington State Department of Agriculture (Parke 2005). The BMPs for California nurseries, developed by the Nursery Committee of the COMTF (Suslow and others 2005) are divided into two categories: exclusion/prevention, and monitoring. Guidelines for Oregon nurseries (Parke and others 2003), Washington nurseries (Parke and others 2004), and California nurseries (Tjosvold and others 2005) have been published. The guidelines are continuously updated as new information becomes available.

A national working group, convened by The Horticultural Research Institute (HRI), the research arm of the American Nursery & Landscape Association (ANLA), developed a menu of nationally applicable BMPs for *P. ramorum* in nurseries. The group comprised diverse representatives from the nursery industry and key technical and research experts from the USDA Agricultural Research Service (ARS), the USDA APHIS, the Cooperative State Research Education and Extension Service (CSREES) and representatives of state Departments of Agriculture through the National Plant Board (NPB). The national working group evaluated and fine-tuned existing BMP plans from California, Oregon, and other regions. The product (*Voluntary Nursery Industry Best Management Practices for* Phytophthora ramorum—*Introduction or Establishment in Nursery Operations* Version 1.0) is available at http://www.hriresearch.org/docs/Publications/HRI%20Publications/VoluntaryIndustryBestManagementPracticesPramorumweb1.pdf. The publication contains biosecurity guidelines, created by and for nursery growers, to reduce the risks associated with *P. ramorum*. The control of the pathogen is based on the insertion of multiple hurdles to prevent the introduction of the pathogen into nursery operations (Suslow 2008b).

The Oregon Department of Agriculture (ODA) has developed a Grower Assisted Inspection Program (GAIP) to help reduce the risk of nursery plants from becoming infected with *P. ramorum*. The objective of the GAIP is to assist nurseries to self monitor for *Phytophthora* species and mitigate pathogen problems using appropriate management practices. The program uses the best cultural practices (BCP) developed by researchers at Oregon State University for their online *Phytophthora* course. Standard operating procedures, structured from the BCP and best available science with modifications specific to each nursery, are used as appropriate. (http://www.oregon.gov/ODA/PLANT/NURSERY/gaip.shtml). Oregon

State University applied an approach based on Hazard Analysis of Critical Control Points (HACCP) for systematically detecting sources of *Phytophthora* contamination in four Oregon nurseries. The goal was to adapt the HACCP approach to identify critical control points (CCPs) for *Phytophthora* contamination in commercial nursery production systems. Critical control points are the best points, steps, or procedures at which significant hazards of contamination can be prevented or reduced to minimum hazard. Critical control points identified in the nurseries were (1) placement of healthy container-grown plants on contaminated soil/gravel substrates (all nurseries), (2) use of contaminated irrigation water (nurseries A and C only), and (3) use of contaminated used pots (all nurseries) (Parke and others 2010a).

Oregon State University Extended Campus (Ecampus) developed an online training course for the management of *Phytophthora* in nurseries (Parke and others 2010b). The "*Phytophthora* Online Course: Training for Nursery Growers" provides access to nursery personnel and the public. The course includes three modules: biology, symptoms, and diagnosis; disease management; and *Phytophthora ramorum*. The course, accessed at (http://ecampus.oregonstate.edu/phytophthora), is available in Spanish as well as English.

The first national U.S. nursery site for invasive species research is being established in Marin County, California. The site, The National Ornamentals Research Site at Dominican University of California (NORS-DUC), is a secure site modeled to reflect a nursery for the purpose of performing studies on nursery stock in a "real world" environment while ensuring high-level safeguards to prevent the escape of plant pests. Initial studies will focus on understanding and controlling the long-range spread of *P. ramorum* through infested nursery stock shipments.

The British Columbia Nursery and Landscape Association has developed a *P. ramorum* certification program for nursery growers, silviculture, and floriculture industries (British Columbia Nursery and Landscape Association 2005). The objective is to minimize the risk of importing and moving the pathogen in the province. The program includes mandatory sampling and testing for *P. ramorum*, workshops for nursery staff, implementation of BMPs, and an audit by an independent organization. In the United Kingdom, a *Practical Guide for the Nursery and Garden Centre Industry* has been produced (http://www.fera.defra.gov.uk/plants/publications/plantHealth/documents/pramnurs.pdf).

Eradication

If the disease is caught early enough, eradication is the current USDA policy to respond to new isolated occurrences of *P. ramorum*. Eradication efforts may be applied to large geographic areas, to smaller areas such as forest stands or nurseries, or to individual host plants. Efforts to eliminate, destroy, or reduce inoculum, including sanitation efforts, can be included in eradication strategies. Eradication of any disease can only be successful if the pathogen is detected early and its distribution is limited. If eradication is not feasible, then attempts to control, manage, and mitigate impacts are considered.

From Forests

Eradication efforts in Oregon—

In July 2001, *P. ramorum* was discovered at nine disease centers in mixed tanoak (*Lithocarpus densiflorus* (Hook. & Arn.) Rehd.)/Douglas-fir (*Pseudotsuga menziesii* (Mirb.) Franco) forests near Brookings, Oregon (Goheen and others 2002b). Aerial photos of the area indicated that the pathogen had been present at one of the sites since about 1997. The pathogen was isolated from stem cankers on tanoak and from foliage and shoots of native *Rhododendron* and *Vaccinium*. All lands within 1.6 km of the disease centers, an approximately 2331-ha area, were subjected to Oregon and APHIS quarantines that prohibited the transport of host materials. Since the fall of 2001, state and federal agencies have attempted to eradicate *P. ramorum* from those infested sites by cutting and burning all infected host plants and a buffer of adjacent apparently uninfected plants (Goheen and others 2004; Hansen and Sutton 2006; Kanaskie and others 2004, 2010a). The Oregon program now consists of early detection, delimitation of infested areas, treatment, research and monitoring, and host reduction in areas of probable disease spread. Following treatment, sites are monitored by baiting of streams and rainwater with leaves of tanoak and rhododendron, baiting of soils with pear fruits and tanoak and rhododendron leaves, and examining sprouting host plants for infection (Hansen and Sutton 2006). Between 2001 and 2008, more than 971 ha were treated at a cost of over $4 million (Kanaskie and others 2009).

During the first 4 years of the eradication effort, the number of new infested sites and infected trees remained steady or decreased each year, indicating modest success at containment and eradication (fig. 14). In 2005, the number of new infected trees and the area infested began increasing. Delays in completing treatments and consecutive years of unusually wet spring and early summer weather contributed to spread of the disease, resulting in expansion of the quarantine zone from 6734 ha to 41 956 ha in 2008 (Kanaskie and others 2008a, 2010a).

Results of the Oregon program indicate modest to moderate success at eradication and good success at containment of the pathogen to a relatively small area, thereby reducing damage to forests and minimizing the economic impact of quarantine regulations (Kanaskie and others 2006b, 2008a, 2010a; Goheen and others 2010).

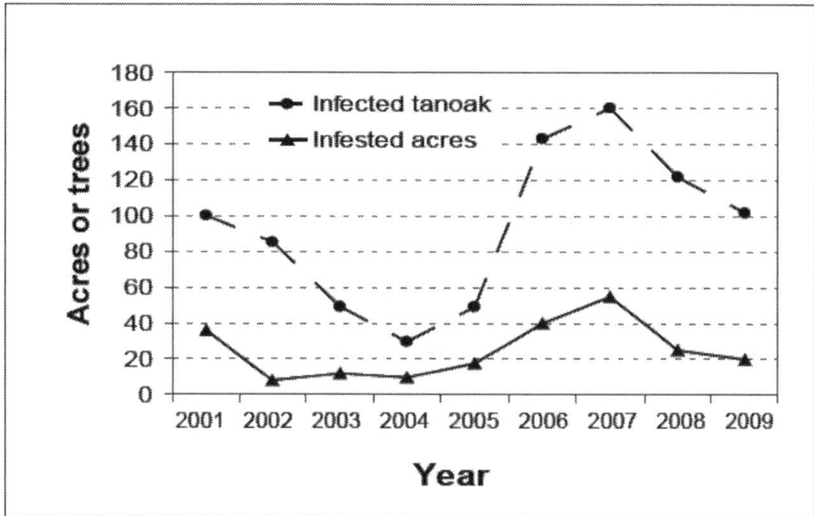

Figure 14—Sudden oak death trends in southern Curry County, Oregon, 2001 to 2009.

Efforts in northern California to slow the spread—

In contrast to the eradication efforts in Oregon forests, the strategies in California forests have been, by necessity, aimed not at elimination, but at efforts to slow the spread. These efforts involve reducing inoculum through sanitation, removal of reservoirs of inoculum, and removal of hosts or alternate hosts.

An infestation of *P. ramorum* in an area of about 518 ha of coast redwood (*Sequoia sempervirens* (D. Don) Endl.) forests near the town of Redway in a residential setting in Humboldt County, California, was confirmed in July 2002. Because eradication was not feasible, efforts were made to slow the spread of the disease there. The area was treated in February 2004 by removing infested tanoaks (Valachovic and others 2006). Additional areas of tanoak mortality in riparian forest settings near Redway and nearby Garberville were confirmed later in 2004. Because clearcutting was not an option owing to adverse environmental impacts, the residential setting, and other considerations, removal of hosts, including California bay laurel (*Umbellularia californica* (Hook. & Arn.) Nutt.) and madrone (*Arbutus menziesii* Pursh), to reduce inoculum was tested at various sites (Valochovic and others 2008) as part of an overall management program. Experimental silvicultural control efforts over 48.6 ha were implemented in 2006. The treatments included California bay laurel and tanoak removal (sporulating hosts of *P. ramorum*) in combination with pile and broadcast burning (Valachovic and others 2008).

Efforts to manipulate forest stands by pruning, host removal, thinning, and other actions to reduce incidence and impact of *P. ramorum* are underway in several other California locations, including the Big Sur area. To reduce the spread of *P. ramorum*, infected and symptomatic tanoaks were removed in fall 2009 from MacKerricher State Park campground north of Fort Bragg in Mendocino County. The Park infestation, first identified in spring 2009, is the first known occurrence of the disease along the northern Mendocino coast. The objective was not eradication, but a proactive and precautionary measure intended to help reduce the spread of the pathogen by reducing inoculum. After the trees were cut, the boles, branches, and leaves were burned in an air curtain incinerator. Other projected management actions for the site include the use of Agri-Fos® on selected tanoaks surrounding the site, as well as planting of Bishop pine (*Pinus muricata* D. Don) seedlings as part of a site rehabilitation effort (see http://nature.berkeley.edu/comtf/pdf/Monthly%20 Reports/COMTF_Report_November_2009.pdf).

From European Woodlands, Parks, and Gardens

In Europe, when *P. ramorum* is found in natural and seminatural environments, the official EU requirement is that appropriate measures be taken to at least contain the harmful organism. Measures used in the European Union include prohibition on the movement of infected plants and parts of plants, destruction by removing and burning or composting of the plant material, prevention of regrowth, and restricting access to the outbreak area (OJEC 2007).

In the United Kingdom, measures that are applied to outbreaks in the semi-natural or natural environment include (Sansford and Woodhall 2007):

- Prohibition on movement of the infected plant and parts of the plant (e.g., must not be used for propagation purposes or foliage purposes).
- Destruction of infected plants and susceptible plants within an appropriate cordon sanitaire [quarantine line] and associated plant debris.
- Prevention of regrowth.
- For infected trees, required felling or pruning depending on the part of the tree infected and the extent of infection.
- Measures required to prevent reinfection at the site (e.g., prohibition on planting susceptible plants in contaminated soil, removal or sterilization of contaminated soil).

In the United Kingdom, significant rhododendron clearance programs have been completed and are ongoing. Through 2007, more than 60 ha of rhododendrons have been cleared from woodlands in each of Cornwall and south Wales. Measures applied at garden/woodland outbreaks are aimed at containment with a view toward eradication. Experiments in historical gardens have shown that completely removing infected rhododendrons and other foliar hosts can prevent new plant infections.

In one garden, no new plant infections have been recorded 4 years after all the significant numbers of infected plants were removed (Turner 2007a); even though it can still be detected in soil and water courses, these levels of contamination appear to be epidemiologically insignificant. In soil, the pathogen is most likely surviving as chlamydospores. This type of spore maintains the pathogen in the U.K. environment for at least 2 years. Removal of foliar hosts protects susceptible trees from infection. Pruning out infections from infected foliar hosts (*Rhododendron*) in the United Kingdom has not proven overly effective, even with the use of fungicides applied prior to pruning to help protect cut surfaces from reinfection (Sansford and others 2009). The U.K. government has provided £25 million over 5 years (2009 through 2013) to help contain and eradicate *P. ramorum* and *P. kernoviae* in historical gardens, woodlands, heathlands, and from nurseries and retailers in England and Wales.

In the Netherlands, eradication of *P. ramorum* from an infested public green was attempted by cutting back all infected rhododendrons to 30 cm. As an experiment, the remaining parts of the plants were treated with thiophanate–methyl, glyphosate, or left untreated, and the removal of plant debris and humus or plant debris only was tested. The regrowth and occurrence of new infections were monitored (Aveskamp and others 2006). The pathogen survived in the sandy soil for at least 1 year, and cutting back the rhododendron shrubs to 30 cm was not sufficient to eradicate *P. ramorum* from the infested public green. Measures taken in the Netherlands therefore now focus on containment.

From Nurseries

United States—

In U.S. nurseries, eradication of the pathogen is the primary objective of the USDA APHIS strategic plan (USDA APHIS 2005b). Through protocols for tracing infected plants and mitigating infested nurseries, *P. ramorum* may be eliminated from nursery stock. Successful eradication can be demonstrated through scientifically valid survey and sampling plans. The implementation of clean stock programs and best management practices for nurseries can ensure that nursery stock moving in commerce is free of *P. ramorum*.

A study of the federal confirmed nursery protocol (USDA APHIS 2004), which outlined the destruction of infected nursery stock, safe disposal of contaminated containers and growing media, and subsequent testing of the remaining plants onsite, was conducted in Oregon during an attempt to eradicate the pathogen in imported, infected nursery stock (Osterbauer and others 2004). *Phytophthora ramorum* was not detected in plants at the nurseries after the destruction of the originally infected plant material. The confirmed nursery protocol has apparently been used successfully in many nurseries, with the failures attributed to instances where *P. ramorum* survived in soil.

Canada—

The Canadian Food Inspection Agency (CFIA) conducts annual surveys for *P. ramorum* and has in the past detected the presence of the pathogen on plants in a number of retail/wholesale nurseries in the southern coastal area of British Columbia. Of the 4,314 samples taken at 60 sites in the 2008 National Nursery Survey, 24 were positive for *P. ramorum*. Samples originated from 9 retail nurseries and 12 landscape sites (http://www.inspection.gc.ca/english/plaveg/pestrava/surv/sit2008e.shtml#phyram). Detections are followed by immediate eradication efforts. Eradication protocols for propagative nurseries (http://www.inspection.gc.ca/english/plaveg/hort/pi-010e.shtml) and retail nurseries (http://www.inspection.gc.ca/english/plaveg/hort/pi-011e.shtml) confirmed with *P. ramorum* have been developed. When *P. ramorum* is found at a retail nursery, all plants found infected, all hosts within 4 m of the infested plants, and all high-risk host plants (plants in the genera *Camellia, Kalmia, Pieris, Rhododendron*, and *Viburnum*) within the retail nursery are placed under quarantine. Following extensive sampling for the pathogen, all plants identified as infested as well as all host plants within 2 m of the infested plants are destroyed (CFIA 2009). Extensive surveys and trace-forward and trace-back activities are conducted to ensure the organism has been eliminated. When the CFIA detects a plant infested with *P. ramorum* and takes regulatory action—such as ordering disposal and treatments, or imposing restrictions or prohibitions—individuals or companies may apply for compensation under the "*Phytophthora ramorum* compensation regulations."

European Union—

Eradication is being attempted in the European Union by destroying all infected plants within a 2-m (6.6-ft) radius of a diseased plant and holding all susceptible plants within a 10-m (32.8-ft) radius plus any remaining plants from the same consignment as the diseased plants for further assessment (Sansford and others 2009, Slawson and others 2006). Release of these plants is allowed following two negative visual inspections during 3 months of active growth.

The eradication and containment actions required against *P. ramorum* in EU nurseries are:

- Destruction by burning or deep burial (infected plants, susceptible plants within a 2-m radius of infected plants and associated plant debris).

- Disinfection of surfaces.
- Prohibition on movement of susceptible plants within a 10-m radius of infected plants and remaining plants in infested lot for at least 3 months.
- Prohibition on use of *Phytophthora* fungicides during the holding period.
- Advise the cessation of overhead irrigation.
- Trace-back and trace-forward of related plant material.

In the case of a finding at a nursery, the following is required as a minimum (Sansford and Woodhall 2007):

- Destruction of infected plants and all susceptible plants within a 2-m radius of the infected plants (from May 2007 this will include the destruction of associated growing media and plant debris, plus appropriate phytosanitary measures applied to the growing surface).
- A quarantine period of 3 months of active growth for all susceptible plants within 10 m of the infected plants and any remaining plants from the affected batch.
- For plants under quarantine, treatments that might suppress symptom development are prohibited during the quarantine period.
- For plants under quarantine, at least two official inspections must be carried out during the quarantine period.
- All other susceptible plants at the place of production should be subject to intensive official reinspection during this period (from May 2007, appropriate phytosanitary measures will have to be taken on the growing surface within a 2-m radius of infected plants).

Additional measures that have been taken by individual EU member states include (Sansford and Woodhall 2007):

- No treatment that could suppress symptoms should be applied during the quarantine period for all susceptible plants at the place of production.
- Where the infected plant is soil-grown, no host plant may be grown in the same area or the area immediately surrounding an infected plant for 3 years.
- A survey of plants within a 500-m radius around an infected place of production.
- After a finding, regular checks of all other susceptible plants at the place of production, including testing of plants and soil.
- Hygiene measures for container-grown plants, disinfection/destruction of cloth, pots, and any other associated material.

Slawson and others (2006) reported some success with eradication in the United Kingdom of 462 outbreaks (376 at nurseries and garden centers and 86 on managed and unmanaged land) recorded through December 2004; 82 percent were eradicated from nursery and retail facilities, and 27 percent were eradicated from managed and unmanaged lands. Modeling work has indicated that in the United Kingdom, the nursery trade has the characteristics of a scale-free network in which major nodes predominate (Pautasso and others 2008). Such a scale-free network lends itself to the current regulatory controls, which focus on plant passporting of key genera and wholesale producers. Conversely, removal of controls would potentially result in rapid epidemic spread throughout such a scale-free network. In the Netherlands, the EU actions to prevent the introduction and spread of *P. ramorum* appear to be successful in nurseries, but less so in woodland areas (Steeghs and de Gruyter 2006). Steeghs and de Gruyter (2006) suggested that because *P. ramorum* is known from about 25 to 30 field sites in the country, complete eradication would not be possible. In the United Kingdom, measures applied to outbreaks in the seminatural or natural environment continue to aim at containment with a view to eradication (Inman 2009).

Heat Treatments

Various heat treatment experiments have been done to determine efficacy in eradicating *P. ramorum* from infested host material.

Effects of composting on pathogen viability—
Composting is considered an effective treatment option for sanitization of *P. ramorum*-infected plant material (Garbelotto 2003a). Swain and others (2002, 2006) demonstrated that composting effectively eliminates *P. ramorum* from green waste. In laboratory heat treatment tests, wood chips and cankered stems from coast live oak and infected California bay laurel leaves were all noninfectious after a 2-week exposure at 55 °C. These same types of infectious plant materials were also used in field composting trials using both windrow and forced-air methods. All plant material extracted from compost piles was free from *P. ramorum* after 2 weeks, based on isolation and polymerase chain reaction (PCR) assay. The absence of *P. ramorum* DNA led the authors to conclude that the pathogen was absent and not merely suppressed or dormant. Aveskamp and Wingelaar (2006) demonstrated that the tunnel-composting process (heating plant material to a minimum of 60 °C for at least 10 hours under controlled conditions, with hot air flowing through the plant debris during the process) eliminated *P. ramorum* from infected *Rhododendron* leaves and shoots among *Rhododendron* plant debris.

Plant material infested with *P. ramorum* and brought into composting facilities may present a contamination risk to users of finished compost (Swain and Garbelotto 2006). Isolating sources of fresh plant material from curing and finished compost at facilities producing compost for commercial sale or transport out of quarantined areas is necessary to eliminate contamination.

Effect of heat treatments on pathogen viability—

Harnik and others (2004) showed that *P. ramorum* is highly heat tolerant and could be reisolated from artificially inoculated California bay laurel leaves placed at 55 °C for up to 1 week. The pathogen was not recovered after 2 weeks at 55 °C. Because the prolonged heat treatments are impractical for bay leaves intended to be sold commercially as a spice, the authors developed a treatment involving a gradual and progressive heating process combined with the application of a moderate vacuum (0.133 kPa) that could be completed in 22 hours; the treatment eliminated the recovery of *P. ramorum*, and had no negative effect on the quality of the bay leaves.

Jennings (2006) reported that a 30-minute dry heat treatment at 60 °C was required to achieve complete kill of *P. ramorum*. However, rhododendron, viburnum, and camellia plants were completely killed after a 20-minute dry heat treatment at 55 °C. The authors found an adverse effect on *P. ramorum* infections using a longer treatment period (130 minutes at 45 °C) on detached leaves, but whole plant treatment was ineffective in controlling symptom development (Jennings 2006). Moist, steam heat is apparently more effective than dry heat. Linderman and Davis (2006c) recovered *P. ramorum* sporangia or chlamydospores from soilless potting media up to 6 months after being added. Aerated steam pasteurization at 50 °C or higher for 30 minutes was an effective means of eradicating *P. ramorum* as well as other pathogens from the infested media and contaminated containers without destroying the containers.

Conifer bark requires either fumigation or heat treatment at 56 °C for 30 minutes before it can enter the EU from non-European countries. Tubajika and others (2008) found that a treatment at 56 °C for 30 minutes might not be adequate to kill *P. ramorum* in wood of tanoak. However, the results were inconclusive, particularly because the detection of *P. ramorum* in the controls was low. Swain and others (2006) showed that a 1-hour exposure at 55 °C was required to no longer detect *P. ramorum* in wood chips and cankered stems of coast live oak.

Protection

Protection strategies—those that provide a chemical, physical, spatial, or temporal barrier to infection—are used when the pathogen is present and infection will likely occur without the intervention of protective measures. Most barriers are chemical.

Chemical

A range of pesticides are available for use on *P. ramorum*. These include protective/preventive fungicides (products that remain on the host surface, protecting it from infection for a period of time; they do not enter the plant tissue), and systemic/curative fungicides (products that are absorbed into the plant and are fairly mobile within the plant; some have curative properties, i.e., the ability to stop infection progress). The mode of action of a fungicide can be fungicidal (kills the pathogen) or fungistatic (inhibits the growth of the pathogen).

Treatment of oaks and tanoak, bark applications—

It was recognized early on that, although fungicidal treatment of host trees in the forest environment would likely not be practical, treatment of individual high-value trees in the urban environment could be feasible and beneficial. Tests (Garbelotto and Rizzo 2001, Garbelotto and others 2002c) determined that many of the standard chemicals used to control other *Phytophthora* spp. (Erwin and Ribeiro 1996, Hardy and others 2001) were effective against *P. ramorum*. Metalaxyl, Al-fosetyl, copper sulfate, copper hydroxide, and phosphonate were effective against *P. ramorum* in vitro (Garbelotto and Rizzo 2001), and three chemical compounds reduced *P. ramorum* growth rate in potted coast live oak saplings (Garbelotto and others 2002c). Saplings injected with phosetyl-Al, metalaxyl, and phosphorous acid had significantly smaller cankers than untreated saplings or saplings injected with copper sulfate pentahydrate.

Garbelotto and others (2003b) evaluated a variety of commercially available chemicals effective against other *Phytophthora* species on coast live oak (*Quercus agrifolia* Née) and tanoak. Application methods included trunk injections, soil drenches, topical applications, and foliar sprays. Treatments with phosphonate compounds significantly reduced lesion size in both oaks (*Quercus* spp.) and tanoaks. Injecting the chemicals into the trunk of the tree was the most effective method. Treatment of the tree prior to infection was significantly more effective at controlling the pathogen than treatment after infection. Phosphonate-treated trees remained resistant to new *P. ramorum* infections for at least 3 months.

Additional field experiments evaluated the effectiveness of phosphonate chemical treatments for control of *P. ramorum* in tanoak and Shreve oak (*Q. parvula* Greene var. *shrevei* (C.H. Mull.) Nixon) (Schmidt and others 2006). Native stands of mature, uninfected trees were treated with Agrifos® systemic fungicide and subsequently inoculated with *P. ramorum*. Injections as well as topical applications of Agrifos with Pentrabark™ (Agrichem, Medina, Ohio) surfactant were evaluated. The injection and topical phosphonate treatments significantly reduced lesion size in tanoaks and Shreve oaks compared to untreated control trees. A combined treatment of injection and topical application methods was most effective in Shreve oak.

Gabelotto and others (2007) developed and tested bark application of a range of phosphite fungicides in combination with the organosilicate surfactant Pentrabark on coast live oak. Soil drenches and bark application of all phosphites without surfactant were ineffective. On the other hand, preventive injections of all phosphites and bark applications of phosphites amended with Pentrabark were consistently effective in suppressing bark colonization by *P. ramorum* without causing phytotoxicity.

Kanaskie and others (2006a) compared the efficacy of phosphonate (Agrifos) injected into the sapwood with application in combination with Pentrabark surfactant to the trunks of tanoak trees on *P. ramorum* lesion development. Lesion size was significantly smaller in the injected trees than in the bark-spray application or control trees. Also, the European isolate caused larger lesions than the North American isolate.

Phosphonate (Agrifos) treatments were effective in slowing both infection and growth rates for at least 18 months (Garbelotto and Schmidt 2009). Conversely, an alternative method consisting of an azomite soil amendment and bark lime wash (a previously untested, and unregistered, treatment) was ineffective, and did not reduce either growth or infection rates.

Agrifos is registered for oaks in California and Oregon. In California, Agrifos is currently recommended as a preventive treatment for use on high-value trees and on trees around high-use facilities. Preventive treatment, before infection has occurred, is more effective than curative treatments. Trees with advanced symptoms of *P. ramorum* infection (such as multiple bleeding areas, extensive beetle attack, evidence of decay, or a sparse or brown canopy) will not benefit from treatment. Two application methods are available, injection under the bark directly into the sapwood and topical application of the product, mixed with PentraBark penetrating surfactant, onto the trunk of the tree. Both methods are effective at controlling the growth of *P. ramorum* in oaks and tanoaks. The phosphite is translocated systemically and broken down into phosphonic acid, which triggers a defense response in the plant. The host response prevents infection and slows down the growth of cankers. Applications should be made when the tree is actively transpiring. Avoid treating trees during very hot or very cold weather, or when new leaves are emerging. Currently in northern California, two applications in the first year are recommended, one fall treatment in November or December and a second treatment approximately 6 months later. Subsequent treatments should be made once every year, preferably in the fall, alternating between injection and topical application methods. Information on tree treatment, including current recommendations, is summarized at http://nature.berkeley.edu/garbelotto/english/treatment.php.

Treatment of oaks and tanoak, foliar applications—

In early studies, foliar treatment of oaks and tanoaks using phosphonates only provided short-lived protection and caused phytotoxicity (Garbelotto 2004). On coast live oak, foliar application of phosphonates amended with surfactants was effective only at times and always caused phytotoxicity (Garbelotto and others 2007). The practicality and efficacy of aerial application of Agrifos for control *P. ramorum* in Oregon tanoak forests is being tested (Kanaskie and others 2010b). Preliminary results indicate small but significant reductions in growth of *P. ramorum* in Agrifos-sprayed trees, comparable to the results obtained from bole injection.

Treatment of foliar hosts—

Numerous chemicals to protect foliar hosts from *P. ramorum* infection have been tested. In most cases, fungicides known to be effective against other species of *Phytophthora* were evaluated. The literature on these studies is summarized in table 5.

Treatment of water and soil—

Treatment of recycled irrigation water with surfactants (Yakabe and Macdonald 2005), or with mefenoxam and Agrifos (Stringfellow and Reddy 2005), has eliminated *P. ramorum*. Hydrogen peroxide (Jet 5) and sodium hypochlorite (10 percent) effectively (at label recommended rates) decontaminated water inoculated with *P. ramorum* sporangia (Sansford and Woodhall 2007). In laboratory trials, two algaecides with copper-based active ingredients (copper carbonate [Captain®]; copper-triethanolamine and copper hydroxide [K-Tea®]) were toxic to zoospores, sporangia, and chlamydospores of *P. ramorum* and to zoospores of six other species of *Phytophthora* (Colburn and Jeffers 2010).

Yakabe and MacDonald (2008) tested chemicals (chloropicrin, 1,3-dichloropropene, dichloropropene with chloropicrin, metam sodium, iodomethane, dazomet, dimethyldisulphite, peroxyacetic acid with hydrogen dioxide and zerotol) in artificially infested soil in jars to determine their effectiveness as potential soil treatments. After 2 weeks or the "label minimum re-entry period" (harvest interval), *P. ramorum* was not detected in soils treated with chloropicrin, dichloropropene with chloropicrin, metam sodium, iodomethane, or dazomet. The remaining chemicals reduced the number of viable propagules, but did not eliminate the pathogen. Dazomet (158.8 kg/ 0.4 ha or 350 lb/acre) incorporated throughout the soil profile at three ornamental nurseries with infested sites in California eliminated the pathogen from treated areas (Yakabe and MacDonald 2008). Metalaxyl-M, added as a soil drench to sterile compost inoculated with *P. ramorum* sporangia, eliminated the pathogen (Turner and others 2006).

Table 5—Fungicides tested on foliar hosts of *Phytophthora ramorum* for prevention of infection

Citation	Fungicide	*P. ramorum* host	Efficacy/comments
Becker and others 2010	Subdue Maxx®, Aliette®	*Rhododendron*	All were effective foliar treatments for the protection of healthy rhododendrons.
Chastagner and Hansen 2003; Chastagner and others 2005, 2006a	Mefenoxam (Subdue MAXX®)	Douglas-fir (*Pseudotsuga menziesii* var. *menziesii*)	Pre-bud-break drench completely prevented infection.
	Dithane®, Gavel®, Maneb®, and Polyram®	Douglas-fir	Post-bud-break spray applications provided 100 percent control.
	Champ Formula 2F®, Reason®, Daconil Ultrex®, Stature®, and IKF – 916®	Douglas-fir	Post-bud-break spray applications reduced infection by 70 to 100 percent.
	Latron CS-7®	Douglas-fir	Post-bud-break spray applications reduced infection by 67 to 100 percent.
	Phostrol™	Douglas-fir	Post-bud-break spray applications reduced infection by 71 to 75 percent.
	Silwet L-77®	Douglas-fir	Post-bud-break spray applications had no effect on infection.
Chastagner and others 2008a	Mancozeb (Dithane 75 DF®), mancozeb + zoxamide (Gavel 75 DF®), dimethomorph (Stature DM®), cyazofamid (Ranman®), maneb (Maneb 75 DF®), metiram (Polyram 80 DF®), fenamidone (Fenstar®), chlorothalonil (Daconil Ultrex®), potassium phosphite (V-10161®), pyraclostrobin (Insignia 20W®), and mefenoxam (Subdue MAXX®)	Noble fir (*Abies procera*), grand fir (*A. grandis*)	Foliar application to seedlings protected foliage from infection by an EU1 A1 or NA1 A2 isolate.

Table 5—Fungicides tested on foliar hosts of *Phytophthora ramorum* for prevention of infection (continued)

Citation	Fungicide	*P. ramorum* host	Efficacy/comments
Chastagner and others 2008a	Maneb®, mancozeb + zoxamide, mefenoxam, cyazafamid, dimethomorph and mancozeb	*Rhododendron* x "Nova Zembla"	Effective treatments in controlling disease development on both wounded and nonwounded *Rhododendron* leaves.
Garbelotto and Rizzo 2001, Garbelotto and others 2002c	Phosetyl-Al, metalaxyl, phosphorous acid	Coast live oak (*Quercus agrifolia*)	Injection of potted saplings resulted in significantly smaller cankers than untreated saplings or saplings injected with copper sulfate pentahydrate.
Goheen and others 2006b	Dimethomorph (Stature®) and phosphonate (Agrifos®)	*Rhododendron macrophyllum*, *Vaccinium ovatum*, California bay laurel (*Umbellaria californica*), tanoak (*Lithocarpus densiflorus*)	Neither fungicide provided complete protection following foliar application.
Harnik and Garbelotto 2006	Metalaxyl (Subdue®), phosphorus acid (Agrifos400®), copper hydroxide (Champ®)	In vitro	All three chemicals were effective in inhibiting hyphal growth, sporangia production, and zoospore germination.
Harnik and Garbelotto 2006	Copper hydroxide (Champ®)	California bay laurel	Foliar application prevented infection up to 6 weeks after treatment.

Table 5—Fungicides tested on foliar hosts of *Phytophthora ramorum* for prevention of infection (continued)

Citation	Fungicide	*P. ramorum* host	Efficacy/comments
Heungens and others 2006	Metalaxyl, dimethomorf, cyazofanid, fosphetal Al, cymoxanil and mancozeb	*Rhododendron*	Metalaxyl, dimethomorf, and cyazofamid resulted in near-complete avoidance of stem infections; fosetyl-Al and cymoxanil had intermediate effects; mancozeb was the least effective. Protective effects best when lower leaf surface treated day before zoospore inoculation.
Linderman and Davis 2006a	Menfenoxam (Subdue Maxx®), SA 110201 (Sipcam Agro USA, Inc.)	*Rhododendron* (cv Nova Zembla)	Drench and foliar applications were effective. Inoculating detached leaves was comparable to inoculating intact plants to evaluate chemical and biological agents against *Phytophthora* species.
Orlikowski 2004b	Phosetyl Al, furalaxyl, fenamidone + phosetyl Al, propamocarb + phosetyl Al, oxadixyl + mancozeb, cymoxanil + famoxate	*Rhododendron*	All six fungicides significantly inhibited the pathogen and development of twig blight in lab and glasshouse trials, with furalaxyl the most effective.
Tjosvold and others 2006a	Mefenoxam (Subdue Maxx®), dimethomorph (Stature DM®), pyraclostrobin (Insignia®), fenamidone	*Rhododendron* "Cunningham's White" and R. "Irish Lace"	Foliar application provided preventive control; post-infection treatments were not effective.

Table 5—Fungicides tested on foliar hosts of *Phytophthora ramorum* for prevention of infection (continued)

Citation	Fungicide	*P. ramorum* host	Efficacy/comments
Turner and others 2006	Metalaxyl-M (SL 567A), dimethomorph/mancozeb (Invader®), cymoxanil/ mancozeb (Curzate M68®), fenamidone/ mancozeb (Sonata®), etridiazole (Standon Etridiazole 35®), azoxystrobin (Amistar®) and famoxadone/ cymoxanil (Tanos®)	*Rhododendron*, *Viburnum*	Foliar application of metalaxyl-M, azoxystrobin and fenamidone/mancozeb on *Rhododendron* completely inhibited symptom development when applied as protectants either 4 or 7 days prior to inoculation. On *Viburnum*, only metalaxyl-M was completely effective at all protectant timings. Fenamidone/mancozeb was effective when applied 4 days prior to inoculation, but not when applied 3 days earlier. Fungicides were generally less effective when applied as eradicants. The most effective was metalaxyl-M, completely inhibiting disease development when applied 4 days after inoculation. None of the fungicides completely controlled disease development on *Viburnum* when applied after the same period.
Wagner and others 2008	Dimethomorph (Acrobat®), copper-octanoate (Cueva®), and mancozeb + fenamidone (Gemini®), Mancozeb alone (Dithane Ultra® WP), Propineb (Antracol® WG), azoxystrobin (Ortiva®), propamacarb (Previcur N®), and cyazofamid (Ranman®)	In vitro	Dimethomorph, copper-octanoate, and mancozeb + fenamidone inhibited mycelium growth and zoospore germination. Mancozeb alone did not inhibit mycelial growth effectively. Propineb, azoxystrobin, propamacarb, and cyazofamid had no effect on mycelial growth and zoospore germination.

Pathogen resistance to metalaxyl-M—

Development of resistance to systemic fungicides has occurred with other *Phytophthora* spp. and is a concern with *P. ramorum*. Some *P. ramorum* isolates obtained from ornamental nursery plants in the United Kingdom have shown resistance to metalaxyl-M (Turner and others 2008b). In Belgium, Heungens and others (2006) identified a strain of *P. ramorum* with decreased sensitivity to metalaxyl-M. Resistance for five European isolates to metalaxyl-M has been reported (Wagner and others 2006, 2008). The isolates all originated from nurseries. Alternating the use of metalaxyl-M with a different fungicide is recommended to reduce the probability of resistance development.

Masking of symptoms by systemic fungicides—

The use of fungicides to control *P. ramorum* has raised concerns that fungicide residues may affect the ability to isolate the pathogen from infected tissue or mask symptom development, making it difficult to detect infected plants during routine visual inspections. Shishkoff (2005) investigated whether fosetyl-aluminium, mefonoxam, or propamocarb hydrochloride have a masking effect on infected *Rhododendron* shoots. The pathogen was recovered following inoculation from control and from fosetyl-Al- and propanocarb-treated lesions at high frequencies (64 to 100 percent) immediately after treatment, with recovery of the pathogen declining thereafter. The pathogen could not be recovered from mefonoxam-treated lesions until 3 to 5 weeks after treatment, when low frequencies (3 to 13 percent) were found. In all of the treatments, symptoms were not suppressed; lesions were easily visible. The pathogen was easily recovered from stem tissue 3 to 5 weeks after treatment, and sometimes isolated from buds, fallen leaves, and roots. Turner and others (2006) reported that *P. ramorum* could not be recovered from *Rhododendron* and *Viburnum* leaves 10 days after protectant and eradicant applications of metalaxyl-M, metalaxyl-M with fluazinam, metalaxyl-M with mancozeb, metalaxyl-M with chlorothalanil, and propamocarb hydrochloride with fenamidone. Results indicated that the chemicals had killed the pathogen and was not merely fungistatic. However, Chastagner and others (2010) occasionally isolated *P. ramorum* from asymptomatic rhododendron tissue inoculated and then treated with Subdue MAXX® and Insignia®, suggesting that those fungicides may pose a high risk of masking symptom development.

Effects of tree essential oils on the pathogen—

Manter and others (2006) reported that 140 mg/kg of essential oil from the wood of Alaska yellow-cedar (*Chamaecyparis nootkatensis* (D. Don) Spach), Port-Orford-cedar (*C. lawsoniana* (A. Murr.) Parl.), incense-cedar (*Calocedrus decurrens*

(Torr.) Florin), or western juniper (*Juniperus occidentalis* Hook.) strongly inhibited zoospore germination and hyphal growth of *P. ramorum* in culture. Field tests (Manter and others 2008) suggested that heartwood chips from western redcedar (*Thuja plicata* Donn ex D. Don), incense-cedar, and yellow-cedar placed over forest litter reduced inoculum potential of the pathogen, and thus, potential for spread.

Biological

Biological agents are also being tested as protectants. The surfactant-producing bacterium *Pseudomonas fluorescens* strain SS101, known to cause zoospore lysing, resulted in significantly less infection of detached California bay laurel leaves by *P. ramorum* (Cohen and others 2006), but results were highly variable.

Linderman and Davis (2006a) found that bacterial antagonists (*Bacillus brevis* and *Paenibacillus polymyxa*) significantly inhibited all *Phytophthora* species tested in vitro, but were ineffective in inoculation assays of leaves dipped in a cell suspension of each antagonist 24 hours prior to inoculation with *P. ramorum* or other *Phytophthora* species. Elliott and Shamoun (2008) found that the bacteria *Streptomyces lydicus* strain WYEC 108 (Actinovate®) and *Bacillus subtilis* (as found in Rhapsody® and Sonata®), applied to detached *Rhododendron* leaves 24 hours before wounding and inoculation with *P. ramorum*, inhibited lesion development. Treatment of whole plants with Rhapsody and Actinovate resulted in some degree of protection to the leaves against *P. ramorum* and reduced the number of foliar lesions; effects of Sonata were not significantly different than treatment of plants with water (Becker and others 2010).

The soil fungus *Trichoderma* spp. may provide some control of the soil phase of *P. ramorum*. Widmer (2008) reported that several isolates of *Trichoderma* were mycoparasitic to *P. ramorum* in vitro, attacking the sporangia and chlamydospores. Laboratory assays by Elliott and Shamoun (2008) gave similar results.

Natural Plant Products

Caffeic acid added to V8 juice agar inhibited zoospore germination and sporangial germination (Widmer 2008). Application of rice bran extract containing derivatives of caffeic acid applied to *Rhododendron* leaves prior to infection reduced leaf necrosis (Widmer 2008). Agar and soil leachate amended with grapefruit extract inhibited colony growth and sporulation of *P. ramorum* (Orlikowski 2004a). Spraying *Rhododendron* inoculated with *P. ramorum* with the grapefruit extract inhibited the spread of necrosis on stems and leaves. Pre- and post-inoculation spraying of *Rhododendron* with chitosan also suppressed the disease (Orlikowski 2004a).

Soil Amendments

Klinger and Zingaro (2006) suggested that symptoms associated with dying oaks in *P. ramorum*-infested areas are sometimes the same as those associated with an increase in soil acidity (reportedly due to mosses, industrial pollution such as acid rain, acid fog, and other factors), and that the soil acidification weakens trees and disposes them to attack by secondary organisms. Thus soil amendments containing calcium (applied as lime wash) and other ingredients (usually azomite as a fertilizer) to offset soil acidification have been recommended as treatment for *P. ramorum*-infected trees. Scientifically valid studies to support the recommendation are lacking. Garbelotto and Schmidt (2009) reported that an azomite soil amendment and bark lime wash treatment was not effective in reducing either growth or infection rates of *P. ramorum*. Increased soil acidity in infested areas has apparently not been demonstrated. The addition of calcium does have numerous effects on trees and on *Phytophthora* in vitro and in vivo, both positive and negative (Balci and Halmschlager 2003, Campanella and others 2002, Kim and others 1997, Messenger and others 2000, Simpfendorfer and Harden 2000, Von Broembsen and Deacon 1997). Treatment of potted coast live oak trees inoculated with *P. ramorum* with azomite soil amendment and bark lime wash had no effect on bark lesion size or infection rates compared to controls (Garbelotto and Schmidt 2009).

Aluminum-amended peatmoss suppressed chlamydospore production and reduced populations of *P. ramorum* in laboratory trials (Fichtner and others 2008c).

Compost Teas

The use of a liquid tea made from compost to protect hosts of *P. ramorum* is gaining support among some organic growers and home gardeners. Compost tea, made by steeping compost in water with other natural ingredients for at least 24 hours, increases the growth of microbes, which may inhibit harmful organisms. The tea is sprayed on leaves or used as a soil drench, depending on the part of the plant to be protected. The theory is that microbial compounds in the tea destroy harmful microbes that attempt to invade plants. Experimental evidence of efficacy in treating *P. ramorum* hosts is lacking. Linderman and Davis (2006c) treated rhododendron leaves with *Paenibacillus polymyxa* taken from compost, and then exposed the plant to *P. ramorum*. The *P. polymyxa* did not protect the plant from damage.

Resistance

A program to develop trees genetically resistant to a pathogen is long term and expensive, and has been undertaken in North America for only a few pathogens (Sniezko 2006). One successful example of a resistance breeding program for a

Phytophthora species is the *P. lateralis* program for Port-Orford-cedar. A genetics white paper developed by the COMTF (Dodd and others 2006) points out the commitment and resources needed to develop a tree resistance program.

Information on the variation in virulence/aggressiveness of *P. ramorum* and the types of genetic resistance in the various host species is limited.

Resistance in California Bay Laurel and Coast Live Oak

Studies (Dodd and others 2005, 2008; Garbelotto and others 2003a, Hüberli and others 2002) indicated that individuals of California bay laurel and coast live oak display differential levels of resistance to *P. ramorum*. Hüberli and others (2002) found a range of resistance, as measured by leaf lesions formed on California bay laurel leaves collected from throughout the geographic range of the pathogen, following inoculation with *P. ramorum* zoospores. Dodd and others (2005) found significant heritable variation in lesion size on branch cuttings of coast live oak in response to inoculation with *P. ramorum*, and suggested that the variability was controlled by several gene loci. Beals and Dodd (2006) found a fairly uniform genetic structure in coast live oak throughout its range, with 96 percent of the molecular variance occurring within populations. Results suggest that searches for *Phytophthora*-resistant genotypes could be limited to smaller areas of the species' distribution.

The susceptibility of California bay laurel varies geographically. Meshriy and others (2006) reported differences in susceptibility to *P. ramorum* among populations of *U. californica*, with trees from Oregon being less susceptible, as exhibited by smaller lesions following zoospore inoculation of detached leaves, than those from California. They found only slight variation among populations from California. The genotypes of the two California bay laurel populations appear to differ, and there are physiological differences in the leaf surfaces of California bay laurel and Oregon myrtlewood (the common name used in Oregon for *U. californica*). The thicker cuticles of Oregon myrtlewood may reduce the potential for leaf infection.

Based on data from lab susceptibility trials and field infection data collected from 97 trees from 12 populations in northern California, Anacker and others (2008) found that experimental lesion size and field infection levels differed significantly among both California bay laurel trees and populations. The phenotypic trait of leaf area was significantly related to lab lesion size, where bigger leaves produced bigger lesions. Variability in lesion size produced in the lab and infection levels in the field were significantly related to amplified fragment length polymorphism (AFLP) markers, suggesting a genetic basis to resistance. They also identified markers associated with phenotypic traits putatively involved in conferring resistance, including leaf toughness and leaf water content.

Resistance in Tanoak

Hayden and Garbelotto (2006) demonstrated differences in resistance among tanoak individuals and populations, suggesting the existence of quantitative resistance to *P. ramorum* in tanoak populations and individuals. Bark and wounded leaf-inoculated tanoak saplings grown from acorns collected in the Six Rivers National Forest showed significant variability in lesion size among individuals, with stem lesion area positively correlated with leaf lesion area. In their study, growing conditions also had an effect with trees in south-facing rows of the lath house having smaller lesions than those in north-facing rows. Additional inoculations of seedlings (using detached leaves and seedling tips) from nine sites revealed variable resistance with significant heritability (Hayden and others 2010).

Resistance in Viburnum

Grünwald and others (2006a) found a considerable range of resistance in the genus *Viburnum*. They evaluated nine species of field-grown *Viburnum* (23 cultivars) for resistance to *P. ramorum* in detached leaf tests. They obtained significant differences between cultivars in percentage of leaf area affected ($P < 0.001$), with no significant differences owing to isolates or interactions between isolates and cultivars. The percentage of leaf area affected ranged from 95 percent in extremely susceptible cultivars (cvs. *V. burkwoodii* cv. unkown, *V. plicatum* var. *tomentosum* cv. Mariesii, and *V. trilobium* cvs. Alfredo and Bailey), to between 25 and 90 percent in a moderately susceptible group (cvs. *V. burkwoodii* cv. Mohawk, *V. lantana* cv. Mohican, *V. opulus* cvs. Compacta and Hanum, *V. lentago* cv. unknown, *V. sargentii* cv. Onandaga, *V. trilobium* cv. Redwing) to less than 15 percent infection in the most resistant group (*V. dentatum* cvs. Autumn Jazz, Blue Muffin, Chicago Lustre, and Burgundy; *V. opulus* cv. Sterile, *V. plicatum* cvs. Newport, Popcorn, Shasta, and Shoshon; *V. nudum* cv. Winterthur, *V. trilobium* cv. Wentworth).

Resistance in Lilac

Grünwald and others (2006b) evaluated the relative susceptibility of 25 species and cultivars of lilac to *P. ramorum* using detached leaf assays. The cultivars tested had significantly different percentage of leaf area affected. Cultivars *Syringa vulgaris* cv. Ellen Willmott, *Syringa* x *prestoniae* cv. Minuet, and *S. vulgaris* cv. Katherine Havemeyer had less than 20 percent leaf area affected and were the most resistant.

Resistance in Rhododendron

Tooley and others (2002) found that leaves of *Rhododendron* "P.J.M.," *R. maximum*, and *R. carolinianum* dipped in suspensions of *P. ramorum* sporangia developed lesions on less than 10 percent of the leaf area compared to a highly susceptible cultivar like Cunningham's White that developed up to 50 percent leaf area infected with the most virulent isolate tested.

De Dobbelaere and others (2006) screened 63 *Rhododendron* species (21 species and 42 hybrids) for their susceptibility to *P. ramorum*. Four inoculation methods (wounded or nonwounded detached leaves and wounded or nonwounded branches) were used. Methods involving nonwounded tissue were used to estimate the ability of the hosts to resist tissue penetration. Methods involving wounded tissue evaluated the resistance to pathogen growth inside leaf tissue. Significant differences in disease susceptibility were observed between species as well as between hybrids with all methods used. Inoculation of wounded leaves and stems showed that most species and hybrids were susceptible to some extent. Inoculation of nonwounded leaves or stems resulted in more variation in susceptibility, with little to no infection occurring in a few hybrids. The results suggested that if significant resistance is present, it probably occurs at the level of tissue penetration.

Linderman and others (2006) tested different species of *Phytophthora* or isolates of *P. ramorum* (both mating types) by inoculating detached leaves of "Nova Zembla" rhododendron, lilac (*Syringa vulgaris* L.), or doublefile viburnum (*Viburnum plicatum* Thunb. var. *tomentosum*). Plant species within genera or cultivars within species varied in susceptibility to isolates of *P. ramorum* and other species of *Phytophthora*. *Phytophthora ramorum*, *P. citricola*, *P. citrophthora*, and *P. nicotianae* were the most virulent pathogens on most of the host plants inoculated. Some plants were susceptible to several species of *Phytophthora*, whereas others were susceptible only to *P. ramorum*.

Resistance in *Vaccinium*

Parke and others (2002b, 2002c) compared the potential susceptibility of wild *Vaccinium* species and of commercial *Vaccinium* crops such as blueberry (*Vaccinium* spp.), cranberry (*V. macrocarpon* Aiton), and lingonberry (*V. vitis-idaea* L. ssp. *minus* (Lodd.) Hultén) in detached leaf assays. A wide range of disease responses—from resistant (cranberry) to highly susceptible (lingonberry)—was observed among the *Vaccinium* species and among cultivars.

Survey and Monitoring

For the disease management strategies discussed here to be implemented correctly and efficaciously, it is essential to know the distribution and incidence of the pathogen. Detection efforts are done through surveys and monitoring. Monitoring to detect *P. ramorum* presence is a critical component of the USDA national *P.*

ramorum management strategy (USDA APHIS 2005b). The national strategic plan strives to prevent artificial spread of *P. ramorum* through prevention, detection and monitoring, and control and management. The objective of the detection and monitoring component of the strategy is to rapidly and accurately determine where the pathogen and disease are located and to reliably verify pathogen presence or absence in areas considered to be uninfested. The plan discusses detection and monitoring needs such as port inspections, nursery surveys, aerial and roadside surveys in wildland and urban forest settings, forest inventory and monitoring plots, and public employees trained to look for the disease.

Aerial and ground-based surveys and image analysis are used in California and Oregon forests and woodlands containing host species to determine the distribution and incidence of *P. ramorum*. In addition, research information on hosts, likely pathways of pathogen movement, and favorable climatic conditions are being used in a risk-based analysis to plan surveys to detect *P. ramorum* (Goheen 2003). For information on remote sensing and other specific image analysis projects, see the University of California Web site http://kellylab.berkeley.edu/oakmapper/. The USDA FS Western Wildland Environmental Threat Assessment Center has an ongoing project to evaluate the use of hyperspectral imagery for previsual detection of *P. ramorum*-infected tanoak trees. Preliminary results suggest that identifying infected tanoaks may be possible, but not in situations where the infected trees are below the tree canopy (http://gis.fs.fed.us/wwetac/projects/completed/hyperspectral.html).

Forest Survey and Monitoring in California

California's *P. ramorum* monitoring program focuses on early detection. Aerial and ground-based surveys of uninfested areas within minimally infested counties or counties with no known occurrence of *P. ramorum* but sharing a common border with infested counties are conducted, and ground-based early-detection surveys in high-risk uninfested areas are done (Mai and others 2006, Mark and Jirka 2002, Meentemeyer and others 2006). Early detection efforts include monitoring of streams and rivers throughout infested and at-risk areas of California by baiting with rhododendron leaves (Aram and Rizzo 2010, Murphy and others 2006).

Forest Survey and Monitoring in Oregon

Several *P. ramorum* detection surveys are conducted each year in at-risk forest areas by the Oregon Department of Forestry and the USDA Forest Service (USDA FS) (Goheen and others 2006a). The forest range of tanoak is systematically surveyed from a fixed-wing aerial survey plane, and suspicious trees are mapped. Followup helicopter surveys provide a closer look at symptomatic trees and enable more precise mapping. All suspected trees are checked from the ground and samples collected for confirmation. In addition, annual ground surveys check the perimeters of previously treated areas for newly infected trees. Oregon nurseries, Christmas tree plantations, and other sites are surveyed regularly, as mandated by federal regulations (Osterbauer and others 2004).

Streams in and near the quarantine area in southwest Oregon are monitored for *P. ramorum* using rhododendron and tanoak leaves. The leaf baits are collected and replaced every 2 weeks throughout the year. Collected leaves are assayed by multiplex rDNA internal transcribed spacer polymerase chain reaction (ITS PCR). Initially, both isolation on a selective medium and ITS PCR were used, but ITS PCR was more sensitive. When infected leaves are detected, ground surveys are used to locate infected hosts upstream (Sutton and others 2009).

National Surveys

A national survey of forests at risk is conducted by the USDA FS Forest Health Monitoring program and its cooperators to determine whether the pathogen occurs outside the quarantined areas of California and Oregon. As a first step, the USDA FS produced a risk-based U.S. map identifying sampling polygons. Factors used to assign risk and develop the sampling polygons were (a) presence of known host species, host genera, and closely related genera; (b) locations of nurseries receiving *Rhododendron* spp. stock; (c) length of yearly mesic/moist weather period; and (d) area outside limiting temperature extremes currently associated with *P. ramorum*. Based on these criteria, much of the southern Appalachian and the Pacific coastal regions are currently rated high risk. Additional information on the national survey, including the methods used and a copy of the national risk map, are available in chapter 4.

Both APHIS-PPQ and the states conduct a national survey of nurseries annually through the Cooperative Agricultural Pest Survey program. The USDA FS and states conducted nursery perimeter and general forest detection surveys using terrestrial vegetation survey protocols from 2003 to 2006. Successful pilot testing of stream baiting survey protocols in 11 states during 2006 resulted in full implementation in 2007, and the more cost-effective stream baiting methods and protocols continued to the present (Oak and others 2010). Table 2 in chapter 2 presents nationwide nursery detections of *P. ramorum* by year.

Canadian Surveys

The Canadian Food Inspection Agency (CFIA) conducts annual surveys—targeting importing nurseries, botanical and public gardens, and collections of rhododendron societies—for *P. ramorum*. When *P. ramorum* is found, the nursery site is placed under quarantine and all infected plant material is destroyed. Extensive surveys and trace-forward and trace-back activities are then conducted to ensure the organism has been eliminated (http://www.inspection.gc.ca/english/plaveg/pestrava/phyram/sodmsce.shtml). As stated earlier in this chapter, samples originating from 9 retail nurseries and 12 landscape sites in British Columbia were positive for *P. ramorum* in 2009.

EU Surveys

In the European Union, annual surveys are required and reported by all EU member states as part of the European Union emergency measures for *P. ramorum* (Slawson and others 2008). In the United Kingdom, surveys of the natural and seminatural environment have included the use of water baiting for detecting the pathogen in water-catchment areas (Sansford and others 2009). Detections of the pathogen in England and Wales in retail and nursery sites and in established gardens, woods, and other natural sites are shown in figs. 15 and 16.

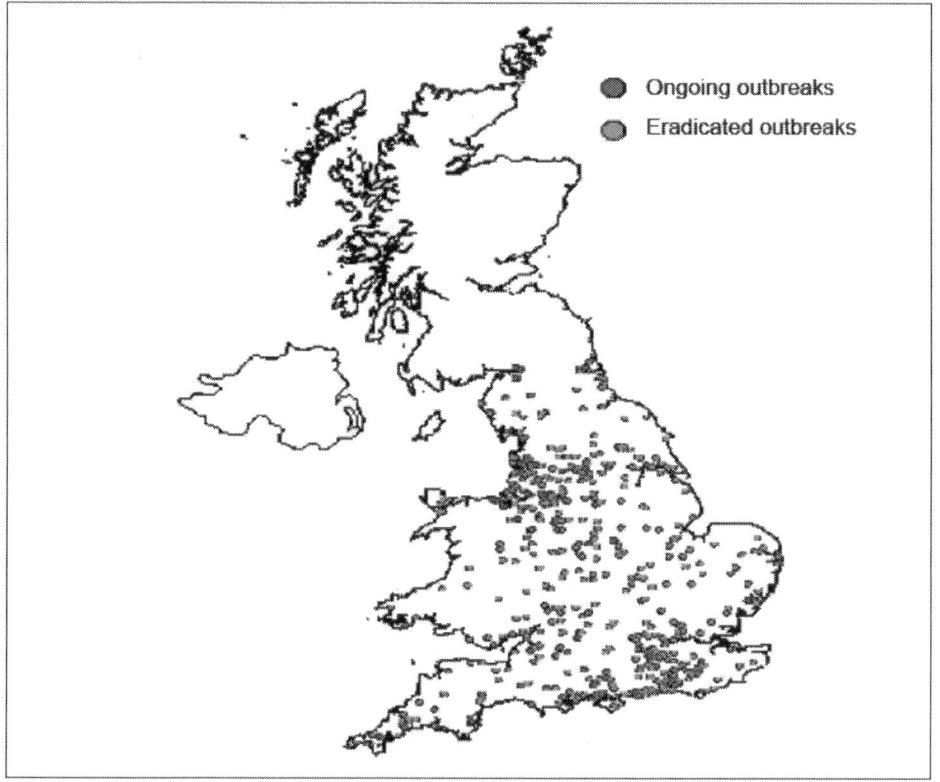

Figure 15—Detection of *Phytophthpra ramorum* at retail and nursery sites in England and Wales, 2002 to 2009. Source: http://www fera.defra.gov.uk/plants/plantHealth/pestsDiseases/documents/pRamorumOutbreakMaps.pdf. (June 2010).

Efforts to model the potential habitat for *P. ramorum* are also important for disease regulation and management. Those modeling efforts are discussed in chapter 4.

Additional Management Actions

Rizzo and others (2005) discussed what they considered to be the necessary components of a management program for *P. ramorum* in California and Oregon forests. In addition to components that have been summarized here (monitoring, eradication, use of fungicides, and prevention of human spread), they add diagnosis, restoration, fire, and stand manipulation. Diagnosis is covered in chapter 2; it is a key aspect of management, as detection and identification are critical to the success of management/control measures. Restoration efforts involving revegetation will be

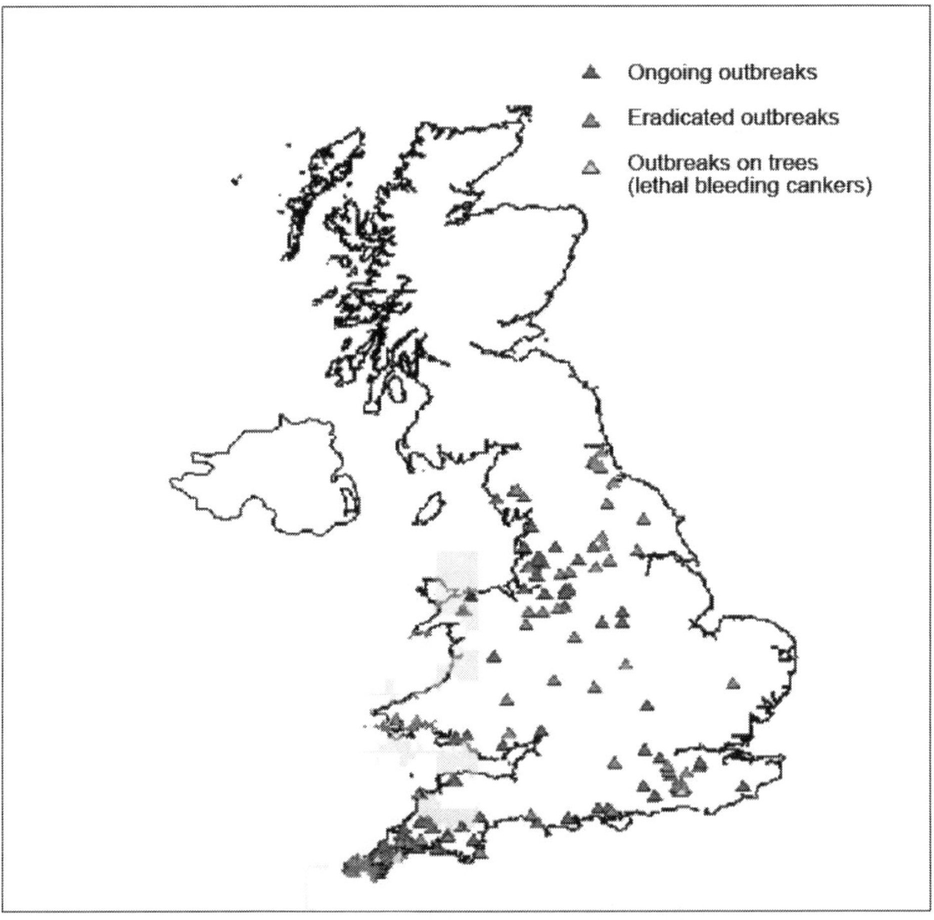

Figure 16—Detection of *Phytophthora ramorum* in gardens, woods, and other natural sites in England and Wales, 2002 to 2009. Source: http://www.fera.defra.gov.uk/plants/plantHealth/pestsDiseases/documents/pRamorumOutbreakMaps.pdf. (June 2010).

dependent on results of host resistance studies. Stand manipulation efforts in California and Oregon are discussed earlier in this chapter under "Eradication." A brief summary of research on fire in relation to *P. ramorum* management follows here.

Fire

Prescribed fire has been used as a tool to restore and maintain natural ecosystems and control tree diseases elsewhere (Brennan and Hermann 1994, Harvey 1994). Because the first reports of *P. ramorum* impact in California forests were in urban areas with a history of fire suppression, some have suggested that the absence of fire may have created stand conditions favoring the pathogen (Moritz and Odin 2005, Rizzo and others 2002b). Moritz and Odion (2005) found a strong negative relationship between *P. ramorum* infections across northern California and the locations of fires since 1950. Their data analysis supported the hypothesis that past fire suppression is somehow important in the spread of the disease. However, in a more detailed study of Sonoma County only, evidence for a negative relationship between the disease and fire history was not as strong (Moritz and Odion 2006), pointing out the complex interactions involved among fire, the disease, and its management at the landscape level. A relationship between fire suppression and disease incidence does not necessarily indicate a causal relationship.

It is unlikely that prescribed fire would be an effective management option in the heavily populated areas of central coastal California. The effects of prescribed fire on *P. ramorum* are being studied in efforts to slow the spread in Sonoma, Mendocino, Humboldt, and Del Norte Counties in north coastal California (Valachovic and others 2010a). In southern Humboldt County, a 20.2-ha infested site was treated by removal of all tanoak and bay laurel trees. Half the site was subsequently underburned. Site monitoring recovered *P. ramorum* from spore traps and soil infrequently, and usually in association with heavy densities of bay laurel sprout clumps or where residual bay and tanoak trees were missed during treatment (Valachovic and others 2008, 2010a). This, together with the Oregon results where *P. ramorum* persisted in underburned sites, suggests that burning can be a tool in cleaning up small infectious material in infested sites, but that the pathogen may persist at low levels. Beh and others (2010) recovered *P. ramorum* from streams in Big Sur areas that had experienced severe wildfire (and no other treatment) the previous season.

Summary

An attempt was made here to compile and summarize the existing literature on management and control of the diseases caused by *P. ramorum*. The pitfalls involved with attempting to summarize the literature associated with an active and evolving area of research such as *P. ramorum* are many. A synthesis of that literature is difficult, as new findings and ongoing projects take time to become public or are published. The reader should make use of the various Web sites available to obtain the most current information. Useful Web sites on regulations and quarantine include an APHIS site http://www.aphis.usda.gov/ for U.S. regulations; the various state regulatory sites such as (http://www.cdfa.ca.gov/phpps/pe/InteriorExclusion/SuddenOakDeath/), and (http://www.oregon.gov/ODA/PLANT/NURSERY/reg_sod.shtml); and the U.K. site (http://www.fera.defra.gov.uk/plants/plantHealth/pestsDiseases/pRamorum.cfm) for international information. Information on recently completed and ongoing studies on eradication, protection, and resistance can be found in monthly reports issued by the COMTF at www.suddenoakdeath.org.

Several recent publications illustrate how control options are being used as part of an overall *P. ramorum* management program. Valachovic and others (2010b) summarized some representative available treatments (including both tested and untested), for Humboldt County in California where tanoak is the primary host (table 6). The treatments were summarized according to the primary *P. ramorum* management goal on that property: (1) minimizing property impacts from the pathogen; (2) strategic protection of tanoak islands, old-growth tanoak, or particular geographic areas; and (3) suppression of *P. ramorum* and limitation of spread.

Table 6—Matrix of *Phytophthora ramorum* management goals and possible treatments

Minimize property impacts	Strategic protection of oak/tanoak islands, old-growth trees, or geographic area	Suppression of *P. ramorum* and limiting spread
Dead tree removal	Manual removal of bay laurel only	Manual removal of bay laurel and tanoak (± prescribed underburning)
Reforestation	Agri-fos® application	Modified fuel hazard reduction removal (± bay girdling)
Maintain some tanoak, with thinning (manually or with Agri-fos)	Combination of manual removal of bay laurel and Agri-fos application	Herbicide host removal (bay laurel and tanoak)

Source: Valachovic and others 2010b.

Redwood National and State Parks in northern California are developing a sudden oak death management plan before the disease arrives in the parks (Bueno and others 2010). The goal is to slow the arrival of *P. ramorum* by implementing preventive measures; to prepare for its arrival by conducting early detection for the pathogen and modeling the potential niche of its most important hosts; and to address the actions needed to confront the disease once it arrives. The Redwood Parks management plan (Bueno and others 2010) summarizes the actions available to manage *P. ramorum* in California forests (table 7).

Table 7—Sudden oak death strategic planning efforts at Redwood National and State Parks

Strategy	Goal	Action
Current efforts (*P. ramorum* not present)		
Prevention	To keep *P. ramorum* out of RNSP as long as possible	Education/outreach, best management practices, information signs, public Web page, sanitation, gravel high-risk areas
Early detection	To find the pathogen before it becomes established in the landscape	Stream baiting, ground surveys, aerial surveys, host modeling
Management planning	To develop and implement a sound management strategy to combat this disease in the park	Communicate with regulatory agencies, adjacent landowners, and interested public on the full array of options available for managing the disease consistent with park values and authority
Future potential efforts after *P. ramorum* arrives in park		
Eradication	To eliminate pathogen before it spreads to uninfested sites	Set quarantine area; some combination of herbicide, cut, burn; monitor treated sites
Protection/ containment	To strengthen important trees near infection sites and to prevent human and natural transmission of the pathogen	Chemical treatments: Agri-fos–tanoaks Physical treatments: Host removal in potential spread areas (buffers) Trail closures Cleaning stations
Restoration/ conservation	To conserve ecologically important oaks and tanoaks in the landscape, rehabilitate infection sites and minimize ecological impacts	Plant resistant hosts (if available); plant conifers and other species Identify tanoak refuges and protect through physical and chemical buffers

Source: Adapted from Bueno and others 2010.

Chapter 6: Economic and Environmental Impacts of *Phytophthora ramorum*

Introduction

The introduction and establishment of the exotic pathogen *Phytophthora ramorum* into native forest ecosystems of California and Oregon; into the nursery/ornamental trade of the United States, Canada, and Europe; and into European gardens and landscapes have had significant economic and environmental impacts. Establishment of the pathogen in areas such as the hardwood forests of the Eastern United States where known susceptible hosts occur will have additional impacts.

This chapter is not intended to be an economic analysis, but rather summarizes the literature on the economic and environmental impacts of *P. ramorum*. The economic impacts section discusses the resources at risk (benefits of hosts/products) and the costs of *P. ramorum* in forests and woodlands, urban forests, and Christmas tree plantations; on forest products other than timber and other forest values; in the nursery industry; and in the cut flower and foliage industry. The environmental impacts section summarizes the literature on the benefits provided by ecosystems and the effects of *P. ramorum* (potential for ecosystem destabilization, reduction in biodiversity, reduction or elimination of keystone species, reduction or elimination of endangered or threatened species) on recreation and on wildlife.

Economic Impacts

Forests/Woodlands, United States

Resources at risk—

California oak woodlands contain about 5 billion ft^3 (142 million m^3) of wood with a stumpage value over $275 million (Kliejunas 2003). The 5.8 billion ft^3 (164 million m^3) of oaks (*Quercus* spp.) in nearby California timberlands are worth over $500 million for forest products alone (Kliejunas 2003). Oak products exported from California from 1996 through 2000 averaged almost $50 million per year (USITC 2005). In the United States as a whole, the export market value of red oak logs and lumber in 2002 was over $300 million (USITC 2005).

In Oregon, the annual timber harvest value (mostly Douglas-fir [*Pseudotsuga menziesii* (Mirb.) Franco]) of the four southwest Oregon counties (Josephine, Coos, Curry, and Douglas) where tanoak (*Lithocarpus densiflorus* (Hook. & Arn.) occurs, based on 2006 data, is $1.68 billion per year (Kanaskie and others 2008b). Although neither tanoak nor coast live oak (*Quercus agrifolia* Née) is a commercial timber tree in California or Oregon, tanoak is harvested in Oregon for the chip market when prices warrant.

Costs—

The major impact of *P. ramorum* in forests of the United States has occurred in the mixed-evergreen and redwood-tanoak forests of coastal central California. Although damage on coast redwood (*Sequoia sempervirens* (Lamb. ex D. Don) Endl.) and Douglas-fir from *P. ramorum* is limited to foliage and small branches, regulatory actions to prevent spread of the pathogen (for example, requiring removal of small branches, washing soil from logs) could impact (presumably in the form of lost markets) the redwood and Douglas-fir industry in California at an estimated $50 million a year (USDA 2005). As an example, 2009 was the first year in over 20 years with an abundant redwood cone crop. Seed collection costs were increased by the need to comply with *P. ramorum* regulations that prohibit movement of redwood twigs and needles out of the infested coastal California counties. Every cone had to be clipped by hand, costing an estimated $100 per bushel for the 300 bushels collected (Frankel 2009). Any regulations imposed to limit spread may also affect timber harvest and trade in the commercial Douglas-fir forests in Oregon, Washington, and western Canada.

In Oregon, potential losses of at least $100 million per year in stumpage value (lost harvest) are estimated if eradication is not successful and *P. ramorum* spreads uncontrolled in southwest Oregon (Kanaskie and others 2008b). Between 2001 and the end of 2008, eradication treatments in Curry County, Oregon, were completed on approximately 2,400 ac (971 ha) of forest at a cost of $4.3 million (Kanaskie and others 2008a, 2008b). Additional costs to monitor and manage the eradication program (environmental documentation for treatment, for example) have been incurred.

An economic analysis was performed including three control scenarios in Oregon forests—continue the current control program (removal and destruction of all host plants within a 100-m radius when current monitoring discovers an infected plant), increase the control program in an attempt to eradicate the pathogen from Oregon forests within 5 years (increase the level of monitoring and control), and no control program (monitoring only) (Hall and Albers 2009). The analysis assumed that each policy would affect costs by altering the rate of spread of the pathogen and thus determine the rate of increase in the quarantine area. Costs to agencies as a result of program implementation and costs to the forest products industry as a result of *P. ramorum* quarantine regulation were projected out for 20 years under the three scenarios. A variety of other costs were not included (a reduction in Oregon's forest product export market, a reduction in the nontimber forest product market, and increased production costs for producers utilizing *P. ramorum* host plants). The estimated costs and benefits associated with each program are

Table 8—Estimated costs and benefits associated with control programs in Oregon forests

Control program	Cost	Benefit
	Million dollars	
None	21.3 to 1,238.5	0
Current	27.5 to 33.4	-6.2 to 1,205.1
Eradication	30.4 to 31.5	-9.1 to 1,207.0

summarized in table 8. The wide range in benefit estimates (from negative $9 million to positive $1.2 billion) results from basing the estimates largely on the uncertain spread rate of *P. ramorum* in Oregon forests.

The economic value of Eastern U.S. timber species would be significantly reduced if *P. ramorum* were to become established there. Two oak species (*Quercus rubra* L. and *Q. falcata* Michx.) native to the Eastern United States were found naturally infected in Europe (Brasier and others 2004a), and susceptibility of other Eastern U.S. tree species (*Q. alba* L., *Q. laurifolia* Michx., *Q. nigra* L., *Q. pagoda* Raf., *Q. phellos* L., *Q. prinus* L., *Q. virginiana* Mill., *Acer saccharum* Marsh., *Juglans nigra* L.) has been experimentally demonstrated (Brasier and others 2002, Linderman and others 2007, Tooley and Kyde 2007). The potential economic threat from the pathogen to commercial timber production from oak hardwood forests in the United States has been estimated as exceeding $30 billion (Kliejunas 2003).

The pathogen has affected international trade. Numerous countries have placed restrictions on the movement of affected plants and plant parts from the United States (Rizzo and Garbelotto 2003), thus reducing potential markets for forest hosts of *P. ramorum*. Worldwide, the European Union pest risk analysis for *P. ramorum* (Sansford and others 2009: appendix 4) lists 68 countries for which *P. ramorum* is either on their lists of regulated pests or mentioned in their legislation.

Forests/Woodlands, Canada and Europe

To date, no tree species have become affected in woodlands or forests in Canada, and no timber plantations have become affected in the European Union. Because widespread mortality in forests in Canada, the United Kingdom, and the European Union has not occurred, potential economic losses owing to *P. ramorum* have not been quantitatively estimated. The estimated annual value of timber in the United Kingdom is (in 2003 figures) about £36 million (Sansford and Woodhall 2007). Kehlenbeck (2008) estimated that in the "Northern European Tree Host System" (broadly defined as trees with stem cankers in association with infected rhododendron in the Netherlands and the United Kingdom) present impacts are moderate and restricted to few areas where *Rhododendron* are associated with tree hosts and environmental impact is caused. Kehlenbeck (2008) estimated the potential impact to be not more than moderate where no widely distributed foliar hosts of Northern European forests occur. In the "Southern European Tree Host System," present impacts are minimal, but potential impact is predicted to be major if *P. ramorum* were introduced and spread in the unique Mediterranean laurel and *Q. ilex* L. forests (Sansford and others 2009).

If *P. ramorum* were to become established in timber plantations in the European Union, there is a potential risk of tree death of a range of species including beech (*Fagus sylvatica* L.) and oak (*Quercus* spp.), as trees of these species have died from the pathogen in the United Kingdom and the Netherlands. Based on climatic conditions most similar to California and Oregon, the areas most likely to become affected are northwest Spain, northern Portugal, southwest England, and parts of Italy and western Albania. The long-term impact was estimated to be minor to moderate in the absence of controls (Sansford and others 2009).

The United Kingdom has provided £25 million for a 5-year program (2009 to 2014) to contain and eradicate *P. ramorum* and *P. kernoviae* in historical gardens, woodlands, heathlands, and from nurseries and retailers in England and Wales. As part of that program, a control strategy for *P. ramorum* will include removal of the sporulating host *Rhododendron ponticum* L. from woodlands, heathlands, and public gardens. Based on work in Cornwall, United Kingdom, the costs of clearance for *R. ponticum* (as a control strategy for both *P. ramorum* and *P. kernoviae*) are estimated at £7,000 per ha for woodland and £10,000 per ha for public gardens (Sansford and others 2009). However, in some situations removal is seen as a benefit, as it would lead to an increase in biodiversity of woodlands and heathlands. Sansford and others (2009) presented an analysis indicating that the biodiversity benefits from undertaking clearance of understory *R. ponticum* for disease control is £3 million over 20 years. Removal of *R. ponticum* from heathlands is also seen as a benefit because biodiversity and heathland condition would improve. Sansford and others (2009) calculated a benefit (as a reduction in heathland loss) of £20,000 over 20 years.

Urban Forests

Resources at risk—

In coastal central California, the value of oak woodland suitable for residential development has been estimated at $20,000 per ac (0.4 ha); rangeland with at least 40 oaks per ac (0.4 ha) was worth 27 percent more than open land (Standiford 2000). In southwestern Oregon, mature black oak trees can increase property values by $5,000 to $30,000 (Osterbauer 2003).

Costs—

Kovacs and others (unpublished data[1]) found a decrease in property values in the north Bay Area (Marin County) of California with proximity to areas affected by *P. ramorum* (proximity to oak woodlands, confirmed infections, aerial-observed oak mortality, or arborist-reported oak mortality). They found a 2 to 5 percent lower value for properties within a quarter mile of oak woodlands infested with *P. ramorum*, and a 5 to 8 percent lower value for properties with confirmed infected trees; the property value rebounds when infected trees are removed.

Tree mortality resulting from *P. ramorum* increases risk from tree failure and more intensive fires because of increased fuel loads from dead trees. In California, landowners in the infested areas have to pay for the costly removal of dead trees to protect homes and property. Kovacs and others (see footnote 1) estimated a removal and treatment cost of $20.5 million over a 10-year period (1998 to 2007) in urban areas of Marin County, California. A survey of arborists in Marin County, California, found that the average cost of oak tree removal was $1,700 per tree; average cost of pruning or removal of California bay trees was $600 (see footnote 1). In Oregon, the cost for removal of a single dead tree from a homeowner's property was as high as $3,000 (Osterbauer 2003). Economic losses from removal of infected Quercus trees may be partially offset by utilization of the material for wood products (Shelly and others 1996).

Two small (less than 1 ha) fires (one in Napa County and one in Sonoma County) have been caused by dead trees (*P. ramorum*-infected) snapping and hitting power lines (Frankel 2008). Power company cost of dead tree removal to prevent power line damage is extremely variable depending on accessibility, tree size, and other factors. Estimates in the Big Sur region of coastal central California begin at about $600 per tree. During a 3-year period (April 2002 through March 2005), the state of California spent $1.5 million on hazard tree removal in five *P. ramorum*-infested counties (Marin, Sonoma, Alameda, Santa Cruz, and Monterey). Additional costs of the hazard tree program included $205,000 for hazard tree assessment and about $71,000 for restoration (Jones 2009). In 2009, the Santa Clara Fire Safe Council received a $150,000 grant for removal of hazard trees resulting from *P. ramorum*-caused mortality (Frankel 2009).

Preventive treatments of oaks in urban areas with the systemic fungicide Agri-fos® are expensive as well as potentially harmful to the environment if used incorrectly. A limited survey of arborists in Marin County, California, found 1,400 customers with treatments in the seven companies surveyed, at an average cost of

---

[1] K. Kovacs and J. Englin, University of Nevada, Reno; T. Holmes, USDA FS, Southern Research Station, Research Triangle Park; J. Alexander, UC Cooperative Extension, Marin County.

$115 per treatment (see footnote 1). The current recommendation is for reapplication each year, so these costs to homeowners (but benefits to arborist companies) may accumulate over time.

A strategic plan for Sonoma County, California (Bell and others 2008), summarizes needed funds for an effective *P. ramorum* management program in the first and subsequent years (table 9). Estimated costs are for hazardous tree management, practices to slow the spread, education of agencies and publics, and fuels reduction in the urban/wildland interface.

Christmas Tree Plantations

Resources at risk—

Nationwide, the Christmas tree industry had a wholesale value of $520 million in 2003 (Cave and others 2008, Jerado 2004). Of that value, Oregon produced $158 million, Washington $60 million, and California $10.4 million (Jerado 2004, USDA 2005).

Costs—

Expansion of establishment of *P. ramorum* in the industry and resulting regulation on trade would likely have significant, but unknown, economic impact. A major Christmas tree species, Douglas-fir, is a host of *P. ramorum*. Other Christmas tree species have been found naturally infected (grand fir [*Abies grandis* (Douglas ex D. Don) Lindl.], white fir [*A. concolor* (Gord. & Glend.) Lindl. ex Hildebr.], red fir [*A. magnifica* A. Murr.]) or susceptible in laboratory trials (Chastagner and others 2006b). The pathogen has been detected in Christmas tree plantations in the

Table 9—Summary of needs and costs, *Phytophthora ramorum* management in Sonoma County, California

	Estimated costs	
Anticipated needs	Year 1	Subsequent years
	Thousand dollars	
Fire fuels reduction/mitigation	2,000.0	2,060.0
Tree removal and treatment/forest health	867.1	639.1
Education and outreach	313.1	296.1
Develop fuel model	200.0	0
Hazardous and infected tree survey	614.2	122.6
Staff training	36.5	37.6
Develop sudden oak death protocols	30.0	0
Fire fuels survey and mitigation plan	30.0	0
Fire department funds	16.2	162
Total	4,107.1	3,171.6

infested area of California, but primarily only in the vicinity of infected California bay laurel (*Umbellularia californica* (Hook. & Arn.) Nutt.) or other sporulating hosts (Chastagner and others 2008d). In one instance, Chastagner and others (2008b) found infection of a few white fir and Douglas-fir Christmas trees under a black walnut (*Juglans nigra* L.) tree that was infected with mistletoe (*Phoradendron serotinum* subsp. *macrophyllum*); the mistletoe was a host of *P. ramorum*. However, their data and the inability of *P. ramorum* to spread from conifer to conifer suggest that there is a very low risk of *P. ramorum* developing in Christmas tree plantations that are not associated with infected high-inoculum producing plants, such as California bay laurel. Regulating small branches and twigs of affected species essentially limits movement of host Christmas trees out of regulated areas.

Forest Products Other Than Timber

Resources at risk—

Products crafted from native materials in coastal California, Oregon, and Washington forests are economically significant. High-value uses for hardwood hosts of *P. ramorum* include custom furniture, flooring, cooperage, and tool handles (Shelly and others 1996). Other uses for wood from hardwood hosts include firewood, wood chips for pulping, mulch, compost, nongrade lumber, and charcoal (Cave and others 2008). In 2000, the Chetco Ranger District on the Rogue River-Siskiyou National Forest in Oregon sold permits for 51 900 kg of tanoak boughs, 8400 kg of huckleberry (*Vaccinium* spp.) foliage, 5000 kg of madrone (*Arbutus menziesii* Pursh) boughs, 100 huckleberry transplants, and about 49 900 kg of miscellaneous boughs and foliage (Zepeda 2001). The foliage of evergreen huckleberry (*Vaccinium ovatum* Pursh), used as browse by elk, is harvested for use in floral arrangements. In the 1970s, an estimated $1 million worth of foliage was harvested annually in western Washington (Minore 1972). Huckleberries are an important secondary forest product from Pacific Northwest forests. Volume harvested varies. The wholesale price of huckleberries (includes species in addition to *V. ovatum*) ranged from $2.98 to $2.19 per lb (0.45 kg) in 1995 and 1996 (Osterbauer 2003).

Costs—

The economic impacts of *P. ramorum* on forest products other than timber have not been estimated.

Other Forest Values

Other benefits of forests, such as water and watershed protection, grazing, wildlife food and habitat, and recreation (Thomas 1997) are usually considered environmental benefits rather than economic, and are discussed in that section.

Nursery Industry, United States

Resources at risk—

In 2006, the U.S. domestic production of nursery crops was valued at about $12.9 billion. Imports for these crops were $341 million and exports were $287 million (Jerado 2007, as cited in Cave and others 2008). The U.S. ornamental nursery industry is valued at over $13 billion annually, ranking as the third-highest-value crop in the United States. California is the industry's leading producer of horticultural plants, valued at $2 billion a year. Oregon's industry is ranked fifth nationally and ranks second in the production of woody plants (USDA 2005). In 2006, the wholesale value of nursery stock sold in Oregon was $966 million (USDA NASS 2007).

Costs—

The U.S. nursery industry has been strongly affected by *P. ramorum*. Surveys in March 2004 detected *P. ramorum* in two large southern California nurseries that had shipped potentially infected plants to over 1,200 nurseries in 29 states. This finding led to 15 states imposing quarantines on nursery stock from California, resulting in estimated losses of $4.3 million to the nursery industry in California in the first month alone (Frankel 2008). The California Association of Nurseries and Garden Centers estimated that California nurseries lost $25 million in sales in spring 2004 when other states prohibited nursery shipments from California (US GAO 2006). In 2004, the U.S. Department of Agriculture Animal and Plant Health Inspection Service (USDA APHIS) spent approximately $20 million to trace and destroy all suspect stock from the two nurseries (Frankel 2008). Similar shipments of infested nursery stock, but at a smaller scale, occurred from Oregon and Washington nurseries.

The potential loss to the nursery industry and forests in Oregon from *P. ramorum* was estimated to be between $81 million and $310 million per year (for direct control, management, and regulatory compliance costs plus loss of markets) (Cusak and others 2009, Griesbach 2008, Kanaskie and others 2008b, Oregon Invasive Species Council 2008). To comply with federal quarantine regulations, the Oregon Department of Agriculture (ODA) has spent about $3.2 million over a 5-year period (2001 through 2006) on surveys of nurseries for *P. ramorum* (Frankel 2008). In 2007, the ODA needed to inspect over 1,450 nurseries to comply with the quarantine rules (Frankel 2008).

Some of the financial impacts of *P. ramorum* in the nursery industry result from enforcement of regulations and other disease management practices to control pathogen spread. In fiscal year 2006, USDA APHIS estimated spending approximately $6.35 million in *P. ramorum* nursery activities in California,

Oregon, and Washington. Approximately $4.15 million was allocated to inspection, sampling, testing, and certification activities. The remainder of the spending was allocated to national survey, trace-forward and trace-back investigations, eradication, and regulation enforcement activities (USDA APHIS 2007a). For Oregon nurseries, it was estimated that the cost of inspections and certification would increase from $800,000 to $6.5 million per year if the pathogen became widely established in the state (Griesbach 2008). If the disease became endemic in the Oregon nursery industry, Griesbach (2008) estimated that the annual cost of a prophylactic fungicide program targeted at *P. ramorum* would be $3,960 per acre (0.4 ha). Assuming that 10 percent of the 94,250 ac (38 141 ha) in production in Oregon opt for this treatment, the annual cost to the industry would be $37.3 million; if 25 percent of the area is treated, the cost increases to $93.3 million per year.

In addition to the monetary costs of compliance with federal quarantine regulations (compliance agreements and nursery and shipment certifications) borne by the public, the nursery industry has also incurred indirect regulation costs. For example, there could be potential costs associated with sales lost while withholding plants for shipment during inspection and testing (USDA APHIS 2007a). In Oregon, indirect costs owing to loss of sales from customer's perception of the product being associated with or exposed to *P. ramorum* range from $34.1 to $204 million per year (Griesbach 2008).

The number and retail value of plants destroyed in Washington state nurseries because of *P. ramorum* quarantine efforts between 2004 and 2005 were estimated by Dart and Chastagner (2007). Data collected during that period indicated that 17,266 containerized nursery plants were destroyed at 32 nurseries, with an estimated retail value of $423,043. The mean loss per nursery was estimated at $11,188 in 2004 and $11,798 in 2005. Other U.S. states do not record this information (Frankel 2008).

The presence of the pathogen within the nursery and ornamental trade has resulted in loss of markets. Oregon ships 75 percent of its nursery production to other states or countries (Griesbach 2008). In 2001, Canada closed its markets to most plant crops from the states of Oregon and California. Without reopened market access, Oregon nurseries alone faced losses in sales to Canada of $15 to $20 million (Canada Gazette 2007, Frankel 2008). For the most part, Canada's markets were reopened to Oregon growers in 2002 (Regelbrugge 2003).

Additional losses to the nursery industry resulting from *P. ramorum* that have not been fully quantified include surveillance and testing costs, facility and equipment cleaning costs, costs of implementation of best management practices such as use of enzyme-linked immunosorbent assay prescreening tests, and others (Frankel 2008, Sansford and others 2009, Suslow 2006).

Nursery Industry, Canada and Europe

Resources at risk—

In Canada, the value of the British Columbia nursery and floriculture sectors was estimated at $500 million, with approximately $170 million in export sales to the United States (Canada Gazette 2007). Canada's export trade for rhododendrons was valued at $5 million in 2000 (Allen and others 2003).

Costs—

Costs to conduct required *P. ramorum* eradication work (plant destruction, soil treatment, loss of plant inventory) in British Columbia nurseries in the spring of 2007 was estimated at $8.5 million. Since then, other nurseries have tested positive for the pathogen, which required additional eradication measures (Canada Gazette 2007).

The current impact on nurseries in the European Union is considered to be moderate in terms of quality and control costs; including phytosanitary controls, the impact is major (Sansford and others 2009). The potential economic impact for the nursery trade in the European Union (27 member states) is estimated as high (Sansford and others 2009).

Cut Flowers/Foliage

Resources at risk—

Cut flower and foliage sales in the United States exceeded $406 and $542 million, respectively (Jerado 2007, as cited in Cave and others 2008).

Costs—

Although the impact of *P. ramorum* to that industry has apparently been minor, Cave and others (2008) pointed out that there is an increase in flower production from woody ornamentals, and many of those plants are hosts for the pathogen, including *Camellia*, *Hamamelis*, *Kalmia*, *Pieris*, *Rhododendron*, *Rosa*, and *Syringa* (Bachmann 2002).

Environmental Impacts

The ability or potential of an introduced pathogen such as *P. ramorum* to cause environmental damage by disrupting native forest ecosystems is difficult to predict. The potential for environmental impacts to the nursery industry is equally difficult to estimate. Most literature describing environmental damage simply lists factors of the environment that could be affected, and then describes that environment. Factors typically considered under environmental damage include potential for ecosystem destabilization, reduction in biodiversity, reduction or elimination of keystone species, reduction or elimination of endangered or threatened species, and nontarget effects of control measures.

The APHIS pest risk assessment for *P. ramorum* (Cave and others 2008), for example, rated the environmental impact of the pathogen as high based on three aspects: the potential of the pest to disrupt native ecosystems and habitats exhibited within its current geographic range; the need for additional chemical or biological control programs because of the presence of the pest; and the potential of the pest to directly or indirectly impact species listed as Threatened or Endangered (50 CFR § 17.11-12). A high degree of uncertainty was assigned to the rating because of the difficulty in estimating costs that address all of the relevant ecological components, including the environmental costs of prevention, eradication, or suppression by herbicide use; the effects on endangered species and the indirect ecological consequences (changes in locally important ecological processes such as perturbations of hydrologic cycles such as flood control and water supply, waste assimilation, nutrient recycling, conservation and regeneration of soils, crop pollination, and habitat destruction) (Cave and others 2008).

Ecosystem Effects

Resources at risk—

Quercus spp. are considered the most important and widespread of the hardwood trees in the North Temperate Zone, with about 300 species (Pavlik and others 1991). Oak woodlands yield important benefits, including water and watershed protection, grazing, wildlife food and habitat, recreation, and wood products (Monahan and Koenig 2006, Thomas 1997). Oak species are part of forest and savanna woodland ecosystems in Europe and the United States (Global Invasive Species Specialist Group 2006).

Many of the foliar hosts of *P. ramorum* have ecological significance. *Rhododendron* spp. occur worldwide, and some species in the United States are currently listed under the Endangered Species Act. *Vaccinium ovatum*, native to British Columbia, Washington, Oregon, and California (Halverson 1986), is a prominent component of California and Oregon forests dominated by tanoak, canyon live oak (*Quercus chrysolepis* Liebm.) and Pacific madrone (*Arbutus menziesii* Pursh) (Sawyer and others 1977). Evergreen huckleberry is an important browse species for elk in the Coast Range and in southern Oregon. *Vaccinium ovatum* is closely related to blueberries and cranberries as well as other huckleberry species. All of the native huckleberries and blueberries are important to wildlife. The success and timing of berry crops has been tied to the reproductive rate of black bears, and berries are critical energy sources for Neotropical birds at the time of migration. The plants themselves provide extensive cover for mammals and nesting birds as well as important winter browse. *Vaccinium* spp. are widely distributed throughout Europe, Asia, and North America; more than 40 species occur in North America.

Environmental and social benefits provided by U.K. woodlands/forests include open-access free recreation, landscape amenity, biodiversity, and carbon sequestration (Sansford and others 2009, Sansford and Woodhall 2007). Studies to assign values to these benefits and timber values for Great Britain were reviewed by Sansford and Woodhall (2007). The estimated social and environmental benefits of British forests (based on estimated values of the recreational and biodiversity benefits, landscape value, and carbon sequestration) are about £1,022 million per year (2003 figures). Adding the estimated timber value of British forests (about £36 million), gives an estimated value of British forests of about £1,058 million per year (2003 figures).

Costs—

A major effect of *P. ramorum* in California coastal forests has been mortality of tanoak, coast live oak, and California black oak (*Q. kelloggii* Newberry). Meentemeyer and others (2008) estimated 235,678 trees (12 650 m^2 tree basal area) killed by *P. ramorum* in the Big Sur ecoregion (79 366 ha study area), of coastal California. The numbers represent about a 20-percent loss of available host trees. Nonlethal foliar and shoot infections occur on other susceptible forest species. The reduction of oak and tanoak populations in these forests has altered the forest stand structure and composition (Meentemeyer and others 2008c). The USDA FS risk assessment (Kliejunas 2003) pointed out that heavy loss of oaks, or of related susceptible genera, owing to *P. ramorum* infection could result in significant ecological effects, including changes in forest composition, loss of wildlife food and habitat, increased soil erosion, and a significant increase in fuel loads in heavily populated urban-forest interfaces.

A pest risk assessment completed by the Plant Health Risk Assessment Unit of the Canadian Food Inspection Agency (CFIA) in March of 2002, and most recently revised in January 2008, concluded that the potential environmental impacts of *P. ramorum* on most areas of Canada is low. For south coastal British Columbia, the risk is medium (CFIA 2008).

In Europe, any significant loss of oak species to *P. ramorum* could impact soil erosion, hydrology, biodiversity, tourism, and cultural history (Global Invasive Species Specialist Group 2006, Sansford and others 2009). Other hosts of *P. ramorum*—European beech (*Fagus sylvatica* L.) and sweet chestnut (*Castanea sativa* Mill.) for example—are important high forest and plantation trees in Europe (Global Invasive Species Specialist Group 2006).

Although the potential effects of *P. ramorum* on rare and endangered plant species are unknown, Cave and others (2008) listed a number of genera on the APHIS List of Hosts and Associated Plants (*Arctostaphylos confertiflora* Eastw., *A. glandulosa* Eastw. ssp. *crassifolia* (Jeps.) Wells, *A. hookeri* G. Don ssp. *ravenii* P.V. Wells, *A. morroensis* Wies. & Schreib., *A. myrtifolia* Parry, *A. pallida* Eastw., *Prunus geniculata* Harper, *Q. hinckleyi* C.H. Muller, and *Rhododendron chapmanii* Gray) that have species on the U.S. Fish and Wildlife Service (USFWS) Threatened and Endangered Species list. See http://www.fws.gov/endangered/wildlife.html for current listing of plants on the USFWS threatened and endangered list.

Recreational Effects

Resources at risk—

Urban and woodland areas affected by *P. ramorum* in California have many federal, state, county, and city parks and recreational facilities. Marin and Sonoma Counties are prime suburban and recreational areas. The economies of the Big Sur region and Santa Cruz are based largely on tourism and recreation.

Costs—

Regulations and restrictions to prevent spread of *P. ramorum* affect recreational use of infested areas. Public access to areas may be restricted during certain seasons to prevent movement of the pathogen or to protect visitors from hazardous trees killed by *P. ramorum*. The Rogue River–Siskiyou National Forest in southern Oregon closed a popular trail just before Labor Day 2009 in response to detection of *P. ramorum* on a tanoak near the trail. Hazard tree removal from along trails in wilderness areas where chainsaws are prohibited would need to be done with handsaws, thus increasing costs; this also increases the likelihood of trail closures owing to a maintenance backlog in heavily impacted wilderness areas, such as the Ventana Wilderness on the Los Padres National Forest. When visitors are requested or required to take precautions to prevent movement of the pathogen, park and forest staff may be required to provide educational information, staff cleaning areas, and provide appropriate supplies and equipment to remove soil from shoes and vehicles (COMTF 2004c). Recreation may also be affected by a loss of recreational areas in woodland severely infested with *P. ramorum* (Appiah and others 2004).

Wildlife Effects

Resources at risk—

Tanoaks and true oaks provide habitat and food for a variety of wildlife (Standiford 2000). On the other hand, some small mammal species may benefit from loss of trees owing to *P. ramorum*. In California, dusky-footed woodrats (*Neotoma fuscipes*) were projected to benefit from the increased shrub cover, the California parasitic mouse (*Peromyscus californicus*) would benefit from an increase in coarse wood debris and the California brush mouse (*P. boylii*) would benefit from lower tree densities. Two salamander species—Monterey salamander (*Ensatina eschscholtzii*) and slender salamander (*Batrachoseps* spp.)—modeled were likely to be relatively unaffected (Tempel and Tietje 2006).

Costs—

Barrett and others (2006) indicated that the loss of *L. densiflorus*, *Q. kelloggii*, and *Q. agrifolia* would have negative effects on dozens of wildlife species because of the direct loss of these three forest tree species, and the associated loss of food and nesting and den sites. Northern spotted owls (*Strix occidentalis caurina*) are known to nest in tanoak stands in coastal California and Oregon, and when combined with an overstory of large conifers, a component of tanoak may improve habitat for the owls by providing canopy structure and habitat for prey such as wood rats and northern flying squirrels (*Glaucomys sabrinus*) (Niemiec and others 1995). A reduction of the oak overstory would also result in a more open canopy, which would encourage dense shrub cover. In studies on the effect of the disease on insectivorous cavity-nesting birds in stands of coast live oak in the San Francisco area, Apigian and Allen-Diaz (2006) observed a loss of bird nest sites, prey reduction, and loss of foraging substrates in *P. ramorum*-affected plots. Monahan and Koenig (2006) reported a negative impact on populations of five California bird species associated with coast live oak in California. The authors projected that bird populations could be 25 to 68 percent smaller and 13 to 49 percent more variable in infested stands compared to noninfested stands. The greater number of beetles associated with infected trees (McPherson and others 2005) may also affect the feeding patterns of birds.

Fischer and Hadj-Chikh (n.d.) used regional risk models for *P. ramorum* to determine risk of habitat infestation to special status vertebrates in California, Oregon, and Washington. In California, seven amphibians, five birds, seven mammals, and one reptile had more than one-third of their predicted habitat at risk of infestation. The numbers for Oregon were 15 amphibians, 18 birds, 21 mammals, and 2 reptiles; and for Washington, 18 amphibians, 139 birds, 58 mammals, and 16 reptiles.

Program Costs

Government

United States Federal Agency expenditures on *P. ramorum* regulatory, research, management, and related activities from 2000 to 2009 were APHIS, $61 million;

USDA FS, $39.9 million; Agricultural Research Service (ARS), $11.9 million; and Cooperative State Research, Education and Extension Service (CSREES), $1 million (Frankel 2009).

As stated previously, the U.K. Environment Minister will provide £25 million over 5 years (2009 through 2013) to help contain and eradicate *P. ramorum* and *P. kernoviae* from historical gardens, woodlands, heathlands, nurseries, and retailers in England and Wales.

Other

Other expenditures for *P. ramorum* include funds from the states of California, Oregon, and other states for education; state and federal salaries for researchers and forest health protection personnel; private grant and nonprofit funds (for example, the Moore Foundation, Oregon Association of Nurseries, other nursery organizations, the Nature Conservancy); and others.

Summary

The current and estimated potential economic and environmental impacts of *P. ramorum* indicate a significant effect of the introduced pathogen. Current economic impacts to forests/woodlands have occurred primarily in central coastal California and southwestern Oregon. Economic losses there have been minor, as host mortality occurs primarily in nontimber species. Current economic impacts in the European Union are estimated as minor to moderate. Potential economic losses have been estimated to be much greater if the pathogen becomes established in other areas, in particular the commercial forests of the Northwest or Eastern United States. Economic impacts in urban areas include reduction in property value and costs associated with hazard tree removal and fire management. Current economic impacts to the nursery/ornamental industry in the United States are estimated to be in the range of $100 to $300 million. Canada spent about $8.5 million in 1 year on control. Estimated impacts if the pathogen spreads are much higher.

Environmental impacts from *P. ramorum* are not fully known because the introduced pathogen has been affecting forest ecosystems only since the mid-1990s and the nursery industry for less time. Estimates of potential environmental impacts range widely (spanning several orders of magnitude), depending on assumptions made. The potential for *P. ramorum* to impact ecosystems depends on numerous factors, many of which are presently unknown.

Although the benefits and costs of various management scenarios have been estimated (see Hall and Albers 2009, and Friend 2008, for example), a comprehensive cost-benefit analysis of the disease has not been done.

Acknowledgments

Thanks to Douglas McCreary, University of California Center for Forestry and Integrated Hardwood Range Management Program, for administrative support. Thanks also for the review and guidance provided by Susan Frankel, USDA Forest Service, Pacific Southwest Research Station; Everett Hansen, Oregon State University; David Rizzo, University of California-Davis; Alan Inman, UK Food and Environment Research Agency; Ellen Goheen, USDA Forest Service, Forest Health Protection; Jonathan Jones and Glen Fowler, USDA Animal and Plant Health Inspection Service; and Ross Meentemeyer, University of North Carolina, Charlotte.

Funding was provided by the USDA Forest Service, Pacific Southwest Research Station, Sudden Oak Death/*Phytophthora ramorum* Research program.

English Equivalents

When you know:	**Multiply by:**	**To find:**
Micrometers (µm)	0.000039	Inches
Millimeters (mm)	0.0394	Inches
Centimeters (cm)	0.394	Inches
Meters (m)	3.28	Feet
Kilometers (km)	0.6215	Miles
Square meters (m^2)	10.76	Square feet (ft^2)
Square kilometers (km^2)	0.386	Square miles (mi^2)
Hectares (ha)	2.47	Acres (ac)
Cubic meters (m^3)	35.314	Cubic feet (ft^3)
Kilograms per hectare (kg/ha)	0.893	Pounds per acre (lb/ac)
Milligrams per kilogram (mg/kg)	1	Parts per million (ppm)
KiloPascal (kPa)	0.145	Poundforce per square inch (lbf/in^2)
Degrees Celsius (°C)	1.8 and add 32	Degrees Fahrenheit

References

Adams, G.C.; Catal, M.; Trummer, L.; Hansen, E.M.; Reeser, P.; Worrall, J.J. 2008. *Phytophthora alni* ssp. *uniformis* found in Alaska beneath thinleaf alders. Plant Health Progress. DOI: 10.1094/PHP-2008-1212-02-BR.

Alexopoulos, C.J.; Mims, C.W.; Strobel, G.A. 1996. Introductory mycology. 4th ed. New York: Wiley. 868 p.

Allen, E.; Callan, B.; Cree, L.; Sela, S. 2003. The impact of *Phytophthora ramorum* on Canada. Sudden oak death online symposium. www.apsnet.org/online/SOD (Web site of The American Phytopathological Society). DOI: 10.1094/SOD-2003-EA.

Alvarado-Rosales, D.; de L. Saavedra-Romero, L.; Almaraz-Sánchez, A. 2008. Primer reporte de *Phytophthora cinnamomi* Rands. Asociado al Encino (*Quercus* spp.) en Tecoanapa, Guerrero, México. Agrociencia. 42: 565–572.

Alvarado-Rosales, D.; de L. Saavedra-Romero, L.; Almaraz-Sánchez, A.; Tlapal-Bolaños, B.; Trejo-Ramírez, O.; Davidson, J.M.; Kliejunas, J.T.; Oak, S.W.; O'Brien, J.G.; Orozco-Torres, F.; Quiroz-Reygadas, D. 2007. Agentes asociados y su papel en la declinación y muerte de encinos (*Quercus*, Fagacaeae) en el centro-oeste de México. Polibotánica. 23: 1–21.

Anacker, B.L.; Rank, N.E.; Hüberli, D.; Garbelotto, M.; Gordon, S.; Harnik, T.; Whitkus, R.; Meentemeyer, R. 2008. Susceptibility to *Phytophthora ramorum* in a key infectious host: landscape variation in host genotype, host phenotype, and environments factors. New Phytologist. 177: 756–766.

Apigian, K.; Allen-Diaz, B. 2006. SOD-induced changes in foraging and nesting behaviour of insectivorous, cavity-nesting birds. In: Frankel, S.J.; Shea, P.J.; Haverty, M.I., tech. coords. Proceedings of the sudden oak death second science symposium: the state of our knowledge. Gen. Tech. Rep. PSW-GTR-196. Albany, CA: U.S. Department of Agriculture, Forest Service, Pacific Southwest Research Station: 191–192.

Appiah, A.A.; Jennings, P.; Turner, J.A. 2004. *Phytophthora ramorum*: one pathogen and many diseases, an emerging threat to forest ecosystems and ornamental plant life. Mycologist. 18: 145–150.

Aram, K.; Rizzo, D.M. 2010. Status of California's *Phytophthora ramorum* stream survey. In: Frankel, S.J.; Kliejunas, J.T.; Palmieri, K.M., tech. coords. Proceedings of the sudden oak death fourth science symposium. Gen. Tech. Rep. PSW-GTR-229. Albany, CA: U.S. Department of Agriculture, Forest Service, Pacific Southwest Research Station: 283–284.

Aveskamp, M.M.; van Baal, P.J.M.; de Gruyter, J. 2006. Effect of sanitary measures on the survival of *Phytophthora ramorum* in soil. In: Frankel, S.J.; Shea, P.J.; Haverty, M.I., tech. coords. Proceedings of the sudden oak death second science symposium: the state of our knowledge. Gen. Tech. Rep. PSW-GTR-196. Albany, CA: U.S. Department of Agriculture, Forest Service, Pacific Southwest Research Station: 279–284.

Aveskamp, M.; Wingelaar, G. 2006. Elimination of *Phytophthora ramorum* in the tunnel composting process. In: Frankel, S.J.; Shea, P.J.; Haverty, M.I., tech. coords. Proceedings, sudden oak death second science symposium: the state of our knowledge. Gen. Tech. Rep. PSW-GTR-196. Albany, CA: U.S. Department of Agriculture, Forest Service, Pacific Southwest Research Station: 585.

Avila, F.J.; Schoedel, B.; Abad, Z. Gloria; Coffey, M.D.; Blomquist, C. 2010. ELISA and ImmunoStrip® for detection of *Phytophthora ramorum*, *P. kernoviae* and other *Phytophthora* species. In: Frankel, S.J.; Kliejunas, J.T.; Palmieri, K.M., tech. coords. Proceedings of the fourth sudden oak death science symposium. Gen. Tech. Rep. PSW-GTR-229. Albany, CA: U.S. Department of Agriculture, Forest Service, Pacific Southwest Research Station: 95–96.

Bachman, J. 2002. Woody ornamentals for cut flower growers. Appropriate technology transfer for rural areas. National Center for Appropriate Technology. 11 p. http://attra.ncat.org/attra-pub/PDF/woodyornamentals.pdf. (April 2010).

Balci, Y.; Balci, S.; Blair, J.E.; Park, S-Y.; Kang, S.; MacDonald, W.L. 2008. *Phytophthora quercetorum*, a novel species isolated from eastern and north-central USA oak forest soils. Mycological Research. 112: 906–916.

Balci, Y.; Balci, S.; Eggers, J.; MacDonald, W.L.; Juzwik, J.; Long, R.P.; Gottschalk, K.W. 2007. *Phytophthora* spp. associated with forest soils in eastern and north-central U.S. oak ecosystems. Plant Disease. 91: 705–710.

Balci, Y.; Halmschlager, E. 2003. Incidence of *Phytophthora* species in oak forests in Austria and their possible involvement in oak decline. Forest Pathology. 33: 157–174.

Barrett, T.M.; Gatziolis, D.; Fried, J.S.; Waddell, K.L. 2006. Sudden oak death in California: What is the potential? Journal of Forestry. 104: 61–64.

Beals, K.; Dodd, R.S. 2006. Does stand density affect mating system and population genetic structure in coast live oak? In: Frankel, S.J.; Shea, P.J.; Haverty, M.I., tech. coords. Proceedings, sudden oak death second science symposium: the state of our knowledge. Gen. Tech. Rep. PSW-GTR-196. Albany, CA: U.S. Department of Agriculture, Forest Service, Pacific Southwest Research Station: 119–120.

Becker, E.; Sumampong, G.; Shamoun, S.F.; Elliott, M.; Varga, A.; Saad Masri, S.; James, D.; Bailey, K.; Boyetchko, S. 2010. An evaluation of *Phytophthora ramorum* preventative treatments for nursery and forest understory plants in British Columbia, Canada. In: Frankel, S.J.; Kliejunas, J.T.; Palmieri, K.M., tech. coords. Proceedings of the sudden oak death fourth science symposium. Gen. Tech. Rep. PSW-GTR-229. Albany, CA: U.S. Department of Agriculture, Forest Service, Pacific Southwest Research Station: 288–291.

Beh, M.; Frangioso, K.; Oguchi, A.; Aram, K.; Rizzo, D. 2010. *Phytophthora ramorum* recovery from 12 Big Sur watersheds following wildfires in 2008. In: Frankel, S.J.; Kliejunas, J.T.; Palmieri, K.M., tech. coords. Proceedings of the sudden oak death fourth science symposium. Gen. Tech. Rep. PSW-GTR-229. Albany, CA: U.S. Department of Agriculture, Forest Service, Pacific Southwest Research Station: 292.

Bell, L.; Safford, C.; Vossen, P.; Rosevear, J.; Perry, C. 2008. Sonoma County sudden oak death strategic response plan. University of California Cooperative Extension, Sonoma County and the Sonoma County Department of Emergency Services. http://cesonoma.ucdavis.edu/files/48051.pdf. (April 2010).

Berger, P. 2006. Update on diagnostics for *Phytophthora ramorum*. In: Frankel, S.J.; Shea, P.J.; Haverty, M.I., tech. coords. Proceedings, sudden oak death second science symposium: the state of our knowledge. Gen. Tech. Rep. PSW-GTR-196. Albany, CA: U.S. Department of Agriculture, Forest Service, Pacific Southwest Research Station: 47–49.

Berger, P. 2008. Personal communication. Director, Center for Plant Health Science and Technology, U.S. Department of Agriculture, Animal and Plant Health Inspection Service, Raleigh, NC 27606.

Běhalová, M. 2006. Surveys for *Phytophthora ramorum* in the Czech Republic. EPPO Bulletin. 36(2): 393–395. DOI: 10.1111/j.1365-2338.2006.01018.x.

Bienapfl, J.; Zanzot, J.; Murphy, S.; Garbelotto, M.; Rizzo, D. 2005. Isolation of a new lineage of *Phytophthora ramorum* from asymptomatic stems and roots of a commercial lot of rhododendrons in California. Phytopathology. 95: S9.

Bilodeau, G.J.; Hamelin, R.C.; de Cock, A.W.A.M.; Duchaine, C.; Kristjansson, G. 2006. Molecular detection of *Phytophthora ramorum* by real-time PCR using Taqman, SYBR Green, and molecular beacons with three genes. In: Frankel, S.J.; Shea, P.J.; Haverty, M.I., tech. coords. Proceedings, sudden oak death second science symposium: the state of our knowledge. Gen. Tech. Rep. PSW-GTR-196. Albany, CA: U.S. Department of Agriculture, Forest Service, Pacific Southwest Research Station: 139–140.

Bilodeau, G.J.; Lévesque, C.A.; De Cock, A.; Duchaine, C.; Kristjansson, G.; Uribe, P.; Martin, F.N.; Hamelin, R.C. 2007. Molecular detection of *Phytophthora ramorum* by real-time PCR using Taqman, SYBR green and molecular beacons with three genes. Phytopathology. 97: 632–642.

Bilodeau, G.; Pelletier, G.; Pelletier, F.; Lévesque, C.; Hamelin, R.C. 2009. Multiplex real-time polymerase chain reaction (PCR) for detection of *Phytophthora ramorum*, the causal agent of sudden oak death. Canadian Journal of Plant Pathology. 31: 195–210.

Bonants, P.; De Weerdt, M.; Baayen, R.; De Gruyer, R.; Man in't Veld, W.A.; Kroon, L. 2002. Molecular identification and detection of *Phytophthora* species and populations of *P. ramorum*. In: Proceedings of the sudden oak death science symposium. Berkeley, CA: U.S. Department of Agriculture, Forest Service and University of California, Berkeley. http://danr.ucop.edu/ihrmp/sodsymp/paper/paper08.html. (April 2010).

Bonants, P.; Hagenaar-de Weerdt, M.; Van Gent-Pelzer, M.; Lacourt, I.; Cooke, D.; Duncan, J. 1997. Detection and identification of *Phytophthora fragariae* Hickman by the polymerase chain reaction. European Journal of Plant Pathology. 103: 345–355.

Bonants, P.; Verstappen, E.; de Vries, I.; Katarzyna Wiejacha, K.; Ivors, K. 2006. Molecular identification and detection of *Phytophthora ramorum*. In: Frankel, S.J.; Shea, P.J.; Haverty, M.I., tech. coords. Proceedings of the sudden oak death second science symposium: the state of our knowledge. Gen. Tech. Rep. PSW-GTR-196. Albany, CA: U.S. Department of Agriculture, Forest Service, Pacific Southwest Research Station: 135–138.

Borchert, D.M.; Magarey, R.D. 2004. A guide to the use of NAPPFAST. Raleigh, NC: U.S. Department of Agriculture, Animal and Plant Health Inspection Service; North Carolina State University. http://www.nappfast.org/usermanual/nappfast-manual.pdf. (April 2010).

Boutet, X.; Chandelier, A. 2009. Production of viable oospores by *Phytophthora ramorum*. In: Goheen, E.M.; Frankel, S.J., tech. coords. Proceedings of the fourth meeting of the International Union of Forest Research Organizations (IUFRO) Working Party S07.02.09: Phytophthoras in forests and natural ecosystems. Gen. Tech. Rep. PSW-GTR-221. Albany, CA: U.S. Department of Agriculture, Forest Service, Pacific Southwest Research Station: 257–260.

Brasier, C.M. 1999. The role of *Phytophthora* pathogens in forests and semi-natural communities in Europe and Africa. In: Hansen, E.M.; Sutton, W., eds. *Phytophthora* diseases of forest trees. Forest Research Laboratory, Oregon State University, Corvallis, OR: 6–13.

Brasier, C.M. 2003a. Phytophthoras in European forests: their rising significance. In: sudden oak death: How concerned should you be? An international online symposium. http://www.apsnet.org/online/proceedings/SOD/Papers/Brasier/. (April 2010).

Brasier, C.M. 2003b. Sudden oak death exhibits transatlantic differences. Mycological Research. 107: 258–259.

Brasier, C.M. 2009. *Phytophthora* biodiversity: How many *Phytophthora* species are there? In: Goheen, E.M.; Frankel, S.J., tech. coords. Proceedings of the fourth meeting of the International Union of Forest Research Organizations (IUFRO) Working Party S07.02.09: Phytophthoras in forests and natural ecosystems. Gen. Tech. Rep. PSW-GTR-221. Albany, CA: U.S. Department of Agriculture, Forest Service, Pacific Southwest Research Station: 101–115.

Brasier, C.M.; Beales, P.A.; Kirk, S.A.; Denman, S.; Rose, J. 2005. *Phytophthora kernoviae* sp. nov., an invasive pathogen causing bleeding stem lesions on forest trees and foliar necrosis of ornamentals in the UK. Mycological Research. 109: 853–859.

Brasier, C.M.; Cooke, D.E.L.; Duncan, J.M. 1999. Origin of a new *Phytophthora* pathogen through interspecific hybridization. Proceedings National Academy Sciences. 96: 5878–5883.

Brasier, C.M.; Denman, S.; Brown, A.; Webber, J.F. 2004a. Sudden oak death (*Phytophthora ramorum*) discovered on trees in Europe. Mycological Research. 108: 1107–1110.

Brasier, C.M.; Denman, S.; Rose, J.; Kirk, S.A.; Hughes, K.J.D.; Griffin, R.L.; Lane, C.R.; Inman, A.J.; Webber, J.F. 2004b. First report of ramorum bleeding canker on *Quercus falcata* caused by *Phytophthora ramorum*. Plant Pathology. 53: 804.

Brasier, C.; Denman, S.; Webber, J.; Brown, A. 2006a. Sudden oak death: recent developments on trees in Europe. In: Frankel, S.J.; Shea, P.J.; Haverty, M.I., tech. coords. Proceedings, sudden oak death second science symposium: the state of our knowledge. Gen. Tech. Rep. PSW-GTR-196. Albany, CA: U.S. Department of Agriculture, Forest Service, Pacific Southwest Research Station: 31–33.

Brasier, C.M.; Jung, T. 2006. Recent developments in *Phytophthora* diseases of trees and natural ecosystems in Europe. In: Brasier, C.M.; Jung, T.; Osswald, W., eds. Progress in research on *Phytophthora* diseases of forest trees. Proceedings of the third International Union of Forest Research Organization (IUFRO) Working Party 07.02.09. Farnham, UK: Forest Research Agency: 5–16.

Brasier, C.M.; Kirk, S.A. 2001. Comparative aggressiveness of standard and variant hybrid alder phytophthoras, *Phytophthora cambivora* and other *Phytophthora* species on bark of *Alnus*, *Quercus* and other woody hosts. Plant Pathology. 50: 218–229.

Brasier, C.M.; Kirk, S. 2004. Production of gametangia by *Phytophthora ramorum* in vitro. Mycological Research. 108: 823–827.

Brasier, C.M.; Kirk, S.A.; Delcan, J.; Cooke, D.E.L.; Jung, T.; Man in't Veld, W.A. 2004c. *Phytophthora alni* sp. nov. and its variants: designation of emerging heteroploid hybrid pathogens spreading on *Alnus* trees. Mycological Research. 108: 1172–1184.

Brasier, C.M.; Kirk, S.A.; Rose, J. 2006b. Differences in phenotypic stability and adaptive variation between the main European and American lineages of *Phytophthora ramorum*. In: Brasier, C.M.; Jung, T,; Oßwald, W., eds. Proceedings of the third international IUFRO Working Party (S07.02.09) meeting: Progress in research on *Phytophthora* diseases of forest trees. Farnham, UK: Forest Research Agency: 166–173.

Brasier, C.; Kirk, S.; Webber, J. 2007. Report on the probability of sexual recombination between European A1 and American A2 isolates. Deliverable Report 11. Farnham, UK: Forest Research, Central Science Laboratory. EU Sixth Framework Project, RAPRA. On file with: Forest Research Agency, Alice Holt Lodge, Farnham, Surrey GU10 4LH, UK.

Brasier, C.M.; Rose, J.; Kirk, S.A.; Webber, J.F. 2002. Pathogenicity of *Phytophthora ramorum* isolates from North America and Europe to bark of European Fagaceae, American *Quercus rubra*, and other forest trees. In: Proceedings of the sudden oak death science symposium. Berkeley, CA: U.S. Department of Agriculture, Forest Service and University of California, Berkeley. http://danr.ucop.edu/ihrmp/sodsymp/paper/paper09.html. (April 2010).

Brennan, L.A.; Hermann, S.M. 1994. Prescribed fire and forest pests: solutions for today and tomorrow. Journal of Forestry. 92(11): 34–37.

British Columbia Landscape and Nursery Association. 2005. Current issues. Managing *P. ramorum* in BC. http://www.bclna.com/bclna_current_issues.htm. (April 2010).

Brown, A.V.; Brasier, C.M. 2007. Colonization of tree xylem by *Phytophthora ramorum, P. kernoviae* and other *Phytophthora* species. Plant Pathology. 56 (2): 227–241.

Brown, A.; Brasier, C.; Denman, S.; Rose, J.; Kirk, S.; Webber, J. 2006. Distribution and etiology of aerial stem infections of *Phytophthora ramorum* and *Phytophthora kernoviae* at three woodland sites in the U.K. In: Frankel, S.J.; Shea, P.J.; Haverty, M.I., tech. coords. Proceedings of the sudden oak death second science symposium: the state of our knowledge. Gen. Tech. Rep. PSW-GTR-196. Albany, CA: U.S. Department of Agriculture, Forest Service, Pacific Southwest Research Station: 105–108.

Bueno, M.; Deshais, J.; Arguello, L. 2010. Waiting for SOD: sudden oak death and Redwood National and State Parks. In: Frankel, S.J.; Kliejunas, J.T.; Palmieri, K.M., tech. coords. Proceedings of the sudden oak death fourth science symposium. Gen. Tech. Rep. PSW-GTR-229. Albany, CA: U.S. Department of Agriculture, Forest Service, Pacific Southwest Research Station: 297–301.

Bulajić, A.; Jović, J.; Krnjajić, S.; Djekić, I.; Krstić, B. 2009. First report of *Phytophthora ramorum* on *Rhododendron* sp. in Serbia. Plant Pathology. 58: 804. DOI: 10.1111/j.1365-3059.2009.02033.x.

Bulluck, R.; Shiel, P.; Berger, P.; Kaplan, D.; Parra, G.; Li, W.; Levy, L.; Keller, J.; Reddy, M.; Sharma, N.; Dennis, M.; Stack, J.; Pierzynski, J.; O'Mara, J.; Webb, C.; Finley, L.; Lamour, K.; McKemy, J.; Palm, M. 2006. A comparative analysis of detection techniques used in U.S. regulatory programs to determine presence of *Phytophthora ramorum* in *Camellia japonica* "Nucio's Gem" in an infested nursery in southern California. Plant Health Progress. DOI: 10.1094/PHP-2006-1016-01-RS.

California Oak Mortality Task Force [COMTF]. 2002. Sudden oak death best management practices in zone of infestation regulated areas. http://nature.berkeley.edu/comtf/pdf/Management%20Guidelines%202002.pdf. (April 2010).

California Oak Mortality Task Force [COMTF]. 2004a. A guide for collecting in forests: simple precautions to prevent the spread of Sudden Oak Death. http://nature.berkeley.edu/comtf/pdf/Plant%20collectors_Sept2004.pdf. (April 2010).

California Oak Mortality Task Force. [COMTF]. 2004b. A guide for plant gatherers: simple precautions to prevent the spread of sudden oak death. http://nature.berkeley.edu/comtf/pdf/Tribal%20gatherers_Sept2004.pdf. (April 2010).

California Oak Mortality Task Force [COMTF]. 2004c. A guide for recreational users: simple precautions to prevent the spread of sudden oak death. http://nature.berkeley.edu/comtf/pdf/Recreational_Sept2004.pdf. (April 2010).

California Oak Mortality Task Force [COMTF]. 2004d. A safety message for firefighters: precautions regarding sudden oak death. http://nature.berkeley.edu/comtf/pdf/Firefighters_Sept2004.pdf. (April 2010).

California Oak Mortality Task Force [COMTF]. 2005. Sudden oak death guidelines for arborists. http://nature.berkeley.edu/comtf/pdf/arborist%206-05.pdf. (April 2010).

California Oak Mortality Task Force [COMTF]. 2006a. A Christmas tree grower's guide to sudden oak death (*Phytophthora ramorum*). http://nature.berkeley.edu/comtf/pdf/ChristmasTreeGuide11-20-06.pdf. (April 2010).

California Oak Mortality Task Force [COMTF]. 2006b. A homeowner's guide to sudden oak death. http://nature.berkeley.edu/comtf/pdf/HomeownerGuide.05.06.pdf. (April 2010).

California Oak Mortality Task Force [COMTF]. 2006c. Sudden oak death guidelines for forestry. http://nature.berkeley.edu/comtf/pdf/ForestryGuideNov2006.pdf. (April 2010).

California Oak Mortality Task Force [COMTF]. 2007. November newsletter. http://nature.berkeley.edu/comtf/pdf/Monthly%20Reports/COMTF_Report_November_2007.pdf. (April 2010).

California Oak Mortality Task Force [COMTF]. 2009. August newsletter. http://nature.berkeley.edu/comtf/pdf/Monthly%20Reports/COMTF_Report_August_2009.pdf. (April 2010).

Campanella, V.; Ippolito, A.; Nigro, F. 2002. Activity of calcium salts in controlling *Phytophthora* root rot of citrus. Crop Protection. 21: 751–756.

Canada Gazette. 2007. Regulations amending the *Phytophthorá ramorum* compensation regulations. Canada Gazette Part II. 141(26): 2623–2628.

Canadian Food Inspection Agency [CFIA]. 2008. Phytosanitary requirements to prevent the entry and spread of *Phytophthora ramorum*. Directive D-01-01. Ottawa, Canada: Canadian Food Inspection Agency. http://www.inspection.gc.ca/english/plaveg/protect/dir/d-01-01e.shtml. (April 2010).

Canadian Food Inspection Agency [CFIA]. 2009. PI-011-Eradication protocol for retail nurseries confirmed with *Phytophthora ramorum*. Ottawa, Ontario: Canadian Food Inspection Agency. http://www.inspection.gc.ca/english/plaveg/hort/pi-011e.shtml. (April 2010).

Cave, G.L.; Randall-Schadel, B.R; Redlin, S.C. 2005. Risk analysis for *Phytophthora ramorum* Werres, de Cock & In't Veld, causal agent of phytophthora canker (sudden oak death), ramorum leaf blight, and ramorum dieback. Raleigh, NC: U.S. Department of Agriculture, Animal and Plant Health Inspection Service, Plant Protection and Quarantine. 82 p.

Cave, G.L.; Randall-Schadel, B.R.; Redlin, S.C. 2008. Risk analysis for *Phytophthora ramorum* Werres, de Cock & In't Veld, causal agent of phytophthora canker (sudden oak death), ramorum leaf blight, and ramorum dieback. Revision 1. Raleigh, NC: U.S. Department of Agriculture, Animal and Plant Health Inspection Service, Plant Protection and Quarantine. 88 p.

Chastagner, G.; DeBauw, A.; Riley, K. 2010. Effect of fungicides on the isolation of *Phytophthora ramorum* from symptomatic and asymptomatic rhododendron leaf tissue. In: Frankel, S.J.; Kliejunas, J.T.; Palmieri, K.M., tech. coords. Proceedings of the sudden oak death fourth science symposium. Gen. Tech. Rep. PSW-GTR-229. Albany, CA: U.S. Department of Agriculture, Forest Service, Pacific Southwest Research Station: 302–304.

Chastagner, G.A.; DeBauw, A.; Riley, K.; Dart, M. 2008a. Effectiveness of fungicides in protecting conifers and rhododendrons from *Phytophthora ramorum*. In: Frankel, S.J.; Kliejunas, J.T.; Palmieri, K.M., tech. coords. Proceedings of the sudden oak death third science symposium. Gen. Tech. Rep. PSW-GTR-214. Albany, CA: U.S. Department of Agriculture, Forest Service, Pacific Southwest Research Station: 325–333.

Chastagner, G.A.; Hansen, E.M. 2003. Identification of fungicides to control sudden oak death. Christmas Tree Lookout. 36(3): 7–9.

Chastagner, G.A.; Hansen, E.M.; Riley, K.L.; Sutton, W. 2004. Susceptibility of conifer shoots to infection by *Phytophthora ramorum*. Phytopathology. 94: S16.

Chastagner, G.A.; Hansen, E.M.; Riley, K.L.; Sutton, W. 2005. Effectiveness of fungicides in protecting Douglas-fir shoots from infection by *Phytophthora ramorum*. Phytopathology. 94: S16.

Chastagner, G.A.; Hansen, E.M.; Riley, K.L.; Sutton, W. 2006a. Effectiveness of fungicides in protecting Douglas-fir shoots from infection by *Phytophthora ramorum*. In: Frankel, S.J.; Shea, P.J.; Haverty, M.I., tech. coords. Proceedings of the sudden oak death second science symposium: the state of our knowledge. Gen. Tech. Rep. PSW-GTR-196. Albany, CA: U.S. Department of Agriculture, Forest Service, Pacific Southwest Research Station: 239.

Chastagner, G.A.; Hansen, E.M.; Riley, K.L.; Sutton, W. 2006b. Susceptibility of conifer shoots to infection by *Phytophthora ramorum* In: Frankel, S.J.; Shea, P.J.; Haverty, M.I., tech. coords. Proceedings of the sudden oak death second science symposium: the state of our knowledge. Gen. Tech. Rep. PSW-GTR-196. Albany, CA: U.S. Department of Agriculture, Forest Service, Pacific Southwest Research Station: 77.

Chastagner, G.A.; Riley, K.; Dart, N. 2008b. *Phytophthora ramorum* isolated from California bay laurel inflorescences and mistletoe; possible implications relating to disease spread. In: Frankel, S.J.; Kliejunas, J.T.; Palmieri, K.M., tech. coords. Proceedings of the sudden oak death third science symposium. Gen. Tech. Rep. PSW-GTR-214. Albany, CA: U.S. Department of Agriculture, Forest Service, Pacific Southwest Research Station: 169–171.

Chastagner, G.A.; Riley, K.; Dart, N. 2008c. Risk of spread of *Phytophthora ramorum* in Christmas trees. In: Thomsen, I.M.; Rasmussen, H.N.; Sørensen, J.M., eds. Proceedings of the 8th international Christmas tree research and extension conference. Forest and Landscape Working Papers No. 26-2008. Hørsholm, Denmark: University of Copenhagen: 46–48.

Chastagner, G.A.; Riley, K.; Dart, N. 2008d. Spread and development of *Phytophthora ramorum* in a California Christmas tree farm. In: Frankel, S.J.; Kliejunas, J.T.; Palmieri, K.M., tech. coords. Proceedings of the sudden oak death third science symposium. Gen. Tech. Rep. PSW-GTR-214. Albany, CA: U.S. Department of Agriculture, Forest Service, Pacific Southwest Research Station: 199–200.

Cohen, M.; Condeso, E.; Anacker, B.; Rank, N.; Mazzola, M. 2006. Biologically-based means for control of Oomycete phytopathogens. In: The sixth California oak symposium: today's challenges, tomorrow's opportunities. Berkeley, CA: University of California. http://danr.ucop.edu/ihrmp/symposium_abstracts.html. (April 2010).

Colburn, G.C.; Jeffers, S.N. 2010. Efficacy of commercial algaecides to manage species of *Phytophthora* in suburban waterways. In: Frankel, S.J.; Kliejunas, J.T.; Palmieri, K.M., tech. coords. Proceedings of the sudden oak death fourth science symposium. Gen. Tech. Rep. PSW-GTR-229. Albany, CA: U.S. Department of Agriculture, Forest Service, Pacific Southwest Research Station: 223–224.

Colburn, G.C.; Sechler, K.E.; Shishkoff, N. 2005. Survivability and pathogenicity of *Phytophthora ramorum* chlamydospores in soil. Phytopathology. 95: S20.

Collins, B.R.; Parke, J.L.; Lachenbruch, B.; Hansen, E.M. 2009. The effects of *Phytophthora ramorum* infection on hydraulic conductivity and tylosis formation in tanoak sapwood. Canadian Journal of Forest Research. 39(9): 1766–1776.

Commission of European Communities. 2004. Commission decision of 29 April 2004 amending decision 2002/757/EC on provisional emergency phytosanitary measures to prevent the introduction into and the spread within the community of *Phytophthora ramorum* Werres, De Cock & Man in't Veld sp.nov. http://www.furs.si/law/EU/zvr/zakonodaja_CIRCA/EU_circa/nadzor_les_phytophthora/32004_426_EC.pdf#search=%222002%2F757%2FEC%20ramorum%22. (April 2010).

Condeso, T.E.; Meentemeyer, R.K. 2007. Effects of landscape heterogeneity on the emerging forest disease sudden oak death. Journal of Ecology. 95: 364–375.

Cooke, D.E.L.; Drenth, A.; Duncan, I.M.; Wagels, G.; Brasier, C.M. 2000a. A molecular phylogeny of *Phytophthora* and related Oomycetes. Fungal Genetics and Biology. 30: 17–32.

Cooke, D.E.L.; Duncan, I.M.; Williams, N.A.; Hagenaar-de Weerdt, M.; Bonants, P.J.M. 2000b. Identification of *Phytophthora* species on the basis of restriction enzyme fragment analysis of the internal transcribed spacer regions of ribosomal RNA. OEPP/EPPO Bulletin. 30: 519–523.

Cooper, M.; Cushman, H. 2006. Effects of recreation on the dispersal of exotic forest pathogen, *Phytophthora ramorum*. In: The sixth California oak symposium: today's challenges, tomorrow's opportunities. http://danr.ucop.edu/ihrmp/symposium_abstracts.html. (April 2010).

Crandall, B.S.; Gravatt, G.F.; Ryan, M.M. 1945. Root disease of *Castanea* species and some coniferous and broadleaf nursery stocks, caused by *Phytophthora cinnamomi*. Phytopathology. 35: 162–180.

Cusak, C.; Harte, M.; Chan, S. 2009. The economics of invasive species. ORESU-G-09-001. Corvallis, OR: Oregon Sea Grant. 12p. http://www.oregon.gov/OISC/docs/pdf/economics_invasive.pdf. (April 2010).

Cushman, J.H.; Cooper, M.; Meentemeyer, R.K.; Benson, S. 2008. Human activity and the spread of *Phytophthora ramorum*. In: Frankel, S.J.; Kliejunas, J.T.; Palmieri, K.M., tech. coords. 2008. Proceedings of the sudden oak death third science symposium. Gen. Tech. Rep. PSW-GTR-214. Albany, CA: U.S. Department of Agriculture, Forest Service, Pacific Southwest Research Station: 179–180.

Cushman, J.H.; Meentemeyer, R. 2006a. The importance of humans in the dispersal and spread of *Phytophthora ramorum* at local, landscape, and regional scales. In: Frankel, S.J.; Shea, P.J.; Haverty, M.I., tech. coords. Proceedings, sudden oak death second science symposium: the state of our knowledge. Gen. Tech. Rep. PSW-GTR-196. Albany, CA: U.S. Department of Agriculture, Forest Service, Pacific Southwest Research Station: 161–163.

Cushman, J.H.; Meentemeyer, R.K. 2006b. Human activity and spread of the pathogen that causes sudden oak death. In: The sixth California oak symposium: today's challenges, tomorrow's opportunities. http://danr.ucop.edu/ihrmp/symposium_abstracts.html. (April 2010).

Dart, N.L.; Chastanger, G.A. 2007. Estimated economic losses associated with the destruction of plants due to *Phytophthora ramorum* quarantine efforts in Washington State. Plant Health Progress. DOI: 10.1094/PHP-2007-0508-02-RS. http://www.puyallup.wsu.edu/ppo/pdf/EstimatedLosses.pdf. (April 2010).

Davidson, J.M.; Fichtner, E.; Patterson, H.; Falk, K.; Rizzo, D. 2005a. Mechanisms underlying differences in inoculum production by *Phytophthora ramorum* in mixed-evergreen versus tanoak-redwood forests in California. In: Frankel, S.J.; Shea, P.J.; Haverty, M.I., tech. coords. Proceedings of the sudden oak death second science symposium: the state of our knowledge. Gen. Tech. Rep. PSW-GTR-196. Albany, CA: U.S. Department of Agriculture, Forest Service, Pacific Southwest Research Station: 500.

Davidson, J.M.; Maloney, P.E.; Wickland, A.C.; Morse, A.C.; Jensen, C.E.; Rizzo, D.M. 2002a. Transmission of *Phytophthora ramorum* via *Umbellularia californica* (California bay) leaves in California oak woodlands. In: Proceedings of the sudden oak death science symposium, the state of our knowledge. Berkeley, CA:.U.S. Department of Agriculture, Forest Service and University of California, Berkeley. http://danr.ucop.edu/ihrmp/sodsymp/paper/paper06.html. (April 2010).

Davidson, J.M.; Maloney, P.E.; Wickland, A.C.; Rizzo, D.M. 2003a. Forest composition influences transmission of *Phytophthora ramorum* (sudden oak death) in California oak woodlands. Ecological Society of America Annual Meeting. Abstract 88.

Davidson, J.M.; Patterson, H.A.; Rizzo, D.M. 2008. Sources of inoculum for *Phytophthora ramorum* in a redwood forest. Phytopathology. 98: 860–866.

Davidson, J.M.; Rizzo, D.M.; Garbelotto, M.; Tjosvold, S.; Slaughter, G.W. 2002b. *Phytophthora ramorum* and sudden oak death in California. II. Transmission and survival. In: Standiford, R.B.; McCreary, D.; Purcell, K.L., tech. coords. Proceedings of the fifth symposium on oak woodlands: oaks in California's changing landscape. Gen. Tech. Rep. PSW-GTR-184. Albany, CA: U.S. Department of Agriculture, Forest Service, Pacific Southwest Research Station: 741–749.

Davidson, J.M.; Shaw, C.G. 2003. Pathways of movement for *Phytophthora ramorum*, the causal agent of sudden oak death. Sudden oak death online symposium. DOI: 10.1094/SOD-2003-TS.

Davidson, J.M.; Werres, S.; Garbelotto, M.; Hansen, E.M.; Rizzo, D.M. 2003b. Sudden oak death and associated diseases caused by *Phytophthora ramorum*. Plant Health Progress. DOI: 10.1094/PHP-2003-0707-01-DG.

Davidson, J.M.; Wickland, A.C.; Patterson, H.A.; Falk, K.R.; Rizzo, D.M. 2005b. Transmission of *Phytophthora ramorum* in mixed evergreen forest in California. Phytopathology. 95: 587–596.

De Dobbelaere, I.; Heungens, K.; Maeas, M. 2006. Susceptibility levels of *Rhododendron* species and hybrids to *Phytophthora ramorum*. In: Frankel, S.J.; Shea, P.J.; Haverty, M.I., tech. coords. Proceedings, sudden oak death second science symposium: the state of our knowledge. Gen. Tech. Rep. PSW-GTR-196. Albany, CA: U.S. Department of Agriculture, Forest Service, Pacific Southwest Research Station: 79–81.

De Dobbelaere, I.; Heungens, K.; Maes, M. 2008. Effect of environmental and seasonal factors on the susceptibility of different *Rhododendron* species and hybrids to *Phytophthora ramorum*. In: Frankel, S.J.; Kliejunas, J.T.; Palmieri, K.M., tech. coords. Proceedings of the sudden oak death third science symposium. Gen. Tech. Rep. PSW-GTR-214. Albany, CA: U.S. Department of Agriculture, Forest Service, Pacific Southwest Research Station: 95–97.

Delatour, C.; Saurat, C.; Husson, C.; Loos, R.; Schenck, N. 2002. Discovery of *Phytophthora ramorum* on *Rhododendron* sp. in France and experimental symptoms on *Quercus robur*. In: Proceedings of the sudden oak death science symposium. Berkeley, CA: U.S. Department of Agriculture, Forest Service and University of California, Berkeley. http://danr.ucop.edu/ihrmp/sodsymp/poster/poster57.html. (April 2010).

De Merlier, D.; Chandelier, A.; Cavelier, M. 2003. First report of *Phytophthora ramorum* on *Viburnum bodnantense* in Belgium. Plant Disease. 87: 203.

Denman, S.; Kirk, S.A.; Brasier, C.M.; Hughes, K.J.D.; Barton, V.C.; Griffin, R.; Webber, J.F. 2005a. *Phytophthora ramorum* on *Quercus ilex* in the United Kingdom. Plant Disease. 89: 1241.

Denman, S.; Kirk, S.A.; Brasier, C.M.; Webber, J.F. 2005b. In vitro leaf inoculation studies as an indication of tree foliage susceptibility to *Phytophthora ramorum* in the UK. Plant Pathology. 54: 512–521.

Demnan, S.; Kirk, S.A.; Moralejo, E.; Webber, J.F. 2009. *Phytophthora ramorum* and *Phytophthora kernoviae* on naturally infected asymptomatic foliage. EPPO Bulletin. 39: 105–111.

Denman, S.; Orton, E.; Kirk, S.A.; Brasier, C.M. 2006. Sporulation potential of *Phytophthora ramorum* on detached leaves of some susceptible UK trees in vitro. In: Brasier, C.M.; Jung, T.; Oßwald, W., eds. Progress in research on *Phytophthora* diseases of forest trees. Proceedings of the third international IUFRO working party 07.02.09. Farnham, UK: Forest Research: 75–78.

Department for Environment, Food, and Rural Affairs [DEFRA]. 2004. Comparison of *Phytophthora ramorum* (sudden oak death) populations from Europe and USA in support of pest risk assessment, management and policy. Project Report PHO 192. London: Final Project Report. Department for Environment, Food and Rural Affairs. On file with: Research Policy and International Division, Final Reports Unit, DEFRA, Area 301, Cromwell House, Dean Stanley Street, London, SW1P 3JH.

Department for Environment, Food, and Rural Affairs [DEFRA]. 2005a. Non-tree host range and diagnosis of *Phytophthora ramorum* (sudden oak death) in support of pest risk assessment, management and policy. Project Report PH0193S. London: SID 5 research project final report. Department for Environment, Food and Rural Affairs. On file with: Research Policy and International Division, Final Reports Unit, DEFRA, Area 301, Cromwell House, Dean Stanley Street, London, SW1P 3JH.

Department for Environment, Forestry and Rural Affairs [DEFRA]. 2005b. *Phytophthora ramorum* epidemiology: infection, latency and survival. Project Report PH0194. London: Department for Environment, Food and Rural Affairs. On file with: Research Policy and International Division, Final Reports Unit, DEFRA, Area 301, Cromwell House, Dean Stanley Street, London, SW1P 3JH.

Department for Environment, Forestry and Rural Affairs [DEFRA]. 2006. Understanding *Phytophthora ramorum*: key findings from UK research. Pest Note PB 12729. 6 p.

Department for Environment, Food, and Rural Affairs [DEFRA]. 2007. Epidemiology of natural outbreaks of *Phytophthora ramorum*. Project Report PH0195. London: Department for Environment, Food and Rural Affairs. On file with: Research Policy and International Division, Final Reports Unit, DEFRA, Area 301, Cromwell House, Dean Stanley Street, London, SW1P 3JH.

Dodd, R.; Frankel, S.; Grunwald, N.; Hansen, E.; Hayden, K.; Kubisiak, T.; Sniezko, R. 2006. Utilizing genetic information to address *Phytophthora ramorum*/sudden oak death. http://nature.berkeley.edu/comtf/pdf/Bibliography/SODgenpaper.082206.final.pdf. (April 2010).

Dodd, R.S.; Hüberli, D.; Douhovnikoff, V.; Harnik, T.Y.; Afzal-Rafii, Z.; Garbelotto, M. 2005. Is variation in susceptibility to *Phytophthora ramorum* correlated with population genetic structure in coast live oak (*Quercus agrifolia*)? New Phytologist. 165: 203–214.

Dodd, R.S.; Hüberli, D.; Mayer, W.; Harnik, T.Y.; Afzal-Rafii, Z.; Garbelotto, M. 2008. Evidence for the role of syncronicity between host phenology and pathogen activity in the distribution of sudden oak death disease. New Phytologist. 179: 505–514.

Elliott, M.; Shamoun, S. 2008. In vitro testing of biological control agents on A1 and A2 isolates of *Phytophthora ramorum*. In: Frankel, S.J.; Kliejunas, J.T.; Palmieri, K.M., tech. coords. Proceedings of the sudden oak death third science symposium. Gen. Tech. Rep. PSW-GTR-214. Albany, CA: U.S. Department of Agriculture, Forest Service, Pacific Southwest Research Station: 351–354.

Elliott, M.; Sumampong, G.; Varga, A.; Shamoun, S.F.; James, D.; Masri, S.; Brière, S.C.; Grünwald, N.J. 2009. PCR-RFLP markers identify three lineages of the North American and European populations of *Phytophthora ramorum*. Forest Pathology. 39: 266–278.

Englander, L.; Browning, M.; Tooley, P.W. 2006. Growth and sporulation of *Phytophthora ramorum* in vitro in response to temperature and light. Mycologia. 98: 365–373.

Erwin, D.C.; Ribeiro, O.K. 1996. *Phytophthora* diseases worldwide. St. Paul, MN: American Phytopathological Society Press. 592 p.

Fichtner, E.J.; Lynch, S.C.; Rizzo, D.M. 2006. Summer survival of *Phytophthora ramorum* in forest soils. In: Frankel, S.J.; Shea, P.J.; Haverty, M.I., tech. coords. Proceedings of the sudden oak death second science symposium: the state of our knowledge. Gen. Tech. Rep. PSW-GTR-196. Albany, CA: U.S. Department of Agriculture, Forest Service, Pacific Southwest Research Station: 165–166.

Fichtner, E.J.; Lynch, S.C.; Rizzo, D.M. 2007. Detection, distribution, survival, and sporulation of *Phytophthora ramorum* in a California redwood-tanoak forest soil. Phytopathology. 97: 1366–1375.

Fichtner, E.J.; Lynch, S.C.; Rizzo, D.M. 2009a. Survival, dispersal, and soil-mediated suppression of *Phytophthora ramorum* in a California redwood-tanoak forest. Phytopathology. 99: 608–619.

Fichtner, E.J.; Rizzo, D.M.; Kirk, S.; Whybrow, A.; Webber, J. 2008a. Root infections of *Phytophthora ramorum* and *Phytophthora kernoviae* in UK woodlands. Phytopathology. 98: S53.

Fichtner, E.J.; Rizzo, D.M.; Kirk, S.A.; Whybrow, A.; Webber, J. 2009b. Root associations of *Phytophthora ramorum* and *Phytophthora kernoviae* in UK woodlands. In: Goheen, E.M.; Frankel, S.J., tech. coords. Proceedings of the fourth meeting of the International Union of Forest Research Organizations (IUFRO) Working Party S07.02.09: Phytophthoras in forests and natural ecosystems. Gen. Tech. Rep. PSW-GTR-221. Albany, CA: U.S. Department of Agriculture, Forest Service, Pacific Southwest Research Station: 281.

Fichtner, E.J.; Rizzo, D.M.; Lynch, S.C.; Davidson, J.; Buckles, G.; Parke, J. 2008b. Summer survival of *Phytophthora ramorum* in California bay laurel leaves. In: Frankel, S.J.; Kliejunas, J.T.; Palmieri, K.M., tech. coords. Proceedings of the sudden oak death third science symposium. Gen. Tech. Rep. PSW-GTR-214. Albany, CA: U.S. Department of Agriculture, Forest Service, Pacific Southwest Research Station: 357–358.

Fichtner, E.J.; Rizzo, D.M.; Shew, H.D. 2008c. Suppression of *Phytophthora ramorum* in aluminum-amended peatmoss. In: Frankel, S.J.; Kliejunas, J.T.; Palmieri, K.M., tech. coords. Proceedings of the sudden oak death third science symposium. Gen. Tech. Rep. PSW-GTR-214. Albany, CA: U.S. Department of Agriculture, Forest Service, Pacific Southwest Research Station: 359–360.

Fischer, K.; Hadj-Chikh, L. [N.d.]. Sudden oak death and *Phytophthora ramorum* risk for special status vertebrates in California, Oregon and Washington. Executive Summary. Wildlife Conservation Society. On file with: Wildlife Conservation Society, 200 Peregrine Lane, Smith River, CA 95567.

Florance, E.R. 2002. Plant structures through which *Phytophthora ramorum* establishes infections. In: Proceedings of the sudden oak death science symposium, the state of our knowledge. Berkeley, CA: U.S. Department of Agriculture, Forest Service and University of California, Berkeley. http://danr.ucop.edu/ihrmp/sodsymp/paper/paper12.html. (April 2010).

Florance, E.R. 2006. Magnetic resonance imaging (MRI) of oak trees infected with *Phytophthora ramorum* to determine potential avenues of infection to bark. In: Frankel, S.J.; Shea, P.J.; Haverty, M.I., tech. coords. Proceedings of the sudden oak death second science symposium: the state of our knowledge. Gen. Tech. Rep. PSW-GTR-196. Albany, CA: U.S. Department of Agriculture, Forest Service, Pacific Southwest Research Station: 91–99.

Forestry Commission. 2009. *Phytophthora ramorum* briefing note. Farnham, UK: Forest Research Agency. http://www.forestry.gov.uk/pdf/fcsymptomshandoutcombined2.pdf/$file/fcsymptomshandoutcombined2.pdf. (April 2010).

Fowler, G.; Magerey, R.; Colunga, M. 2006. Climate-host mapping of *Phytophthora ramorum*, causal agent of sudden oak death. In: Frankel, S.J.; Shea, P.J.; Haverty, M.I., tech. coords. Proceedings of the sudden oak death second science symposium: the state of our knowledge. Gen. Tech. Rep. PSW-GTR-196. Albany, CA: U.S. Department of Agriculture, Forest Service, Pacific Southwest Research Station: 329–332.

Frankel, S. 2002. Sudden oak death, caused by a new species, *Phytophthora ramorum*. NA-PR-06-01. Newtown Square, PA: U.S. Department of Agriculture, Forest Service, State and Private Forestry, Northeastern Area. 2 p.

Frankel, S.J. 2008. Sudden oak death and *Phytophthora ramorum* in the USA: a management challenge. Australasian Plant Pathology. 37: 19–25.

Frankel, S.J. 2009. Personal communication. Sudden oak death research program manager, Pacific Southwest Research Station. PO Box 245, Berkeley, CA 94701.

Friend, G. 2008. Impact assessment on future management of risks from *Phytophthora ramorum* and *Phytophthora kernoviae*. York, UK: Department for Environment, Food and Rural Affairs. http://www.defra.gov.uk/corporate/consult/phytophthora-ram-kern/impact-assessment.pdf. (April 2010).

Gaastra, W. 1984. Enzyme linked immuno-sorbent assay. In: Walker, J., ed. Methods in microbiology. Clifton, NJ: Humana Press: 349–355.

Garbelotto, M. 2003a. Composting as a control for sudden oak death disease. Biocycle. 44(3): 53–56.

Garbelotto, M. 2003b. Molecular diagnostics of *Phytophthora ramorum*, causal agent of sudden oak death. APS sudden oak death online symposium. The American Phytopathological Society. DOI: 10.1094/SOD-2003-MG.

Garbelotto, M. 2004. Sudden oak death: a tale of two continents. Outlooks on Pest Management. 15: 85–89.

Garbelotto, M.; Davidson, J.M.; Ivors, K.; Maloney, P.E.; Hüberli, D.; Rizzo, D.M. 2003a. Non-oak native plants are the main hosts for the sudden oak death pathogen in California. California Agriculture. 57(1): 18–23.

Garbelotto, M.; Ivors, K.; Hüberli, D.; Bonants, P.; Wagner, A. 2006. Potential for sexual reproduction of *Phytophthora ramorum* in Washington State nurseries. In: Frankel, S.J.; Shea, P.J.; Haverty, M.I., tech. coords. Proceedings, the sudden oak death second science symposium: the state of our knowledge. Gen. Tech. Rep. PSW-GTR-196. Albany, CA: U.S. Department of Agriculture, Forest Service, Pacific Southwest Research Station: 129.

Garbelotto, M.; Rizzo, D.M. 2001. Preliminary studies on chemical and cultural control of *Phytophthora* associated with sudden oak death. Phytopathology. 91(S30): 1057–1065.

Garbelotto, M.; Rizzo, D.M. 2005. A California-based chronological review (1995–2004) of research on *Phytophthora ramorum*, the causal agent of sudden oak death. Phytopathologia Mediterranea. 44(2): 127–143.

Garbelotto, M.; Rizzo, D.M.; Davidson, J.M.; Frankel, S.J. 2002a. How to recognize the symptoms of the diseases caused by *Phytophthora ramorum*, causal agent of sudden oak death. Vallejo, CA: U.S. Department of Agriculture, Forest Service, Pacific Southwest Region. 15 p.

Garbelotto, M.; Rizzo, D.M.; Hayden, K.; Meija-Chan, M.; Davidson, J.M.; Tjosvold, S. 2002b. *Phytophthora ramorum* and sudden oak death in California. III. Pathogen genetics. In: Standiford, R.; McCreary, D., eds. Fifth symposium on California oak woodlands. Gen. Tech. Rep. PSW-GTR-184. Berkeley, CA: U.S. Department of Agriculture, Forest Service, Pacific Southwest Research Station: 765–774.

Garbelotto, M.; Rizzo, D.M.; Marais, L. 2002c. *Phytophthora ramorum* and sudden oak death in California: IV. Preliminary studies on chemical control. In: Standiford, R.; McCreary, D.; Purcell, K.L., tech. coords. 5th symposium on California oak woodlands: oaks in California's changing landscape. Gen. Tech. Rep. PSW-GTR-184. Albany, CA: U.S. Department of Agriculture, Forest Service, Pacific Southwest Research Station: 811–818.

Garbelotto, M.; Schmidt, D.J. 2009. Phosphonate controls sudden oak death pathogen for up to 2 years. California Agriculture. 63: 10–17.

Garbelotto, M.; Schmidt, D.J.; Harnik, T.Y. 2007. Phosphite injections and bark application of phosphite + Pentrabark™ control sudden oak death in coast live oak. Arboriculture and Urban Forestry. 33(5): 309–317.

Garbelotto, M.; Schmidt, D.J.; Tjosvold, S.; Harnik, T.Y. 2003b. Chemical treatment strategies for control of sudden oak death in oaks and tanoaks. Phytopathology. 93: S28.

Garbelotto, M.; Svihra, P.; Rizzo, D.M. 2001. Sudden oak death syndrome fells three oak species. California Agriculture. 55: 9–19.

Geltz, E.; McHugh, J.; Baird, L.; Ghosh, S.; Thut, P.; Kolipinski, M. 2006. Anatomical examination of *Phytophthora ramorum* infection in *Camellia*. In: Frankel, S.J.; Shea, P.J.; Haverty, M.I., tech. coords. Proceedings of the sudden oak death second science symposium: the state of our knowledge. Gen. Tech. Rep. PSW-GTR-196. Albany, CA: U.S. Department of Agriculture, Forest Service, Pacific Southwest Research Station: 512.

Gewasbescherming. 2004. *Phytophthora ramorum* in Amerikaanse eik. Gewasbescherming. 35(2): 126.

Gibbs, J.; van Dijk, C.; Webber, J., eds. 2003. *Phytophthora* disease of alder in Europe. Bulletin 126. Edinburgh: Forestry Commission. 82 p.

Global Invasive Species Specialist Group. 2006. Global Invasive Species Database: *Phytophthora ramorum* (fungus). Auckland, New Zealand: University of Auckland, IUCN Species Survival Commission.

Goheen, E.M. 2003. Detecting, surveying, and monitoring *Phytophthora ramorum* in forest ecosystems. Sudden oak death online symposium. The American Phytopathological Society. DOI: 10.1094/SOD-2003-EG.

Goheen, E.; Hansen, E.; Kanaskie, A.; Sutton, W.; Reeser, P. 2008. Vegetation response following *Phytophthora ramorum* eradication treatments in southwest Oregon forests. In: Frankel, S.J.; Kliejunas, J.T.; Palmieri, K.M., tech. coords. Proceedings of the sudden oak death third science symposium. Gen. Tech. Rep. PSW-GTR-214. Albany, CA: U.S. Department of Agriculture, Forest Service, Pacific Southwest Research Station: 301–303.

Goheen E.M.; Hansen E.M.; Kanaskie A.; McWilliams, M.G. 2002a. Sudden oak death caused by *Phytophthora ramorum* in Oregon. Plant Disease. 86: 441.

Goheen, E.M.; Hansen, E.M.; Kanaskie, A.; McWilliams, M.G.; Osterbauer, N.; Sutton, W. 2002b. Eradication of sudden oak death in Oregon. Phytopathology. 92: S30.

Goheen, E.; Hansen, E.; Kanaskie, A.; McWilliams, M.; Osterbauer, N.; Sutton, W.; Rehms, L. 2004. An eradication strategy for *Phytophthora ramorum* in Oregon coastal forests. Phytopathology. 94: S35.

Goheen, E.M.; Hansen, E.; Kanaskie, A.; Osterbauer, N.; Parke, J.; Pscheidt, J.; Chastagner, G. 2006a. Sudden oak death and *Phytophthora ramorum*: a guide for forest managers, Christmas tree growers, and forest-tree nursery operators in Oregon and Washington. EM 8877. Corvallis, OR: Extension Service, Oregon State University. 16 p.

Goheen, E.M.; Kanaskie, A.; Hansen, E.; Sutton, W.; Reeser, P.; Osterbauer, N. 2010. Eradication effectiveness monitoring in Oregon tanoak forests. In: Frankel, S.J.; Kliejunas, J.T.; Palmieri, K.M., tech. coords. Proceedings of the sudden oak death fourth science symposium. Gen. Tech. Rep. PSW-GTR-229. Albany, CA: U.S. Department of Agriculture, Forest Service, Pacific Southwest Research Station: 233–235.

Goheen, E.M.; Kanaskie, A.; Parke, J.; Roth, M.; Osterbauer, N.; Trippe, A. 2006b. Application of fungicides to protect four hosts from foliar infection by *Phytophthora ramorum* in Curry County, Oregon. In: Frankel, S.J.; Shea, P.J.; Haverty, M.I., tech. coords. Proceedings, sudden oak death second science symposium: the state of our knowledge. Gen. Tech. Rep. PSW-GTR-196. Albany, CA: U.S. Department of Agriculture, Forest Service, Pacific Southwest Research Station: 513–514.

Gibbs, J.; van Dijk, C.; Webber, J., eds. 2003. *Phytophthora* disease of alder in Europe. Bulletin 126. Edinburgh: Forestry Commission. 82 p.

Goss, E.M.; Caarbone, I.; Grünwald, N.J. 2009a. Ancient isolation and independent evolution of the three clonal lineages of the exotic sudden oak death pathogen *Phytophthora ramorum*. Molecular Ecology. 18: 1161–1174.

Goss, E.M.; Larsen, M.; Carbone, I.; Givens, D.R.; Chastagner, G.A.; Grünwald, N.A. 2010. Population genetic analysis reveals ancient evolution and recent migration of *Phytophthora ramorum*. In: Frankel, S.J.; Kliejunas, J.T.; Palmieri, K.M., eds. Proceedings of the sudden oak death fourth science symposium. Gen. Tech. Rep. 229. Albany, CA: U.S. Department of Agriculture, Forest Service, Pacific Southwest Research Station: 116–118.

Goss, E.M.; Larsen, M.; Chastagner, G.A.; Givens, D.R.; Grünwald, N.J. 2009b. Population genetic analysis infers migration pathways of *Phytophthora ramorum* in US nurseries. PLoS Pathogens. 5(9): e1000583.

Griesbach, J.A. 2008. Potential economic impacts of the widespread distribution of *Phytophthora ramorum* to Oregon's nursery and Christmas tree industries: a preliminary economic assessment of failing to eradicate *P. ramorum* from Oregon's forestlands. Unpublished report. On file with: Ascent Agricultural Services, LLC, 4742 Liberty Road S., Salem, Oregon 97302. 3 p. http://www.ascentag.com/pramorum.pdf. (April 2010).

Grünwald, N.J.; Davis, E.A.; Linderman, R.G. 2006a. Variation in phenotype for resistance to *Phytophthora ramorum*, in a range of species and cultivars of the genus *Viburnum*. In: Frankel, S.J.; Shea, P.J.; Haverty, M.I., tech. coords. Proceedings, sudden oak death second science symposium: the state of our knowledge. Gen. Tech. Rep. PSW-GTR-196. Albany, CA: U.S. Department of Agriculture, Forest Service, Pacific Southwest Research Station: 83–85.

Grünwald, N.J.; Goss, E.M.; Ivors, K.; Garbelotto, M.; Martin, F.N. [and others]. 2009. Standardizing the nomenclature for clonal lineages of the sudden oak death pathogen, *Phytophthora ramorum*. Phytopathology. 99: 792–795.

Grünwald, N.J.; Goss, E.M.; Larsen, M.M.; Press, C.M.; McDonald, V.T.; Blomquist, C.L.; Thomas, S.L. 2008a. First report of the European lineage of *Phytophthora ramorum* on *Viburnum* and *Osmanthus* spp. in a California nursery. Plant Disease. 92: 314.

Grünwald, N.J.; Goss, E.M.; Press, C.M. 2008b. *Phytophthora ramorum*: a pathogen with a remarkably wide host range causing sudden oak death on oaks and ramorum blight on woody ornamentals. Molecular Plant Pathology. 9: 729–740.

Grünwald, N.J.; Kitner, M.L.; Larsen, M.M.; Linderman, R.G.; Parke, J.L. 2006b. Evaluation of lilac cultivars for susceptibility to *Phytophthora ramorum*. Biological and Cultural Tests for Control of Plant Diseases. 21: 005.

Grünwald, N.J.; Kitner, M.; Linderman, R.G. 2008c. Effect of flooding on root and foliar disease severity on *Rhododendron* caused by *P. ramorum*. In: Frankel, S.J.; Kliejunas, J.T.; Palmieri, K.M., tech. coords. Proceedings of the sudden oak death third science symposium. Gen. Tech. Rep. PSW-GTR-214. Albany, CA: U.S. Department of Agriculture, Forest Service, Pacific Southwest Research Station: 363–365.

Gundersen, D.E.; Lee, I.M. 1996. Ultrasensitive detection of phytoplasmas by nested-PCR assays using two universal primer pairs. Phytopathologia Mediterranea. 35: 144–151.

Guo, Q.C.; Kelly, M.; Gong, P.; Liu, D. 2007. An object-based classification approach in mapping tree mortality using high spatial resolution imagery. GIScience and Remote Sensing. 44: 24–47.

Guo, Q.; Kelly, M.; Graham, C.H. 2005. Support vector machines for predicting distribution of sudden oak death in California. Ecological Modelling. 182: 75–90.

Hagen, B. 1999. Special report: tanoak/live oak decline. In: Forest Pest Conditions in California–1999. California Forest Pest Council: 11–12.

Hall, K.M.; Albers, H.J. 2009. Economic analysis for the impact of *Phytophthora ramorum* on Oregon forest industries. Unpublished report. On file with: Department of Agricultural and Resource Economics, 213 Ballard Extension Hall, Oregon State University, Corvallis, OR 97331-3601.

Halverson, N.M., comp. 1986. Major indicator shrubs and herbs on national forests of western Oregon and southwestern Washington. R6-TM-229. Portland, OR: U.S. Department of Agriculture, Forest Service, Pacific Northwest Region. 180 p.

Hansen, E. 2003. *Phytophthora* in North American forests. In: Sudden oak death online symposium. http://nature.berkeley.edu/comtf/pdf/Bibliography/hansen2003a.pdf. (April 2010).

Hansen, E. 2007. Personal communication. Professor, Department of Botany and Plant Pathology, Oregon State University, Corvallis, OR 97331.

Hansen, E. 2008a. Alien forest pathogens: *Phytophthora* species are changing world forests. Boreal Environment Research. 13: 33–41.

Hansen, E. 2008b. Rethinking *Phytophthora*—research opportunities and management. In: Frankel, S.J.; Kliejunas, J.T.; Palmieri, K.M., tech. coords. Proceedings of the sudden oak death third science symposium. Gen. Tech. Rep. PSW-GTR-214. Albany, CA: U.S. Department of Agriculture, Forest Service, Pacific Southwest Research Station: 5–14.

Hansen, E.M.; Hesse, C.; Reeser, P.; Sutton, W. 2006a. Using single strand conformational polymorphisms (SSCP) to identify *Phytophthora* species in Oregon forests affected by sudden oak death. In: Frankel, S.J.; Shea, P.J.; Haverty, M.I., tech. coords. Proceedings, sudden oak death second science symposium: the state of our knowledge. Gen. Tech. Rep. PSW-GTR-196. Albany, CA: U.S. Department of Agriculture, Forest Service, Pacific Southwest Research Station: 141–142.

Hansen, E.M.; Kanaskie, A.; Goheen, E.M.; Osterbauer, N.; Sutton, W. 2006b. Epidemiology of *Phytophthora ramorum* in Oregon. In: Frankel, S.J.; Shea, P.J.; Haverty, M.I., tech. coords. Proceedings of the sudden oak death second science symposium: the state of our knowledge. Gen. Tech. Rep. PSW-GTR-196. Albany, CA: U.S. Department of Agriculture, Forest Service, Pacific Southwest Research Station: 27–29.

Hansen, E.M.; Kanaskie, A.; Prospero, S.; McWilliams, M.; Goheen, E.M.; Osterbauer, N.; Reeser, P.; Sutton, W. 2008. Epidemiology of *Phytophthora ramorum* in Oregon tanoak forests. Canadian Journal of Forest Research. 38: 1133–1143.

Hansen, E.M.; Parke, J.L.; Sutton, W. 2005. Susceptibility of Oregon forest trees and shrubs to *Phytophthora ramorum*: a comparison of artificial inoculation and natural infection. Plant Disease. 89: 63–70.

Hansen, E.M.; Reeser, P.W.; Sutton, W.; Winton, L.M. 2003. First report of A1 mating type of *Phytophthora ramorum* in North America. Plant Disease. 87: 1267.

Hansen, E.M.; Rizzo, D.; Garbelotto, M. 2006c. *Phytophthora* species from oak and tanoak forests in California and Oregon. In: Frankel, S.J.; Shea, P.J.; Haverty, M.I., tech. coords. Proceedings, sudden oak death second science symposium: the state of our knowledge. Gen. Tech. Rep. PSW-GTR-196. Albany, CA: U.S. Department of Agriculture, Forest Service, Pacific Southwest Research Station: 63–65.

Hansen, E.M.; Sutton, W. 2006. Persistence of *Phytophthora ramorum* after eradication efforts in Oregon tanoak forests. In: Frankel, S.J.; Shea, P.J.; Haverty, M.I., tech. coords. Proceedings of the sudden oak death second science symposium: the state of our knowledge. Gen. Tech. Rep. PSW-GTR-196. Albany, CA: U.S. Department of Agriculture, Forest Service, Pacific Southwest Research Station: 516.

Hansen, E.; Sutton, W.; Parke, J.; Linderman, R. 2002. *Phytophthora ramorum* and Oregon forest trees—one pathogen, three diseases. In: Proceedings of the sudden oak death science symposium. Berkeley, CA: U.S. Department of Agriculture, Forest Service and University of California, Berkeley. http://danr.ucop.edu/ihrmp/sodsymp/poster/poster07.html. (April 2010).

Hardy, G.E.; Barrett, S.; Shearer, B.L. 2001. The future of phosphite as a fungicide to control the soilborne plant pathogen *Phytophthora cinnamomi* in natural ecosystems. Australasian Plant Pathology. 39: 133–139.

Harnik, T.Y.; Garbelotto, M. 2006. Effect of chemicals on hyphal growth, sporangia production and zoospore germination of *Phytophthora ramorum*. In: Frankel, S.J.; Shea, P.J.; Haverty, M.I., tech. coords. Proceedings, sudden oak death second science symposium: the state of our knowledge. Gen. Tech. Rep. PSW-GTR-196. Albany, CA: U.S. Department of Agriculture, Forest Service, Pacific Southwest Research Station: 517.

Harnik, T.Y.; Mejia-Chang, M.; Lewis, J.; Garbelotto, M. 2004. Efficacy of heat-based treatments in eliminating the recovery of the sudden oak death pathogen (*Phytophthora ramorum*) from infected California bay laurel leaves. HortScience. 39(7): 1677–1680.

Harvey, A.E. 1994. Integrated roles for insects, diseases and decomposers in fire dominated forests of the inland Western United States: past, present and future forest health. Journal of Sustainable Forestry. 2(1/2): 211–220.

Hayden, K.; Garbelotto, M. 2006. Quantitative resistance to *Phytophthora ramorum* in tanoak. In: Frankel, S.J.; Shea, P.J.; Haverty, M.I., tech. coords. Proceedings, sudden oak death second science symposium: the state of our knowledge. Gen. Tech. Rep. PSW-GTR-196. Albany, CA: U.S. Department of Agriculture, Forest Service, Pacific Southwest Research Station: 518.

Hayden, K.; Ivors, K.; Wilkinson, C.; Garbelotto, M. 2006. Taqman chemistry for *Phytophthora ramorum* detection and quantification, with a comparison of diagnostic methods. Phytopathology. 96: 846–854.

Hayden, K.J.; Lundquist, A.; Schmidt, D.J.; Sniezko, R.A.; Frankel, S.; Garbelotto, M. 2010. Tanoak resistance: Can it be used to sustain populations? In: Frankel, S.J.; Kliejunas, J.T.; Palmieri, K.M., tech. coords. Proceedings of the sudden oak death fourth science symposium. Gen. Tech. Rep. PSW-GTR-229. Albany, CA: U.S. Department of Agriculture, Forest Service, Pacific Southwest Research Station: 183–188.

Hayden, K.J.; Rizzo, D.; Tse, J.; Garbelotto, M. 2004. Detection and quantification of *Phytophthora ramorum* from California forests using a real-time polymerase chain reaction assay. Phytopathology. 94: 1075–1083.

Heid, C.A.; Stevens, J.; Livak, K.J.; Williams, P.J. 1996. Real time quantitative PCR. Genome Research. 6: 986–994.

Heiniger, U.; Theile, F.; Stadler, B. 2004. Erstfund von *Phytophthora ramorum* in Switzerland. Scheitzerische Zeitschrift für Forstwesen. 155: 53–54.

Herrero, M.L.; Toppe, B.; Klemsdal, S.S.; Stensvand, A. 2006. First report of *Phytophthora ramorum* in ornamental plants in Norway. Plant Disease. 90: 1458. DOI: 10.1094/PD-90-1458B.

Heungens, K.; De Debbelaere, I.; Maes, M. 2006. Fungicide control of *Phytophthora ramorum* on *Rhododendron*. In: Frankel, S.J.; Shea, P.J.; Haverty, M.I., tech. coords. Proceedings, sudden oak death second science symposium: the state of our knowledge. Gen. Tech. Rep. PSW-GTR-196. Albany, CA: U.S. Department of Agriculture, Forest Service, Pacific Southwest Research Station: 241–257.

Holland, P.M.; Abramson, R.D.; Watson, R.; Gelfand, D.H. 1991. Detection of specific polymerase chain reaction product by utilizing the 5' to 3' exonuclease activity of *Thermus aquaticus* DNA polymerase. Proceedings of the National Academy of Sciences. 88: 7276–7280.

Hüberli, D.; Van Sant, W.; Swain, S.; Davidson, J.; Garbelotto, M. 2002. Resistance of *Umbellularia californica* (bay laurel) to *Phytophthora ramorum*. Sudden oak death science symposium. Berkeley, CA: University of California. http://danr.ucop.edu/ihrmp/sodsymp/paper/paper16.html. (April 2010).

Hughes, K.; Griffin, R.; Tomlinson, J.; Boonham, N.; Barton, V.; Giltrap, P.; Hobden, E.; Walker, L.; Humphries, G.; Barnes, A.; Beales, P.; Inman, A.; Lane, C. 2006a. Comparative evaluation of real-time PCR (Taqman) with isolation for diagnosis of *Phytophthora ramorum*. In: Frankel, S.J.; Shea, P.J.; Haverty, M.I., tech. coords. Proceedings, sudden oak death second science symposium: the state of our knowledge. Gen. Tech. Rep. PSW-GTR-196. Albany, CA: U.S. Department of Agriculture, Forest Service, Pacific Southwest Research Station: 554–555.

Hughes, K.; Tomlinson, J.; Boonham, N.; Ivors, K.; Garbelotto, M.; Barker, I. 2006b. Application of rapid on-site PCR (Taqman) for *Phytophthora ramorum* under U.S. conditions. In: Frankel, S.J.; Shea, P.J.; Haverty, M.I., tech. coords. Proceedings, sudden oak death second science symposium: the state of our knowledge. Gen. Tech. Rep. PSW-GTR-196. Albany, CA: U.S. Department of Agriculture, Forest Service, Pacific Southwest Research Station: 143–144.

Hughes, K.J.D.; Tomlinson, J.A.; Griffin, R.L.; Boonham, N.; Inman, A.J.; Lane, C.R. 2006c. Development of a one-step real-time polymerase chain reaction assay for diagnosis of *Phytophthora ramorum*. Phytopathology. 96: 975–981.

Hunter, R.D.; Meentemeyer, R.K.; Rizzo, D.M.; Gilligan, C.A. 2008. Predicting the spread of sudden oak death in California: spatial-temporal modeling of susceptible-infectious transitions. In: Frankel, S.J.; Kliejunas, J.T.; Palmieri, K.M., tech. coords. Proceedings of the sudden oak death third science symposium. Gen. Tech. Rep. PSW-GTR-214. Albany, CA: U.S. Department of Agriculture, Forest Service, Pacific Southwest Research Station: 277.

Inman, A. 2009. Personal communication. Coordinator, Central Science Laboratory, Department for Environment, Food, and Rural Affairs, Sand Hutton, York, UK.

Inman, A.J.; Hughes, K.J.D.; Beales, P.A.; Lane, C.R.; Rizvi, R.; Barnes, A.V.; Barton, V.; Bowyer. R.J.; Griffin, R. 2005. Non-tree host range and diagnosis of *Phytophthora ramorum* (sudden oak death) in support of pest risk assessment, management and policy. Project Report PH0193S. London: Department of Environment, Food and Rural Affairs. On file with: Research Policy and International Division, Final Reports Unit, DEFRA, Area 301, Cromwell House, Dean Stanley Street, London, SW1P 3JH.

Ioos, R,; Andrieux, A.; Marçais, B.; Frey, P. 2006. Genetic characterization of the natural hybrid species *Phytophthora alni* as inferred from nuclear and mitochondrial DNA analyses. Fungal Genetics and Biology. 43: 511–529.

Ivors, K.; Garbelotto, M. 2002. TaqMan® PCR for detection of *Phytophthora* DNA in environmental plant samples. In: Proceedings of the sudden oak death science symposium. Berkeley, CA: U.S. Department of Agriculture, Forest Service and University of California, Berkeley. http://danr.ucop.edu/ihrmp/sodsymp/poster/poster10.html. (April 2010).

Ivors, K.; Garbelotto, M.; de Vries, I.; Bonants, P. 2006a. Use of microsatellite markers derived from whole genome sequence data for identifying polymorphism in *Phytophthora ramorum*. In: Frankel, S.J.; Shea, P.J.; Haverty, M.I., tech. coords. Proceedings, sudden oak death second science symposium: the state of our knowledge. Gen. Tech. Rep. PSW-GTR-196. Albany, CA: U.S. Department of Agriculture, Forest Service, Pacific Southwest Research Station: 145.

Ivors, K.; Garbelotto, M.; DeVries, I.; Ruyter-Spira, C.; Te Hekkert, B.; Rosenzweig, N.; Bonants, P. 2006b. Microsatellite markers identify three lineages of *Phytophthora ramorum* in US nurseries, yet single lineages in US forest and European nursery populations. Molecular Ecology. 15: 1493–1505.

Ivors, K.I.; Hayden, K.J.; Bonants, P.J.M.; Rizzo, D.M.; Garbelotto, M. 2004. AFLP and phylogenetic analyses of North American and European populations of *Phytophthora ramorum*. Mycological Research. 108: 378–392.

Ivors, K.; Hayden, K.; Garbelotto, M.; Rizzo, D. 2002. Molecular population analyses of *Phytophthora ramorum*. In: Proceedings of the sudden oak death science symposium. Berkeley, CA: U.S. Department of Agriculture, Forest Service and University of California, Berkeley. http://danr.ucop.edu/ihrmp/sodsymp/paper/paper17.html. (April 2010).

Jeffers, S. 2005. Recovery of *Phytophthora ramorum* from soilless mixes around container-grown ornamental plants. Phytopathology. 95: S48.

Jeger, M.J.; Pautasso, M.; Holdenrieder, O.; Shaw, M.W. 2007. Modelling disease spread and control in networks: implications for plant sciences. New Phytologist. 174: 279–297.

Jennings, P. 2006. Investigation of dry-heat treatment methods for sanitisation of *P. ramorum* and *P. kernoviae* on/in plants. SID 5 Research project 2 final report. Sand Hutton, York, UK: Central Science Laboratory. 13 p. http://www.fera.defra.gov.uk/plants/plantHealth/pestsDiseases/documents/research/project2February07.pdf. (April 2010).

Jerado, A. 2004. Floriculture and nursery crops situation and outlook yearbook. FLO-2004. Washington, DC: U.S. Department of Agriculture, Economic Research Service.

Jerado, A. 2007. Floricultural and nursery crops situation and outlook yearbook. FLO-2007. Washington, DC: U.S. Department of Agriculture, Economic Research Service.

Jones, J.M. 2006. APHIS *Phytophthora ramorum* regulatory strategy for nurseries. In: Frankel, S.J.; Shea, P.J.; Haverty, M.I., tech. coords. Proceedings, sudden oak death second science symposium: the state of our knowledge. Gen. Tech. Rep. PSW-GTR-196. Albany, CA: U.S. Department of Agriculture, Forest Service, Pacific Southwest Research Station: 45–46.

Jones, S. 2009. Personal communication. Deputy Chief for Forestry Assistance, Dept. of Forestry and Fire Protection, 1416 9th Street, Sacramento, CA 94244-2460.

Kanaskie, A.; Goheen, E.; Hansen, E.; Osterbauer, N.; McWilliams, M.; Schultz, M.; Savona, S.; Sutton, W.; Reeser, P. 2009. Early detection and eradication of *Phytophthora ramorum* (sudden oak death) in Oregon forests. Phytopathology. 99: S61.

Kanaskie, A.; Goheen, E.; Osterbauer, N.; McWilliams, M.; Hansen, E.; Sutton, W. 2008a. Eradication of *Phytophthora ramorum* from Oregon forests: status after six years. In: Frankel, S.J.; Kliejunas, J.T.; Palmieri, K.M., tech. coords. Proceedings of the sudden oak death third science symposium. Gen. Tech. Rep. PSW-GTR-214. Albany, CA: U.S. Department of Agriculture, Forest Service, Pacific Southwest Research Station: 15–17.

Kanaskie, A.; Hansen, E.; Goheen, E.; Osterbauer, N. 2008b. Sudden oak death eradication in Oregon forests: the final phase. Unpublished report. On file with: Oregon Department of Forestry, 2600 State Street, Salem, OR 97310. 13 p.

Kanaskie, A.; Hansen, E.; Goheen, E. Michaels.; Osterbauer, N.; McWilliams, M.; Laine, J.; Thompson, M.; Savona, S.; Timeus, H.; Woosley, B.; Sutton, W.; Reeser, P.; Schultz, R.; Hilburn, D. 2010a. Detection and eradication of *Phytophthora ramorum* from Oregon forests, 2001–2008. In: Frankel, S.J.; Kliejunas, J.T.; Palmieri, K.M., eds. Proceedings of the sudden oak death fourth science symposium. Gen. Tech. Rep. PSW-GTR-229. Albany, CA: U.S. Department of Agriculture, Forest Service, Pacific Southwest Research Station: 3–5.

Kanaskie, A.; Hansen, E.; Sutton, W. 2006a. Effects of phosphonate treatments on the growth of *Phytophthora ramorum* in tanoak stems. In: Frankel, S.J.; Shea, P. J.; Haverty, M.I., tech. coords. Proceedings, sudden oak death second science symposium: the state of our knowledge. Gen. Tech. Rep. PSW-GTR-196. Albany, CA: U.S. Department of Agriculture, Forest Service, Pacific Southwest Research Station: 259–261.

Kanaskie, A.; Hansen, E.; Sutton, W.; Reeser, P.; Choquette, C. 2010b. Aerial applicaton of Agri-Fos to prevent sudden oak death in Oregon tanoak forests. In: Frankel, S.J.; Kliejunas, J.T.; Palmieri, K.M., tech. coords. Proceedings of the sudden oak death fourth science symposium. Gen. Tech. Rep. PSW-GTR-229. Albany, CA: U.S. Department of Agriculture, Forest Service, Pacific Southwest Research Station: 225–232.

Kanaskie, A.; McWilliams, M.; Mair, J.; Lain, J.; Beeson, J.; Goheen, E.; Schroeter, R.; Hansen, E.; Sutton, W.; Osterbauer, N.; Rehms, L. 2004. Monitoring *Phytophthora ramorum* in Oregon coastal forests. Phytopathology. 99: S48.

Kanaskie, A.; Osterbauer, N.; McWilliams, M.; Goheen, E.; Hansen, E.; Sutton, W. 2006b. Eradication of *Phytophthora ramorum* in Oregon forests—status after 3 years. In: Frankel, S.J.; Shea, P.J.; Haverty, M.I., tech. coords. Proceedings, sudden oak death second science symposium: the state of our knowledge. Gen. Tech. Rep. PSW-GTR-196. Albany, CA: U.S. Department of Agriculture, Forest Service, Pacific Southwest Research Station: 489–490.

Kanaskie, A.; Violet, K.; Hansen, E.; Sutton, W.; Labonte, J. 2002. Monitoring insect activity near sites infested with *Phytophthora ramorum* in southwest Oregon. In: Proceedings of the sudden oak death science symposium, the state of our knowledge. Berkeley, CA: U.S. Department of Agriculture, Forest Service and University of California, Berkeley. http://danr.ucop.edu/ihrmp/sodsymp/poster/poster06.html. (April 2010).

Kehlenbeck, H. 2008. Assessment of potential economic and environmental impacts caused by *Phytophthora ramorum* in Europe. In: Frankel, S.J.; Kliejunas, J.T.; Palmieri, K.M., tech. coords. Proceedings of the sudden oak death third science symposium. Gen. Tech. Rep. PSW-GTR-214. Albany, CA: U.S. Department of Agriculture, Forest Service, Pacific Southwest Research Station: 265–267.

Kelly, M.; Guo, Q.; Liu, D.; Shaari, D. 2007. Modeling the risk of a new invasive forest disease in the United States: an evaluation of five environmental niche models. Computers, Environment and Urban Systems. 31(6): 689–710.

Kelly, M.; Liu, D.; McPherson, B.; Wood, D.; Staniford, R. 2008. Spatial pattern dynamics of oak mortality and associated disease symptoms in a California hardwood forest affected by sudden oak death. Journal of Forest Research. DOI: 10.1007/s10310-008-0083-7.

Kelly, N.M.; Meentemeyer, R.K. 2002. Landscape dynamics of the spread of sudden oak death. Photogrammetric Engineering and Remote Sensing. 68: 1001–1009.

Kelly, M.; Shaari, D.; Guo. Q.; Liu, D. 2004. A comparison of standard and hybrid classifier methods for mapping hardwood mortality in areas affected by "sudden oak death." Photogrammetric Engineering and Remote Sensing. 70: 1229–1239.

Kelly, M.; Shaari, Q.; Guo, Q.; Liu, D. 2006. Modeling risk for SOD nationwide: What are effects of model choice on risk prediction? In: Frankel, S.J.; Shea, P.J.; Haverty, M.I., tech. coords. Proceedings of the sudden oak death second science symposium: the state of our knowledge. Gen. Tech. Rep. PSW-GTR-196. Albany, CA: U.S. Department of Agriculture, Forest Service, Pacific Southwest Research Station: 333–344.

Kessel, G.; Werres, S.; Webber, J. 2007. *P. ramorum* infection process in selected trees and ornamental plants. Deliverable Report 8. Farnham, UK: Forest Research, Central Science Laboratory. EU Sixth Framework Project, RAPRA. On file with: Forest Research Agency, Alice Holt Lodge, Farnham, Surrey GU10 4LH, UK.

Kim, K.D.; Nemec, S.; Musson, G. 1997. Control of *Phytophthora* root and crown rot of bell pepper with composts and soil amendments in the greenhouse. Applied Soil Ecology. 5: 169–179.

Kliejunas, J.T. 2003. A pest risk assessment for *Phytophthora ramorum* in North America. Washington, DC: U.S. Department of Agriculture, Forest Service. Exotic Forest Pest Information System for North America. http://www.suddenoakdeath.org/pdf/RevisedPRA.8.03.pdf. (April 2010).

Klinger, L.; Zingaro, R. 2006. Etiology and evidence of systemic acidification in SOD-affected forests of California. In: Frankel, S.J.; Shea, P.J.; Haverty, M.I., tech. coords. Proceedings, sudden oak death second science symposium: the state of our knowledge. Gen. Tech. Rep. PSW-GTR-196. Albany, CA: U.S. Department of Agriculture, Forest Service, Pacific Southwest Research Station: 181–182.

Koch, F.H.; Smith, W.D. 2008. Mapping sudden oak death nationally using host, climate and pathways data. In: Frankel, S.J.; Kliejunas, J.T.; Palmieri, K.M., tech. coords. Proceedings of the sudden oak death third science symposium. Gen. Tech. Rep. PSW-GTR-214. Albany, CA: U.S. Department of Agriculture, Forest Service, Pacific Southwest Research Station: 280–287.

Kong, P.; Hong, C.; Jeffers, S.N.; Richardson, P.A. 2003a. A species-specific polymerase chain reaction assay for rapid detection of *Phytophthora nicotianae* in irrigation water. Phytopathology. 93: 822–831.

Kong, P.; Hong, C.; Richardson, P.A.; Gallegly, M.E. 2003b. Single-strand-conformation polymorphism of ribosomal DNA for rapid species differentiation in genus *Phytophthora*. Fungal Genetics and Biology. 39: 238–249.

Kong, P.; Hong, C.X.; Tooley, P.W.; Ivors, K.; Garbelotto, M.; Richardson, P.A. 2004. Rapid identification of *Phytophthora ramorum* using PCR-SSCP analysis of ribosomal DNA ITS-1. Letters in Applied Microbiology. 38: 433–439.

Kong, P.; Richardson, P.A.; Hong, C.X. 2003c. Use of single-strand conformation polymorphism of PCR-amplified ribosomal DNA for detection of *Phytophthora ramorum* in plant tissues. Phytopathology. 93: S47.

Kong, P.; Richardson, P.A.; Hong, C.; Kubisiak, T.L. 2006. Single-strand conformation polymorphism analysis of ribosomal DNA detection of *Phytophthora ramorum* directly from plant tissues. In: Frankel, S.J.; Shea, P.J.; Haverty, M.I., tech. coords. Proceedings, sudden oak death second science symposium: the state of our knowledge. Gen. Tech. Rep. PSW-GTR-196. Albany, CA: U.S. Department of Agriculture, Forest Service, Pacific Southwest Research Station: 147.

Kox, L.; De Gruyer, H.; Garbelotto, M.; Van Brouwershaven, I.; Admiraal, I.; Baayen, R. 2002. Validation of a PCR method for detection and identification of *Phytophthora ramorum*. In: Proceedings of the sudden oak death science symposium. Berkeley, CA: U.S. Department of Agriculture, Forest Service and University of California, Berkeley. http://danr.ucop.edu/ihrmp/sodsymp/poster/poster12.html. (April 2010).

Kox, L.F.F.; van Brouwershaven, I.R.; van de Vossenberg, B.T.L.H.; van den Beld, H.E.; Bonants, P.J.M.; de Gruyter, J. 2007. Diagnostic values and utility of immunological, morphological, and molecular methods for in planta detection of *Phytophthora ramorum*. Phytopathology. 97: 1119–1129.

Kroon, L.P.N.M.; Verstappen, E.C.P.; Kox, L.F.F.; Flier, W.G.; Bonants, P.J.M. 2004. A rapid diagnostic test to distinguish between American and European populations of *Phytophthora ramorum*. Phytopathology. 94: 613–620.

Lane, C.R.; Barnes, A.V.; Beales, P.A.; Griffin, R.L.; Hughes, K.J.D.; Inman, A.J.; Townsend, V.C.; Brasier, C.M.; Webber, J.F. 2003a. First report of *Phytophthora ramorum* in the UK. In: 8th International Congress of Plant Pathology, Paper 19.35. Christchurch, NZ: International Congress of Plant Pathology.

Lane, C.R.; Beales, P.A.; Hughes, K.J.D.; Griffin, R.L.; Munro, R.L.; Brasier, C.M.; Webber, J.F. 2003b. First outbreak of *Phytophthora ramorum* in England on *Viburnum tinus*. Plant Pathology. 52: 414.

Lane, C.R.; Hobden, E.; Walker, L.; Barton, V.C.; Inman, A.J.; Hughes, K.J.D.; Swan, H.; Colyer, A.; Barker, I. 2007. Evaluation of a rapid diagnostic field test kit for identification of *Phytophthora* species, including *P. ramorum* and *P. kernoviae* at the point of inspection. Plant Pathology. DOI: 10.1111/j.1365-3059.2007.01615.x.

Lee, S.B.; Taylor, J.W. 1992. Phylogeny of five fungus-like protoctistan *Phytophthora* species, inferred from the Internal Transcribed Spacers of Ribosomal DNA. Molecular Biology and Evolution. 9: 636–653.

Lewis, C.D.; Parke, J.L. 2006. Pathways of infection for *Phytophthora ramorum* in rhododendron. In: Frankel, S.J.; Shea, P.J.; Haverty, M.I., tech. coords. Proceedings of the sudden oak death second science symposium: the state of our knowledge. Gen. Tech. Rep. PSW-GTR-196. Albany, CA: U.S. Department of Agriculture, Forest Service, Pacific Southwest Research Station: 295–297.

Lewis, C.D.; Roth, M.L.; Choquette, C.J.; Parke, J.L. 2004. Root infection of rhododendron by *Phytophthora ramorum*. Phytopathology. 94: S61.

Lilja, A. 2007. Invasive alien species fact sheet: *Phytophthora ramorum*. Online database of the north European and Baltic network on invasive alien species–NOBANIS. http://www.nobanis.org/files/factsheets/Phytophthora_ramorum.pdf. (April 2010).

Linderman, R.G.; Davis, E.A. 2005. Chemical control of *Phytophthora ramorum* on rhododendron and lilac. American Phytopathological Society. 2005 annual meeting. Poster-654. California Oak Mortlity Task Force. http://www.cnr.Berkeley.edu/comtf/html/aps_abstracts_2005.html#poster654. (March 2010).

Linderman, R.G.; Davis, E.A. 2006a. Evaluation of chemical and biological agents for control of *Phytophthora* species on intact plants or detached leaves of rhododendron and lilac. In: Frankel, S.J.; Shea, P.J.; Haverty, M.I., tech. coords. Proceedings, sudden oak death second science symposium: the state of our knowledge Gen. Tech. Rep. PSW-GTR-196. Albany, CA: U.S. Department of Agriculture, Forest Service, Pacific Southwest Research Station: 265–268.

Linderman, R.G.; Davis, E.A. 2006b. Survival of *Phytophthora ramorum* compared to other species of *Phytophthora* in potting media components, compost, and soil. HortTechnology. 16: 502–512.

Linderman, R.G.; Davis, E.A. 2006c. Survival of *Phytophthora* species and other pathogens in soilless media components or soil and their eradication with aerated steam. In: Frankel, S.J.; Shea, P.J.; Haverty, M.I., tech. coords. Proceedings, sudden oak death second science symposium: the state of our knowledge. Gen. Tech. Rep. PSW-GTR-196. Albany, CA: U.S. Department of Agriculture, Forest Service, Pacific Southwest Research Station: 299–302.

Linderman, R.G.; Davis, E.A.; Marlow, J.L. 2006. Response of selected nursery crop plants to inoculation with isolates of *Phytophthora ramorum* and other *Phytophthora* species. HortTechnology. 16: 216–224.

Linderman, R.G.; de Sá, P.B.; Davis, E.A. 2007. Comparative susceptibility of plants native to the Appalachian range of the United States to inoculation with *Phytophthora ramorum*. Plant Health Progress. DOI: 10.1094/PHP-2007-0917-01-RS.

Linzer, R.E.; Rizzo, D.M.; Cacciola, S.O.; Garbelotto, M. 2009. AFLPs detect low genetic diversity for *Phytophthora nemorosa* and *P. pseudosyringae* in the US and Europe. Mycological Research. 113: 298–307.

Liu, D.; Kelly, M.; Gong, P. 2006. A spatial-temporal approach to monitoring forest disease spread using multi-temporal high spatial resolution imagery. Remote Sensing of Environment. 101: 167–180.

Liu, D.; Kelly, M.; Gong, P.; Guo, Q. 2007. Characterizing spatial-temporal tree mortality patterns associated with a new forest disease. Forest Ecology and Management. 253: 220–231.

Lockley, D.; Turner, J.; Humphries, G.; Jennings, P. 2008. Monitoring *Phytophthora ramorum* and *P. kernoviae* in soil and rainwater samples collected at two sites at a Cornish estate. In: Frankel, S.J.; Kliejunas, J.T.; Palmieri, K.M., tech. coords. Proceedings of the sudden oak death third science symposium. Gen. Tech. Rep. PSW-GTR-214. Albany, CA: U.S. Department of Agriculture, Forest Service, Pacific Southwest Research Station: 389–391.

Magarey, R.D.; Fowler, G.A.; Borchert, D.M.; Sutton, T.B.; Colunga-Garcia, M.; Simpson, J.A. 2007. NAPPFAST: an Internet system for the weather-based mapping of plant pathogens. Plant Disease. 91: 336–345.

Magarey, R.; Fowler, G.: Colunga, M.; Smith, B.; Meentemeyer, R. 2008. Climate-host mapping of *Phytophthora ramorum*, causal agent of sudden oak death. In: Frankel, S.J.; Kliejunas, J.T.; Palmieri, K.M., tech. coords. Proceedings of the sudden oak death third science symposium. Gen. Tech. Rep. PSW-GTR-214. Albany, CA: U.S. Department of Agriculture, Forest Service, Pacific Southwest Research Station: 269–275.

Magarey, R.; Fowler, G.; Randall-Schadel, B.; Colunga, M. 2006. Climate and host risk map for sudden oak death risk (*Phytophthora ramorum*). CPHST NAPPFAST SOD Risk Mapping Report Oct. 06 2006. 6 p. On file with: Animal and Plant Health Inspection Service, Plant Protection and Quarantine, Center for Plant Health Science and Technology, Plant Epidemiology and Risk Analysis Laboratory, Raleigh, NC 27603.

Mai, J.A.; Mark, W.; Fischer, L.; Jirka, A. 2006. Aerial and ground surveys for mapping the distribution of *Phytophthora ramorum* in California. In: Frankel, S.J.; Shea, P.J.; Haverty, M.I., tech. coords. Proceedings, sudden oak death second science symposium: the state of our knowledge. Gen. Tech. Rep. PSW-GTR-196. Albany, CA: U.S. Department of Agriculture, Forest Service, Pacific Southwest Research Station: 345–360.

Maloney, P.E.; Kane, S.F.; Jensen, C.E.; Rizzo, D.M. 2002. Epidemiology and ecology of *Phytophthora ramorum* in redwood/tanoak forest ecosystems of the California Coast Range. In: Proceedings of the sudden oak death science symposium, the state of our knowledge. Berkeley, CA: U.S. Department of Agriculture, Forest Service and University of California, Berkeley. http://danr.ucop.edu/ihrmp/sodsymp/paper/paper21.html. (April 2010).

Maloney, P.E.; Lynch, S.C.; Kane, S.F.; Jensen, C.E.; Rizzo, D.M. 2005. Establishment of an emerging generalist pathogen in redwood forest communities. Journal of Ecology. 93(5): 899–905.

Maloney, P.E.; Lynch, S.L.; Kane, S.F.; Jensen, C.E.; Rizzo, D.M. 2007. Disease ecology of *Phytophthora ramorum* in redwood forests in the California coast ranges. In: Standiford, R.B.; Giusti, G.A.; Valachovic, Y.; Zielinski, W.J.; Furniss, M.J., tech. eds. Proceedings of the redwood region forest science symposium: What does the future hold? Gen. Tech. Rep. PSW-GTR-194. Albany, CA: U.S. Department of Agriculture, Forest Service, Pacific Southwest Research Station: 467–468.

Manter, M.; Hansen. E.; Parke, J. 2010. Virulence, sporulation, and elicitin production in three clonal lineages of *Phytophthora ramorum*. In: Frankel, S.J.; Kliejunas, J.T.; Palmieri, K.M., tech. coords. Proceedings of the fourth sudden oak death science symposium. Gen. Tech. Rep. PSW-GTR-229. Albany, CA: U.S. Department of Agriculture, Forest Service, Pacific Southwest Research Station: 88.

Manter, D.K.; Karchesy, J.J.; Kelsey, R.G. 2006. The sporicidal activity of yellow-cedar heartwood, essential oil and wood constituents towards *Phytophthora ramorum* in culture. Forest Pathology. 36: 297–308.

Manter, D.K.; Kelsey, R.G.; Karchesy, J.J. 2008. Antimicrobial activity of extracts and select compounds in the heartwood of seven western conifers toward *Phytophthora ramorum*. In: Frankel, S.J.; Kliejunas, J.T.; Palmieri, K.M., tech. coords. Proceedings of the sudden oak death third science symposium. PSW-GTR-214. Albany, CA: U.S. Department of Agriculture, Forest Service, Pacific Southwest Research Station: 375–378.

Mark, W.; Jirka, A. 2002. Surveying for sudden oak death in California. In: Standiford, R.; McCreary, D.; Purcell, K.L., tech. coords. 5th symposium on California oak woodlands: oaks in California's changing landscape. Gen. Tech. Rep. PSW-GTR-184. Albany, CA: U.S. Department of Agriculture, Forest Service, Pacific Southwest Research Station: 819–823.

Martin, F.N. 2008. Mitochondrial haplotype determination in the Oomycete plant pathogen *Phytophthora ramorum*. Current Genetics. 54: 23–34.

Martin, F.N.; Tooley, P.W. 2003. Phylogenetic relationships of *Phytophthora ramorum*, *P. nemorosa*, and *P. pseudosyringae*, three species recovered from areas in California with sudden oak death. Mycological Research. 107: 1379–1391.

Martin, F.N.; Tooley, P.W. 2004. Identification of *Phytophthora* isolates to species level using restriction fragment length polymorphism analysis of a polymerase chain reaction-amplified region of mitochondrial DNA. Phytopathology. 94: 983–991.

Martin, F.N.; Tooley, P.W.; Blomquist, C. 2004. Molecular detection of *Phytophthora ramorum*, the causal agent of sudden oak death in California, and two additional species commonly recovered from diseased plant material. Phytopathology. 94: 621–631.

Mascheretti, S.; Croucher, P.; Vettraino, A.; Prospero, S.; Garbelotto, M. 2008. Reconstruction of the sudden oak death epidemic in California through microsatellite analysis of the pathogen *Phytophthora ramorum*. Molecular Ecology. 17(11): 2755–2768.

McKelvey, S.; Koch, F.; Smith, B. 2008. Predicting the movement of nursery hosts using a linear network model. In: Frankel, S.J.; Kliejunas, J.T.; Palmieri, K.M., tech. coords. Proceedings of the sudden oak death third science symposium. Gen. Tech. Rep. PSW-GTR-214. Albany, CA: U.S. Department of Agriculture, Forest Service, Pacific Southwest Research Station: 249–256.

McKenney, D.; Campbell, K.; Hopkin, T.; Lawrence, K. [N.d.]. Climatic domain maps for sudden oak death: current climate (1971–2000), and future climate scenarios (Hadleyb2 and CGCM2b), 2011–2040 and 2041–2070 (using confirmed North American sites, California and Oregon only. Plus an extreme minimum temperature model that may indicate North American temperature limits on SOD). http://nature.berkeley.edu/comtf/pdf/sod_biomap_results_05%20V2.pdf. (April 2010).

McKenney, D.W.; Hopkin, A.A.; Campbell, K.L.; Mackey, B.G.; Footit, R. 2003. Opportunities for improved risk assessments of exotic species in Canada using bioclimatic modeling. Environmental Monitoring and Assessment. 88: 445–461.

McLaughlin, I.; Sutton, W.; Hansen, E. 2006. Survival of *Phytophthora ramorum* in tanoak and rhododendron leaves. In: Frankel, S.J.; Shea, P.J.; Haverty, M.I., tech. coords. Proceedings of the sudden oak death second science symposium: the state of our knowledge. Gen. Tech. Rep. PSW-GTR-196. Albany, CA: U.S. Department of Agriculture, Forest Service, Pacific Southwest Research Station: 529.

McPherson, B.A.; Mori, S.; Wood, D.L.; Storer, A.J.; Svihra, P.; Kelly, N.M.; Standiford, R.B. 2005. Sudden oak death in California: disease progression in oaks and tanoaks. Forest Ecology and Management. 213: 71–89.

McPherson, B.A.; Mori, S.R.; Wood, D.L.; Storer, A.J.; Svihra, P.; Kelly, N.M.; Standiford, R.B. 2006. Sudden oak death disease progression in oaks and tanoaks. In: Frankel, S.J.; Shea, P.J.; Haverty, M.I., tech. coords. Proceedings of the sudden oak death second science symposium: the state of our knowledge. Gen. Tech. Rep. PSW-GTR-196. Albany, CA: U.S. Department of Agriculture, Forest Service, Pacific Southwest Research Station: 379–382.

McPherson, B.A.; Rizzo, D.M.; Garbelotto, M.; Svihra, P.; Wood, D.L.; Storer, A.J.; Kelly, N.M.; Palkovsky, N.; Tjosvold, S.A.; Standiford, R.B.; Koike, S.T. 2002a. Sudden oak death in California. Pest Notes. Publication 7498. Agriculture and Natural Resources, University of California. 5 p.

McPherson, B.A.; Standiford, R.B.; Wood, D.L.; Storer, A.J.; Svihra, P. 2002b. Interactions among bark and ambrosia beetles (Coleoptera: Scolytidae) and a novel disease of oaks in California. In: Proceedings of the sudden oak death science symposium, the state of our knowledge. Berkeley, CA: U.S. Department of Agriculture, Forest Service and University of California, Berkeley. http://danr.ucop.edu/ihrmp/sodsymp/poster/poster40.html. (April 2010).

McPherson, B.A.; Wood, D.L.; Storer, A.J.; Svihra, P.; Rizzo, D.M.; Kelly, N.M.; Standiford, R.B. 2000. Oak mortality syndrome: sudden death of oaks and tanoaks. Tree Notes 26. Sacramento, CA: California Department of Forestry and Fire Protection. 6 p.

Meentemeyer, R.K.; Anacker, B.L.; Mark, W.; Rizzo, D.M. 2008a. Early detection of emerging forest disease using dispersal estimation and ecological niche modeling. Ecological Applications. 18: 377–390.

Meentemeyer, R.; Lotz, E.; Rizzo, D.; Buja, K.; Mark, W. 2006. Early detection monitoring of *Phytophthora ramorum* in high-risk forests of California. In: Frankel, S.J.; Shea, P.J.; Haverty, M.I., tech. coords. Proceedings, sudden oak death second science symposium: the state of our knowledge. Gen. Tech. Rep. PSW-GTR-196. Albany, CA: U.S. Department of Agriculture, Forest Service, Pacific Southwest Research Station: 361–363.

Meentemeyer, R.K.; Rank, N.E.; Anacker, B.L.; Rizzo, D.M.; Cushman, J.H. 2008b. Influence of land-cover change on the spread of an invasive forest pathogen. Ecological Applications. 18: 159–171.

Meentemeyer, R.K.; Rank, N.E.; Shoemaker, D.A.; Oneal, C.B.; Wickland, A.C.; Frangioso, K.M.; Rizzo. D.M. 2008c. Impact of sudden oak death on tree mortality in the Big Sur ecoregion of California. Biological Invasions. 10: 1243–1255.

Meentemeyer, R.; Rizzo, D.; Mark, W.; Lotz, E. 2004. Mapping the risk of establishment and spread of sudden oak death in California. Forest Ecology and Management. 200: 195–214.

Meshriy, M.; Hüberli, D.; Harnik, T.; Miles, L.; Reuther, K.; Garbelotto, M. 2006. Variation in susceptibility of *Umbellularia californica* (bay laurel) to *Phytophthora ramorum*. In: Frankel, S.J.; Shea, P.J.; Haverty, M.I., tech. coords. Proceedings, sudden oak death second science symposium: the state of our knowledge. Gen. Tech. Rep. PSW-GTR-196. Albany, CA: U.S. Department of Agriculture, Forest Service, Pacific Southwest Research Station: 87–89.

Messenger, B.J.; Menge, J.A.; Pond, E. 2000. Effects of gypsum soil amendments on avocado growth, soil drainage, and resistance to *Phytophthora cinnamomi*. Plant Disease. 84: 612–616.

Minore, D. 1972. The wild huckleberries of Oregon and Washington: a dwindling resource. PNW-GTR-143. Portland, OR: U.S. Department of Agriculture, Forest Service, Pacific Northwest Forest and Range Experiment Station. 20 p.

Mistretta, P. 1984. Littleleaf disease. Forest Insect and Disease Leaflet 20. Washington, DC: U.S. Department of Agriculture, Forest Service. 6 p.

Monahan, W.B.; Koenig, W.D. 2006. Estimating the potential effects of sudden oak death on oak-dependent birds. Biological Conservation. 127: 146–157.

Moralejo, E.; Denman, S.; Beales, P.; Webber, J. 2007. Report on the ability of key tree and nontree hosts to support inoculum production of *Phytophthora ramorum*. Deliverable Report 27. London: Department of Environment, Food and Rural Affairs. On file with: Research Policy and International Division, Final Reports Unit, DEFRA, Area 301, Cromwell House, Dean Stanley Street, London, SW1P 3JH.

Moralejo, E.; Descals, E. 2006. Multihyphal structures formed by *Phytophthora ramorum* on inoculated leaves of Mediterranean shrubs. In: Frankel, S.J.; Shea, P.J.; Haverty, M.I., tech. coords. Proceedings of the sudden oak death second science symposium: the state of our knowledge. Gen. Tech. Rep. PSW-GTR-196. Albany, CA: U.S. Department of Agriculture, Forest Service, Pacific Southwest Research Station: 530.

Moralejo, E.; Hernández, L. 2002. Inoculation trials of *Phytophthora ramorum* on detached Medíterrean sclerophyll leaves. In: Proceedings of the sudden oak death science symposium, the state of our knowledge. Berkeley, CA: U.S. Department of Agriculture, Forest Service and University of California, Berkeley. http://danr.ucop.edu/ihrmp/sodsymp/paper/paper25.html. (April 2010).

Moralejo, E.; Puig, M.; Garcia, J.A.; Descals, E. 2006. Stromata, sporangiomata and chlamydosori of *Phytophthora ramorum* on inoculated Mediterranean woody plants. Mycological Research. 110: 1323–1332.

Moralejo, E.; Werres, S. 2002. First report of *Phytophthora ramorum* on *Rhododendron* sp. in Spain. Plant Disease. 86: 1052.

Moritz, M.A.; Odion, D.C. 2005. Examining the strength and possible causes of the relationship between fire history and sudden oak death. Oecologia. 144: 106–114.

Moritz, M.A.; Odion, D.C. 2006. Examining the relationship between fire history and sudden oak death patterns: a case study in Sonoma County. In: Frankel, S.J.; Shea, P.J.; Haverty, M.I., tech. coords. Proceedings, sudden oak death second science symposium: the state of our knowledge. Gen. Tech. Rep. PSW-GTR-196. Albany, CA: U.S. Department of Agriculture, Forest Service, Pacific Southwest Research Station: 169–177.

Murphy, S.K.; Lee, C.; Bienapfl, J.; Valachovic, Y.; Rizzo, D.M. 2006. Monitoring *Phytophthora ramorum* distribution in streams within coastal California watersheds. In: Frankel, S.J.; Shea, P.J.; Haverty, M.I., tech. coords. Proceedings, sudden oak death second science symposium: the state of our knowledge. Gen. Tech. Rep. PSW-GTR-196. Albany, CA: U.S. Department of Agriculture, Forest Service, Pacific Southwest Research Station: 531.

Mycological Research News. 2004. Sudden oak death (*Phytophthora ramorum*) discovered on trees in Europe. Mycological Research News. 108: 1108–1109.

Niemiec, S.S.; Ahrens, G.R.; Willits, S.; Hibbs, D.E. 1995. Hardwoods of the Pacific Northwest. Research Contribution 8. Corvallis, OR: Oregon State University, Forest Research Laboratory. 115 p.

North American Plant Protection Organization [NAPPO]. 2006. Ongoing eradication efforts of *Phytophthora ramorum* in 3 retail and 1 wholesale nursery in British Columbia, Canada. Phytosanitary Alert System. Official Pest Report Posted 12 October 2006. http://www.pestalert.org/oprDetail.cfm?oprID=235. (April 2010).

Oak, S.W.; Elledge, A.H.; Yockey, E.K.; Smith, W.D.; Tkacz, B.M. 2008. *Phytophthora ramorum* early detection surveys for forests in the U.S., 2003–2006. In: Frankel, S.J.; Kliejunas, J.T.; Palmieri, K.M., tech. coords. Proceedings of the sudden oak death third science symposium. Gen. Tech. Rep. PSW-GTR-214. Albany, CA: U.S. Department of Agriculture, Forest Service, Pacific Southwest Research Station: 413–416.

Oak, S.W.; Hwang, J.; Jeffers, S.N.; Tkacz, B.M. 2010. *Phytophthora ramorum* in USA streams from the national early detection survey of forests. In: Frankel, S.J.; Kliejunas, J.T.; Palmieri, K.M., tech. coords. Proceedings of the sudden oak death fourth science symposium. Gen. Tech. Rep. PSW-GTR-229. Albany, CA: U.S. Department of Agriculture, Forest Service, Pacific Southwest Research Station: 353–354.

Oak, S.W.; Smith, W.D.; Tkacz, B.M. 2006. *Phytophthora ramorum* detection surveys for forests in the United States. In: Brasier, C.; Jung, T.; Oßwald, W., eds. Proceedings of the third international IUFRO working party S07.02.09 meeting. Progress in research on *Phytophthora* diseases of forest trees. Farnham, Surry, UK: Forest Research: 28–30.

O'Brien, J.; Mielke, M.E.; Oak, S.; Moltzan, B. 2002. Sudden oak death. Oak mortality is caused by a new pathogen, *Phytophthora ramorum*. NA-PR-02-02. Newtown Square, PA: U.S. Department of Agriculture, Forest Service, State and Private Forestry, Northeastern Area. 2 p.

Official Journal of the European Communities [OJEC]. 2002. Commission decision (2002/757/EC) on provisional emergency phytosanitary measures to prevent the introduction into and the spread within the Community of *Phytophthora ramorum* Werres, De Cock & Man in't Veld sp. nov. Official Journal of the European Communities. L252, 20 September 2002: 37–39.

Official Journal of the European Communities. [OJEC]. 2007. Commission decision (2007/201/EC) amending decision 2002/757/EC on provisional emergency phytosanitary measures to prevent the introduction into and the spread within the Community of *Phytophthora ramorum* Werres, De Cock & Man in 't Veld sp. nov. Official Journal of the European Communities. L90, 27 March 2007: 83–85.

Oregon Invasive Species Council. 2008. Oregon invasive species council state-wide summit. 68 p. http://olcvblog.typepad.com/olcvblog/files/finalsummitreport091008.pdf. (April 2010).

Organisation Europeenne et Mediterraneenne pour la Protection des Plants/ European and Mediterranean Plant Protection Organization [OEPP/EPPO]. 2006. *Phytophthora ramorum*. EPPO Bulletin. 36(1): 145–155.

Orlikowski, L.B. 2004a. Biological control of *Phytophthora ramorum* on rhododendron. Communications in Agricultural and Applied Biological Sciences. 69: 687–692.

Orlikowski, L.B. 2004b. Chemical control of rhododendron twig blight caused by *Phytophthora ramorum*. Journal of Plant Protection Research. 44(1): 41–46.

Orlikowski, L.B.; Skrzypczak, Cz.; Szkuta, G. 2004. Zagrożenie roślin przez *Phytophthora ramorum* w Polsce i na świecie. Progress in Plant Protection. 45(2): 966–969.

Orlikowski, L.B.; Szkuta, G. 2002. First record of *Phytophthora ramorum* in Poland. Phytopathologia Polonica. 25: 69–79.

Osterbauer, N.K. 2003. *Phytophthora ramorum* Werres, de Cock & Man in't Veld. Pest risk assessment for Oregon. http://www.suddenoakdeath.org/pdf/SOD_PRA_OR_2=04.pdf. (April 2010).

Osterbauer, N.K.; Griesbach, J.A.; Hedberg, J. 2004. Surveying for and eradicating *Phytophthora ramorum* in agricultural commodities. Plant Health Progress. DOI: 10.1094/PHP-2004-0309-02-RS.

Parke, J. 2005. Nursery guidelines for the exclusion and management of *Phytophthora ramorum* in nurseries. http://extension.oregonstate.edu/emergency/Nursery_Guidelines_Dec2005.pdf. (April 2010).

Parke, J.L.; Bienapfl, J.; Oh, E.; Rizzo, D.; Hansen, E.; Buckles, G.; Lee, C.; Valachovic, Y. 2006a. Natural infection of tanoak seedling roots by *Phytophthora ramorum*. Phytopathology. 96: S90.

Parke, J.L.; Grünwald, N.; Lewis, C.; Fieland, V. 2010a. A systems approach for detecting sources of *Phytophthora* contamination in nurseries. In: Frankel, S.J.; Kliejunas, J.T.; Palmieri, K.M., tech. coords. Proceedings of the sudden oak death fourth science symposium. Gen. Tech. Rep. PSW-GTR-229. Albany, CA: U.S. Department of Agriculture, Forest Service, Pacific Southwest Research Station: 67–68.

Parke, J.L.; Hansen, E.M.; Linderman, R.G. 2002a. Sporulation potential of *Phytophthora ramorum* on leaf disks from selected hosts. In: Proceedings of the sudden oak death science symposium. Berkeley, CA: U.S. Department of Agriculture, Forest Service and University of California, Berkeley. http://danr.ucop.edu/ihrmp/sodsymposium.html. (April 2010).

Parke, J.L.; Lewis, C. 2007. Root and stem infection of *Rhododendron* from potting media infested with *Phytophthora ramorum*. Plant Disease. 91: 1265–1270.

Parke, J.L.; Linderman, R.G; Hansen, E.M. 2002b. Susceptibility of *Vaccinium* to *Phytophthora ramorum*, cause of sudden oak death. Phytopathology. 92: S63.

Parke, J.L.; Linderman, R.G.; Hummer, K.; Hansen, E.M. 2002c. Differential susceptibility to *Phytophthora ramorum* among *Vaccinium* species and cultivars. In: Proceedings of the sudden oak death science symposium, the state of our knowledge. Berkeley, CA: U.S. Department of Agriculture, Forest Service and University of California, Berkeley. http://danr.ucop.edu/ihrmp/sodsymp/poster/poster21.html. (April 2010).

Parke, J.L.; Lucas, S. 2008. Sudden oak death and ramorum blight. The Plant Health Instructor. DOI: 10.1094/PHI-I-2008-0227-01.

Parke, J.L.; Oh, E.: Ochiai, N.; Stone, J.; Hansen, E. 2006b. Recovery and detection of *Phytophthora ramorum* from sapwood of mature tanoak. Phytopathology. 96: S170.

Parke, J.L.; Oh, E.; Voelker, S.; Hansen, E.M.; Buckles, G.; Lachenbruch, B. 2007. *Phytophthora ramorum* colonizes tanoak xylem and is associated with reduced stem water transport. Phytopathology. 97: 1558–1567.

Parke, J.; Pscheidt, J.; Linderman, R. 2003. *Phytophthora ramorum*, a guide for Oregon nurseries. Bulletin EM 8840. Corvallis, OR: Department of Botany and Plant Pathology, Oregon State University Extension Service. 8 p.

Parke, J.; Pscheidt, J.; Linderman, R. 2004. *Phytophthora ramorum*, a guide for Washington nurseries. Corvallis, OR: Department of Botany and Plant Pathology, Oregon State University Extension Service. 8 p.

Parke, J.L.; Pscheidt, J.; Regan, R.; Hedberg, J.; Grünwald, N. 2010b. The *Phytophthora* online course: training for nursery growers. In: Frankel, S.J.; Kliejunas, J.T.; Palmieri, K.M., tech. coords. Proceedings of the sudden oak death fourth science symposium. Gen. Tech. Rep. PSW-GTR-229. Albany, CA: U.S. Department of Agriculture, Forest Service, Pacific Southwest Research Station: 355.

Parke, J.L.; Roth, M.L.; Lewis, C.; Choquette, C.J. 2006c. *Phytophthora ramorum* disease transmission from artificially infested potting media. In: Frankel, S.J.; Shea, P.J.; Haverty, M.I., tech. coords. Proceedings of the sudden oak death second science symposium: the state of our knowledge. Gen. Tech. Rep. PSW-GTR-196. Albany, CA: U.S. Department of Agriculture, Forest Service, Pacific Southwest Research Station: 291–293.

Parke, J.L.; Stamm, E.; Oguchi, A.; Fichtner, E.; Rizzo, D.M. 2008. Viability of *Phytophthora ramorum* after passage through slugs. Phytopathology. 98: S121.

Pautasso, M.; Harwood, T.; Shaw, M.; Xu, X.; Jeger, M. 2008. Epidemiological modeling of *Phytophthora ramorum*: network properties of susceptible plant genera movements in the nursery sector of England and Wales. In: Frankel, S.J.; Kliejunas, J.T.; Palmieri, K.M., tech. coords. Proceedings of the sudden oak death third science symposium. Gen. Tech. Rep. PSW-GTR-214. Albany, CA: U.S. Department of Agriculture, Forest Service, Pacific Southwest Research Station: 257–264.

Pavlik, B.M.; Muick, P.C.; Johnson, S.G.; Popper, M. 1991. Oaks of California. Los Olivos, CA: Cachuma Press and the California Oak Foundation. 184 p.

Pogoda, F.; Werres, S. 2002. Pathogenicity of European and American *P. ramorum* isolates to rhododendron. In: Proceedings of the sudden oak death science symposium. Berkeley, CA: U.S. Department of Agriculture, Forest Service and University of California, Berkeley. http://danr.ucop.edu/ihrmp/sodsymp/poster/poster26.html. (April 2010).

Pogoda, F.; Werres, S. 2004. Histological studies of *Phytophthora ramorum* in *Rhododendron* twigs. Canadian Journal of Botany. 82: 1481–1489.

Prospero, S.; Grünwald, N.J.; Winton, L.M.; Hansen, E.M. 2009. Migrating patterns of the emerging plant pathogen *Phytophthora ramorum* on the west coast of the United States of America. Phytopathology. 99: 739–749.

Prospero, S.; Hansen, E.M.; Grünwald, N.J.; Winton, L.M. 2007. Population dynamics of the sudden oak death pathogen *Phytophthora ramorum* in Oregon from 2001 to 2004. Molecular Ecology. 16: 2958–2973.

Purdue University Center for Environmental and Regulatory Information Systems Export Certification Project. 2007. Product requirements for Australia, Canada, the European Union, Korea and Switzerland. West Lafayette IN: Export Certification Project, Perdue Research Foundation, Purdue University, Indiana.

Ramsfield, T.D.; Dick, M.A.; Beever, R.E.; Horner, I.J.; McAlonan, M.J.; Hill, C.F. 2009. *Phytophthora kernoviae* in New Zealand. In: Goheen, E.M.; Frankel, S.J., tech. coords. Proceedings of the fourth meeting of the International Union of Forest Research Organizations (IUFRO) Working Party S07.02.09: Phytophthoras in forests and natural ecosystems. Gen. Tech. Rep. PSW-GTR-221. Albany, CA: U.S. Department of Agriculture, Forest Service, Pacific Southwest Research Station: 47–53.

Rank, N.; Cushman, H.; Meentemeyer, R.; Rizzo, D. 2010. Establishment of *Phytophthora ramorum* depends on woodland diversity and species composition. In: Frankel, S.J.; Kliejunas, J.T.; Palmieri, K.M., tech. coords. Proceedings of the sudden oak death fourth science symposium. Gen. Tech. Rep. PSW-GTR-229. Albany, CA: U.S. Department of Agriculture, Forest Service, Pacific Southwest Research Station: 356–357.

Regelbrugge, C. 2003. Sudden oak death–U.S. nursery trade impacts. Sudden oak death online symposium. The American Phytopathological Society. DOI: 10.1094/SOD-2003-TS.

Ribeiro, O.K. 1983. Physiology of asexual sporulation and spore germination in *Phytophthora*. In: Erwin, D.C.; Bartnicki-Garcia, S.; Tsao, P.H., eds. *Phytophthora*, its biology, taxonomy, ecology, and pathology. St. Paul, MN: APS Press: 55–70.

Riedel, M.; Julich, S.; Kielpinski, M.; Möller, R.; Fritsche, W.; Wagner, S.; Henkel, T.; Breitenstein, A.; Werres, S. 2010. Chip-based on site diagnosis of *Phytophthora ramorum*. In: Frankel, S.J.; Kliejunas, J.T.; Palmieri, K.M., tech. coords. Proceedings of the fourth sudden oak death science symposium. Gen. Tech. Rep. PSW-GTR-229. Albany, CA: U.S. Department of Agriculture, Forest Service, Pacific Southwest Research Station: 362–364.

Riedel, M.; Wagner, S.; Goetz, M.; Belbahri, L.; Lefort, F.; Werres, S. 2008. Studies on the tissue colonisation in *Rhododendron* by *Phytophthora ramorum.* In: Frankel, S.J.; Kliejunas, J.T.; Palmieri, K.M., tech. coords. Proceedings of the sudden oak death third science symposium. Gen. Tech. Rep. PSW-GTR-214. Albany, CA: U.S. Department of Agriculture, Forest Service, Pacific Southwest Research Station: 485–487.

Rizzo, D.M. 2006. Research on the epidemiology, ecology and management of *Phytophthora ramorum* in California forests. In: Frankel, S.J.; Shea, P.J.; Haverty, M.I., tech. coords. Proceedings of the sudden oak death second science symposium: the state of our knowledge. Gen. Tech. Rep. PSW-GTR-196. Albany, CA: U.S. Department of Agriculture, Forest Service, Pacific Southwest Research Station: 21–25.

Rizzo, D.; Fichtner, E. 2009. *Phytophthora* in forests and natural ecosystems of the Americas. In: Goheen, E.M.; Frankel, S.J., tech. coords. Proceedings of the fourth meeting of the International Union of Forest Research Organizations (IUFRO) Working Party S07.02.09: Phytophthoras in forests and natural ecosystems. Gen. Tech. Rep. PSW-GTR-221. Albany, CA: U.S. Department of Agriculture, Forest Service, Pacific Southwest Research Station: 35–44.

Rizzo, D.M.; Garbelotto, M. 2003. Sudden oak death: endangering California and Oregon forest ecosystems. Frontiers in Ecology and the Environment. 1(5): 197–204.

Rizzo, D.M.; Garbelotto, M.; Davidson, J.M.; Slaughter, G.W.; Koike, S.T. 2002a. *Phytophthora ramorum* and sudden oak death in California. I. Host relationships. In: Standiford, R.; McCreary, D., eds. 5th symposium on California oak woodlands. Gen. Tech. Rep. PSW-GTR-184. Berkeley, CA: U.S. Department of Agriculture, Forest Service, Pacific Southwest Research Station: 733–740.

Rizzo, D.M.; Garbelotto, M.; Davidson, J.M.; Slaughter, G.W.; Koike, S.T. 2002b. *Phytophthora ramorum* as the cause of extensive mortality of *Quercus* spp. and *Lithocarpus densiflorus* in California. Plant Disease. 86: 205–214.

Rizzo, D.M.; Garbelotto, M.; Hansen, E.A. 2005. *Phytophthora ramorum*: integrative research and management of an emerging pathogen in California and Oregon forests. Annual Review of Phytopathology. 43: 309–335.

Rossman, A.Y.; Palm, M.E. 2006. Why are *Phytophthora* and other Oomycota not true Fungi? Outlooks on Pest Management. 17: 217–219.

Sabaratnam, S.; Woodske, D. 2006. Ramorum blight and dieback (sudden oak death). Vancouver, BC: Pest Management, Ministry of Agriculture and Lands, British Columbia. http://www.agf.gov.bc.ca/cropprot/sod.htm. (April 2010).

Sansford, C.E.; Inman, A.J.; Baker, R.; Brasier, C.; Frankel, S.; de Gruyter, J.; Husson, C.; Kehlenbeck, H.; Kessel, G.; Moralejo, E.; Steeghs, M.; Webber, J.; Werres, S. 2009. Report on the risk of entry, establishment, spread and socio-economic loss and environmental impact and the appropriate level of management for *Phytophthora ramorum* for the EU. Deliverable Report 28. Sand Hutton, York, UK: Forest Research, Central Science Laboratory. EU Sixth Framework Project, RAPRA. 310 p. http://rapra.csl.gov.uk/RAPRA-PRA_26feb09.pdf. (April 2010).

Sansford, C.E.; Jones, D.R.; Brasier, C.M. 2003. Revised summary pest risk analysis for *Phytophthora ramorum* for the UK. York, United Kingdom: Forest Research, Central Science Laboratory. 23 p.

Sansford, C.E.; Woodhall, J.W. 2007. Datasheet for *Phytophthora ramorum.* PPP 11824. Sand Hutton, York: Central Science Laboratory, Department of Environment, Forestry, and Rural Affairs. 43 p. http://www.suddenoakdeath.org/pdf/pram_PRA_UK.pdf. (April 2010).

Sawyer, J.O.; Thornburgh, D.A.; Griffin, J.R. 1977. Mixed evergreen forest. In: Barbour, M.G.; Major, J., eds. Terrestrial vegetation of California. New York: John Wiley and Sons: 359–381.

Schaad, N.W.; Frederick, R.D. 2002. Real-time PCR and its application for rapid plant disease diagnostics. Canadian Journal of Plant Pathology. 24: 250–258.

Schena, L.; Hughes, K.J.D.; Cooke, D.E.L. 2006. Detection and quantification of *Phytophthora ramorum*, *P. kernoviae*, *P. citricola*, and *P. quercina* in symptomatic leaves by multiplex real-time PCR. Molecular Plant Pathology. 7(5): 365–379.

Schmidt, D.; Garbelotto, M.; Chambers, D.; Tjosvold, S. 2006. Effects of phosphonate treatments on sudden oak death in tanoak and Shreve's oak. In: Frankel, S.J.; Shea, P.J.; Haverty, M.I., tech. coords. Proceedings, sudden oak death second science symposium: the state of our knowledge. Gen. Tech. Rep. PSW-GTR-196. Albany, CA: U.S. Department of Agriculture, Forest Service, Pacific Southwest Research Station: 263.

Sela, S. 2008. Personal communication, Western forestry specialist, Canadian Food Inspection Agency, Victoria, BC, Canada.

Shearer, B.L.; Smith, I.W. 2000. Diseases of eucalypts caused by soilborne species of *Phytophthora* and *Pythium*. In: Keane, P.J.; Kile, G.A.; Podger, F.D.; Brown, B.N., eds. Diseases and pathogens of eucalypts. Collingwood, Australia: CSIRO Publishing: 259–291.

Shelly, J.; Singh, R.; Langford, C.; Mason, T. 2006. Evaluating the survival of *Phytophthora ramorum* in firewood. In: Frankel, S.J.; Shea, P.J.; Haverty, M.I., tech. coords. Proceedings, sudden oak death second science symposium: the state of our knowledge. Gen. Tech. Rep. PSW-GTR-196. Albany, CA: U.S. Department of Agriculture, Forest Service, Pacific Southwest Research Station: 540.

Shelly, J.; Tietje, W.; McCreary, D. 1996. Resource evaluation for forest products. In: Standiford, R., tech. coord. Guidelines for managing California's hardwood rangelands. Publication 3368. Berkeley, CA: University of California Division of Agriculture and Natural Resources: 82–97. Chapter 8.

Shishkoff, N. 2005. The effect of systemic fungicides on detection by culturing of *Phytophthora ramorum*. Phytopathology 95: S96. http://apsjournals.apsnet.org/doi/pdf/10.1094/PHYTO.2005.95.6.S1. (April 2010).

Shiskoff, N. 2007. Persistence of *Phytophthora ramorum* in soil mix and roots of nursery ornamentals. Plant Disease. 91: 1245–1249.

Shishkoff, N. 2008. Sporulation on plant roots by *Phytophthora ramorum*. Phytopathology. 98: S145.

Shishkoff, N.; Tooley, P. 2004. Persistence of *Phytophthora ramorum* in nursery plants and soil. Phytopathology. 94: S95.

Simpfendorfer, S.; Harden, T.J. 2000. Effect of calcium on the growth and virulence of *Phytophthora clandestine*. Australian Journal of Experimental Agriculture. 40: 47–52.

Slawson, D.; Bennett, L.; Parry, N.; Lane, C. 2006. The current situation with *Phytophthora ramorum* in England and Wales. In: Frankel, S.J.; Shea, P.J.; Haverty, M.I., tech. coords. Proceedings, sudden oak death second science symposium: the state of our knowledge. Gen. Tech. Rep. PSW-GTR-196. Albany, CA: U.S. Department of Agriculture, Forest Service, Pacific Southwest Research Station: 455–457.

Slawson, D.; Blackburn, J.; Bennett, L. 2008. An update on *Phytophthora ramorum* in European nurseries. In: Frankel, S.J.; Kliejunas, J.T.; Palmieri, K.M., tech. coords. Proceedings of the sudden oak death third science symposium. Gen. Tech. Rep. PSW-GTR-214. Albany, CA: U.S. Department of Agriculture, Forest Service, Pacific Southwest Research Station: 31–34.

Smith, A.L.; Hansen, E.M. 2008. The maturation and germination of *Phytophthora ramorum* chlamydospores. In: Frankel, S.J.; Kliejunas, J.T.; Palmieri, K.M., tech. coords. Proceedings of the sudden oak death third science symposium. Gen. Tech. Rep. PSW-GTR-214. Albany, CA: U.S. Department of Agriculture, Forest Service, Pacific Southwest Research Station: 451–454.

Smith, W.; Coulston, J.W.; Goheen, E.M.; Sapio, F.; Gottschalk, K.W.; Frankel, S.; Dunn, P.; Tkacz, B.M. 2002. Development of a national survey protocol for detection of *Phytophthora ramorum*. In: Proceedings of the sudden oak death science symposium. Berkeley, CA: U.S. Department of Agriculture, Forest Service, Pacific Southwest Research Station. http://danr.ucop.edu/ihrmp/sodsymp/paper/paper01.html. (April 2010).

Sniezko, R.A. 2006. Resistance breeding against nonnative pathogens in forest trees—current successes in North America. Canadian Journal of Plant Pathology. 28: S270–S279.

Standiford, R.B. 2000. California's hardwood rangelands: production and conservation values. Oak Fact Sheets No. 89. Berkeley, CA: integrated hardwood range management program, University of California. 4 p.

Steeghs, M.H.C.G. 2008. Contingency planning for *Phytophthora ramorum* outbreaks: progress report work package 7, EU RAPRA project. In: Frankel, S.J.; Kliejunas, J.T.; Palmieri, K.M., tech. coords. Proceedings of the sudden oak death third science symposium. Gen. Tech. Rep. PSW-GTR-214. Albany, CA: U.S. Department of Agriculture, Forest Service, Pacific Southwest Research Station: 313–319.

Steeghs, M.H.C.G.; de Gruyter, J. 2006. *Phytophthora ramorum* experience and approach in the Netherlands. In: Frankel, S.J.; Shea, P.J.; Haverty, M.I., tech. coords. Proceedings, sudden oak death second science symposium: the state of our knowledge. Gen. Tech. Rep. PSW-GTR-196. Albany, CA: U.S. Department of Agriculture, Forest Service, Pacific Southwest Research Station: 367–369.

Stokstad, E. 2004. Nurseries may have shipped sudden oak death pathogen nationwide. Science. 303: 1959.

Storer, A.J.; Keirnan, K.E.; Palkovsky, N.K.; Hagen, B.W.; Slaughter, G.W., Kelley N.M.; Svihra, P. 2002. Diagnosis and monitoring of sudden oak death. Pest Alert No. 6. Novato, CA: University of California, Marin County Cooperative Extension. 13 p.

Stringfellow, B.; Reddy, M.B. 2005. Control of *Phytophthora* in nursery recycled and fresh inlet irrigation water by Agrifos systemic fungicide treatment. Phytopathology. 95: S100.

Suslow, K. 2006. *Phytophthora ramorum*—economic impacts and challenges for the nursery industry. In: Frankel, S.J.; Shea, P.J.; Haverty, M.I., tech. coords. Proceedings of the sudden oak death second science symposium: the state of our knowledge. Gen. Tech. Rep. PSW-GTR-196. Albany, CA: U.S. Department of Agriculture, Forest Service, Pacific Southwest Research Station: 41–44.

Suslow, K. 2008a. Determining the effectiveness of the federal order/interim rule on *Phytophthora ramorum* in nurseries. In: Frankel, S.J.; Kliejunas, J.T.; Palmieri, K.M., tech. coords. Proceedings of the sudden oak death third science symposium. PSW-GTR-214. Albany, CA: U.S. Department of Agriculture, Forest Service, Pacific Southwest Research Station: 27–30.

Suslow, K. 2008b. Recommended industry best management practices for the prevention of *Phytophthora ramorum* introduction in nursery operations. In: Frankel, S.J.; Kliejunas, J.T.; Palmieri, K.M., tech. coords. Proceedings of the sudden oak death third science symposium. PSW-GTR-214. Albany, CA: U.S. Department of Agriculture, Forest Service, Pacific Southwest Research Station: 115–128.

Suslow, K.; Kosta, K.; Raabe, G.; Cohen, S. 2005. Best management practices for the California nursery industry for sudden oak death (SOD) biosecurity. http://nature.berkeley.edu/comtf/pdf/NurseryBMP.pdf. (April 2010).

Sutton, W.; Hansen, E.M.; Reeser, P.W.; Kanaskie, A. 2009. Stream monitoring for detection of *Phytophthora ramorum* in Oregon tanoak forests. Plant Disease. 93: 1182–1186.

Svihra, P. 1999a. Sudden death of tanoak, *Lithocarpus densiflorus*. Pest Alert No. 1. Novato, CA: University of California Cooperative Extension, Marin County. 2 p.

Svihra, P. 1999b. Tan oak and coast live oak under attack. Oaks 'n' folks. 14(2): 1 p.

Svihra, P. 1999c. Western oak bark beetles and ambrosia beetles, killers of live oaks. Pest Alert No. 3. Novato, CA: University of California Cooperative Extension, Marin County. 2 p.

Svihra, P. 2001. Diagnosis of SOD: case study of a scientific process. California Agriculture. 55(1): 12–14, 16.

Swain, S.; Garbelotto, M. 2006. Extended abstract on the potential for *Phytophthora ramorum* to infest finished compost. In: Frankel, S.J.; Shea, P.J.; Haverty, M.I., tech. coords. Proceedings, sudden oak death second science symposium: the state of our knowledge. Gen. Tech. Rep. PSW-GTR-196. Albany, CA: U.S. Department of Agriculture, Forest Service, Pacific Southwest Research Station: 483–486.

Swain, S.; Harnik, T.; Mejia-Chang, M.; Creque, J.; Garbelotto, M. 2002. Survivability of *Phytophthora ramorum* in the composting process. Sudden oak death science symposium. Berkeley, CA: University of California. http://danr.ucop.edu/ihrmp/sodsymp/paper/paper31.html. (April 2010).

Swain, S.; Harnik, T.; Mejia-Chang, M.; Hayden, K.; Bakx, W.; Creque, J.; Garbelotto, M. 2006. Composting is an effective treatment option for sanitization of *Phytophthora ramorum*-infected plant material. Journal of Applied Microbiology. 101: 815–827.

Swiecki, T.J. 2001. Observations and comments on oak and tanoak dieback and mortality in California. Vacaville, CA: Phytosphere Research. http://www.phytosphere.com/tanoakobservations/tanoak.html. (April, 2010).

Swiecki, T.J.; Bernhardt, E.A. 2001. Evaluation of stem water potential and other tree and stand variables as risk factors for *Phytophthora ramorum* canker development in coast live oak and tanoak. Vacaville, CA: Phytosphere Research. Prepared for State and Private Forestry, Forest Service, U.S. Department of Agriculture, Vallejo, CA. http://phytosphere.com/publications/Phytophthora_case-control.htm. (April 2010).

Swiecki, T.J.; Bernhardt, E.A. 2004. *Phytophthora ramorum* canker (sudden oak death) in coast live oak and tanoak: factors affecting disease risk, disease progression, and failure potential. Vacaville, CA: Phytosphere Research. Prepared for Pacific Southwest Research Station, Forest Service, U.S. Department of Agriculture, Berkeley, CA. http://phytosphere.com/publications/Phytophthora_case-control2004.htm. (April 2010).

Swiecki, T.J.; Bernhardt, E.A. 2006. *Phytophthora ramorum* canker (sudden oak death) in coast live oak and tanoak, 2000–2005: factors affecting disease risk, disease progression, and failure potential. Vacaville, CA: Phytosphere Research. Prepared for Pacific Southwest Research Station, Forest Service, U.S. Department of Agriculture, Berkeley, CA. 39 p. http://phytosphere.com/publications/Phytophthora_case-control2006.htm. (April 2010).

Swiecki, T.J.; Bernhardt, E. 2008. Increasing distance from California bay reduces the risk and severity of *Phytophthora ramorum* canker in coast live oak. In: Frankel, S.J.; Kliejunas, J.T.; Palmieri, K.M., tech. coords. Proceedings of the sudden oak death third science symposium. Gen. Tech. Rep. PSW-GTR-214. Albany, CA: U.S. Department of Agriculture, Forest Service, Pacific Southwest Research Station: 181–194.

Tainter, F.H.; O'Brien, J.G.; Hernandez, A.; Orozco, F.; Rebolledo, O. 2000. *Phytophthora cinnamomi* as a cause of oak mortality in the state of Colima, Mexico. Plant Disease. 84: 394–398.

Tempel, D.; Tietje, W. 2006. Potential effects of sudden oak death on the small mammal and herpetofaunal communities in San Luis Obispo County coast live oak (*Quercus agrifolia*) woodlands. In: Frankel, S.J.; Shea, P.J.; Haverty, M.I., tech. coords. Proceedings of the sudden oak death second science symposium: the state of our knowledge. Gen. Tech. Rep. PSW-GTR-196. Albany, CA: U.S. Department of Agriculture, Forest Service, Pacific Southwest Research Station: 233–236.

Thomas, J.D. 1997. California's oak woodlands: where we have been, where we are, where we need to go. In: Pillsbury, N.H.; Verner, J.; Titje, W.D., tech. coords. Proceedings of a symposium on oak woodlands: ecology, management, and urban interface issues. Gen. Tech. Rep. PSW-GTR-160. Albany, CA: U.S. Department of Agriculture, Forest Service, Pacific Southwest Research Station: 3–9.

Tjosvold, S.A.; Buermeyer, K.R.; Bloomquist, C.; Frankel, S. 2005. Nursery guide for diseases of *Phytophthora ramorum* on ornamentals: diagnosis and management. Publication 8156. Davis, CA: Division of Agriculture and Natural Resources, University of California, Davis. 20 p.

Tjosvold, S.A.; Chambers, D.L.; Davidson, J.M.; Rizzo, D.M. 2002a. Incidence of *Phytophthora ramorum* inoculum found in soil collected from a hiking trail and hiker's shoes in a California park. In: Proceedings of the sudden oak death science symposium, the state of our knowledge. Berkeley, CA: U.S. Department of Agriculture, Forest Service and University of California, Berkeley. http://danr.ucop.edu/ihrmp/sodsymp/poster/poster46.html. (April 2010).

Tjosvold, S.A.; Chambers, D.L.; Davidson, J.M.; Rizzo, D.M. 2002b. Incidence of *Phytophthora ramorum* inoculum found in streams running through areas of high incidence of sudden oak death in Santa Cruz County. In: Proceedings of the sudden oak death science symposium, Berkeley, CA: U.S. Department of Agriculture, Forest Service, Pacific Southwest Research Station. http://danr.ucop.edu/ihrmp/sodsymp/poster/poster24.html. (April 2010).

Tjosvold, S.A.; Chambers, D.L.; Koike, S. 2006a. Evaluation of fungicides for the control of *Phytophthora ramorum* infecting *Rhododendron*, *Camellia*, *Viburnum*, and *Pieris*. In: Frankel, S.J.; Shea, P.J.; Haverty, M.I., tech. coords. Proceedings, sudden oak death second science symposium: the state of our knowledge. Gen. Tech. Rep. PSW-GTR-196. Albany, CA: U.S. Department of Agriculture, Forest Service, Pacific Southwest Research Station: 269–271.

Tjosvold, S.A.; Chambers, D.L.; Koike, S.; Fichtner, E. 2006b. Epidemiology of *Phytophthora ramorum* infecting rhododendrons under simulated nursery conditions. In: Frankel, S.J.; Shea, P.J.; Haverty, M.I., tech. coords. Proceedings of the sudden oak death second science symposium: the state of our knowledge. Gen. Tech. Rep. PSW-GTR-196. Albany, CA: U.S. Department of Agriculture, Forest Service, Pacific Southwest Research Station: 459–461.

Tjosvold, S.A.; Chambers, D.L.; Tse, J.; Davidson, J.M.; Garbelotto, M.; Koike, S.T. 2002c. Evaluation of a novel diagnostic procedure to detect the presence of *Phytophthora ramorum* by sampling ooze from infected cankers. In: Proceedings of the sudden oak death science symposium, the state of our knowledge. Berkeley, CA: U.S. Department of Agriculture, Forest Service and University of California, Berkeley. http://danr.ucop.edu/ihrmp/sodsymp/poster/poster23.html. (April 2010).

Tomlinson, J.A.; Barker, I.; Boonham, N. 2007. Faster, simpler, more-specific methods for improved molecular detection of *Phytophthora ramorum* in the field. Applied and Environmental Microbiology. 73: 4040–4047.

Tomlinson, J.A.; Boonham, N.; Hughes, K.J.D.; Griffin, R.L.; Barker, I. 2005. On-site DNA extraction and real-time PCR for detection of *Phytophthora ramorum* in the field. Applied and Environmental Microbiology. 71: 6702–6710.

Tooley, P.; Browning, M.; Berner, D. 2008. Recovery of *P. ramorum* following exposure to temperature extremes. Plant Disease. 92: 431–437.

Tooley, P.W.; Kyde, K.L. 2003. Susceptibility of some eastern oak species to sudden oak death caused by *Phytophthora ramorum*. Phytopathology. 93: S84.

Tooley, P.W; Kyde, K.L. 2007. Susceptibility of some eastern forest species to *Phytophthora ramorum*. Plant Disease. 91: 435–438.

Tooley, P.W.; Kyde, K.L.; Englander, L. 2002. Infectivity of *Phytophthora ramorum* on selected Ericaceous host species. Phytopathology. 92: S81.

Tooley, P.W.; Kyde, K.L.; Englander, L. 2004. Susceptibility of selected Ericaceous ornamental host species to *Phytophthora ramorum*. Plant Disease. 88: 993–999.

Tooley, P.W.; Martin, F.N.; Carras, M.M.; Frederick, R.D. 2006. Real-time fluorescent polymerase chain reaction detection of *Phytophthora ramorum* and *Phytophthora pseudosyringae* using mitochondrial gene regions. Phytopathology. 96: 336–345.

Tubajika, K.M.; Singh, R.; Shelly, J.R. 2008. Preliminary observations of heat treatment to control *Phytophthora ramorum* in infected wood species: an extended abstract. In: Frankel, S.J.; Kliejunas, J.T.; Palmieri, K.M., tech. coords. Proceedings of the sudden oak death third science symposium. Gen. Tech. Rep. PSW-GTR-214. Albany, CA: U.S. Department of Agriculture, Forest Service, Pacific Southwest Research Station: 477–480.

Turner, J. 2007a. Personal communication. Central Science Laboratory, Department for Environment, Food and Rural Affairs, Sand Hutton, York, YO41 1LZ.

Turner, J. 2007b. *Phytophthora ramorum* and *Phytophthora kernoviae*: development of post eradication strategies for management/treatment of contaminated substrates and inoculum at outbreak sites. Annual Project Report (PH0414) 2006-2007. Sand Hutton, York, UK: Forest Research. On file with: Central Science Laboratory, Department for Environment, Food and Rural Affairs, Sand Hutton, York, YO41 1LZ.

Turner, J.; Jennings, P. 2006. Epidemiology of *Phytophthora ramorum* in relation to risk and policy. Project Work Package 3 Report—January to December 2005. Sand Hutton, York, UK: Forest Research. On file with: Central Science Laboratory, Department for Environment, Food and Rural Affairs, Sand Hutton, York, YO41 1LZ.

Turner, J.; Jennings, P. 2008. Report indicating the limiting and optimal environmental conditions for production, germination and survival of sporangia and zoospores. Deliverable Report 7. Sand Hutton, York, UK: Forest Research. On file with: Central Science Laboratory, Department for Environment, Food and Rural Affairs, Sand Hutton, York, YO41 1LZ.

Turner, J.; Jennings, P.; Humphries, G. 2005. *Phytophthora ramorum* epidemiology: sporulation potential, dispersal, infection and survival. Project Report PH0194. Sand Hutton, York, UK: Forest Research. On file with: Central Science Laboratory, Department for Environment, Food and Rural Affairs, Sand Hutton, York, YO41 1LZ.

Turner, J.; Jennings, P.; Humphries, G.; Parker, S.; McDonough, S.; Stonehouse, J.; Lockley, D.; Slawson, D. 2008a. Natural outbreaks of *Phytophthora ramorum* in the UK—current status and monitoring update. In: Frankel, S.J.; Kliejunas, J.T.; Palmieri, K.M., tech. coords. Proceedings of the sudden oak death third science symposium. Gen. Tech. Rep. PSW-GTR-214. Albany, CA: U.S. Department of Agriculture, Forest Service, Pacific Southwest Research Station: 43–48.

Turner, J.; Jennings, P.; McDonough, S.; Liddell, D.; Stonehouse, J. 2006. Chemical control of *Phytophthora ramorum* causing foliar disease in hardy nursery stock in the United Kingdom. In: Frankel, S.J.; Shea, P.J.; Haverty, M.I., tech. coords. Proceedings, sudden oak death second science symposium: the state of our knowledge. Gen. Tech. Rep. PSW-GTR-196. Albany, CA: U.S. Department of Agriculture, Forest Service, Pacific Southwest Research Station: 273–274.

Turner, J.; Jennings, P.; Werres, S.; Wagner, S. 2008b. Report on response of isolates of *P. ramorum* exposed to fungicides commonly used to control *Phytophthora* diseases in nurseries. Deliverable Report 5. Sand Hutton, York, UK: Forest Research, Central Sciences Laboratory. EU Sixth Framework Project, RAPRA.

U.S. Department of Agriculture [USDA]. 2005. Plant diseases caused by *Phytophthora ramorum*—a national strategic plan for USDA. http://www.aphis.usda.gov/plant_health/plant_pest_info/pram/downloads/pdf_files/usdaprstratplan.pdf. (April 2010).

U.S. Department of Agriculture, Animal and Plant Health Inspection Service [USDA APHIS]. 2004. Nursery protocol for nurseries with plants infected with *Phytophthora ramorum* (sudden oak death). Confirmed Nursery Protocol. Version 4.2. Riverdale, MD: Invasive species and pest management. http://nature.berkeley.edu/comtf/pdf/confirmed_nursery_protocol.pdf. (April 2010).

U.S. Department of Agriculture, Animal and Plant Health Inspection Service [USDA APHIS]. 2005a. Emergency federal order restricting movement of nursery stock from California, Oregon, and Washington nurseries. Riverdale, MD: Plant Protection and Quarantine. http://www.doacs.state.fl.us/pi/enpp/pathology/images/fedorder12-21-04sodl.pdf. (April 2010).

U.S. Department of Agriculture, Animal and Plant Health Inspection Service [USDA APHIS]. 2005b. Plant diseases caused by *Phytophthora ramorum*: A national strategic plan for USDA. September 14, 2005. 18 p. http://www.aphis.usda.gov/plant_health/plant_pest_info/pram/downloads/pdf_files/usdaprstratplan.pdf. (April 2010).

U.S. Department of Agriculture, Animal and Plant Health Inspection Service [USDA APHIS]. 2007a. *Phytophthora ramorum*; quarantine and regulations. Federal Register 7 CFR Part 301. Vol. 72 (38): 8585–8604.

U.S. Department of Agriculture, Animal and Plant Health Inspection Service [USDA APHIS] 2007b. Update on PPQ diagnostics for SOD: diagnostic procedures approved by APHIS and diagnostic analyses performed by APHIS PPQ for *Phytophthora ramorum*. Revised 6 May 2007. http://www.aphis.usda.gov/plant_health/plant_pest_info/pram/downloads/pdf_files/diagnosticssummary6-07.pdf. (April 2010).

U.S. Department of Agriculture, Animal and Plant Health Inspection Service [USDA APHIS]. 2009. Official regulatory protocol for *Phytophthora ramorum* detections in residential or landscaped commercial settings. Confirmed Residential Protocol. Version 2.0. Riverdale, MD: Plant Protection and Quarantine. http://www.aphis.usda.gov/plant_health/plant_pest_info/pram/downloads/pdf_files/residential-protocol-final%20.pdf. (April 2010).

U.S. Department of Agriculture, Forest Service. 2004. Sudden oak death: protecting America's woodlands from *Phytophthora ramorum*. FS-794. Arlington, VA: U.S. Department of Agriculture, Forest Service, State and Private Forestry, Forest Health Protection. 16 p.

U.S. Department of Agriculture, National Agricultural Statistics Service [USDA NASS]. 2007. Nursery crops 2006 summary. Sp Cr 6-3 (07). Washington, DC: Agricultural Statistics Board. http://usda.mannlib.cornell.edu/usda/current/NursProd/NursProd-09-26-2007.pdf. (April 2010).

U.S. Government Accountability Office [US GAO]. 2006. Invasive forest pests: lessons learned from three recent infestations may aid in managing future efforts. GAO-06-353. Washington, DC: Report to the Chairman, Committee on Resources, House of Representatives. 118 p.

U.S. International Trade Commission [USITC]. 2005. Interactive Tariff and Trade Dataweb. United States International Trade Commission. http://dataweb.usitc.gov. (April 2010).

Václavík, T.; Kanaskie, A.; Goheen, E.; Ohmann, J.; Hansen, E.; Meentemeyer, R. 2010. Mapping the risk of sudden oak death in Oregon: prioritizing locations for early detection and eradication. In: Frankel, S.J.; Kliejunas, J.T.; Palmieri, K.M., tech. coords. Proceedings of the sudden oak death fourth science symposium. Gen. Tech. Rep. PSW-GTR-229. Albany, CA: U.S. Department of Agriculture, Forest Service, Pacific Southwest Research Station: 126–132.

Valachovic, Y.; Lee, C.; Glebocki, R.; Scanlon, H.; Varner, J.P.; Rizzo, D. 2010a. Understanding the long term fire risks in forests affected by sudden oak death. In: Frankel, S.J.; Kliejunas, J.T.; Palmieri, K.M., tech. coords. Proceedings of the sudden oak death fourth science symposium. Gen. Tech. Rep. PSW-GTR-229. Albany, CA: U.S. Department of Agriculture, Forest Service, Pacific Southwest Research Station: 262–270.

Valachovic, Y.; Lee, C.; Marshall, J.; Scalon, H. 2010b. Forest treatment strategies for *Phytophthora ramorum*. In: Frankel, S.J.; Kliejunas, J.T.; Palmieri, K.M., tech. coords. Proceedings of the sudden oak death fourth science symposium: the state of our knowledge. Gen. Tech. Rep. PSW-GTR-229. Albany, CA: U.S. Department of Agriculture, Forest Service, Pacific Southwest Research Station: 239–248.

Valachovic, Y.; Lee, C.; Marshall, J.; Scanlon, H. 2008. Wildland management of *Phytophthora ramorum* in northern California forests. In: Frankel, S.J.; Kliejunas, J.T.; Palmieri, K.M., tech. coords. Proceedings of the sudden oak death third science symposium. Gen. Tech. Rep. PSW-GTR-214. Albany, CA: U.S. Department of Agriculture, Forest Service, Pacific Southwest Research Station: 305–312.

Valachovic, Y.; Lee, C.; Rizzo, D.; Marshall, J.; Bienapfl, J.; Murphy, S. 2006. *Phytophthora ramorum* research and control in north coastal California. In: Frankel, S.J.; Shea, P.J.; Haverty, M.I., tech. coords. Proceedings, sudden oak death second science symposium: the state of our knowledge. Gen. Tech. Rep. PSW-GTR-196. Albany, CA: U.S. Department of Agriculture, Forest Service, Pacific Southwest Research Station: 543–544.

Venette, R.C.; Cohen, S.D. 2006. Potential climatic suitability for establishment of *Phytophthora ramorum* within the contiguous United States. Forest Ecology and Management. 231: 18–26.

Vettraino, A.M.; Huberli, D.; Garbelotto, M. 2008. *Phytophthora ramorum* infection of coast live oak leaves in Californian forests and its capacity to sporulate in vitro. Australasian Plant Pathology. 37: 72–73.

Von Broembsen, S.L.; Deacon, J.W. 1997. Calcium interference with zoospore biology and infectivity of *Phytophthora parasitica* in nutrient irrigation solutions. Phytopathology. 87: 522–528.

Wagner, S.; Kaminski, K.; Keitz, W.V.; Werres, S. 2006. Influence of Metalaxyl-M on *Phytophthora ramorum*. In: Brasier, C.M.; Jung, T.; Oßwald, W., eds. Proceedings of the third international IUFRO working party (S07.02.09) meeting: progress in research on *Phytophthora* diseases of forest trees. Farnham, UK: Forest Research, Central Sciences Laboratory.

Wagner, S.; Kaminski, K.; Werres, S. 2008. Evaluation of fungicides for control of *Phytophthora ramorum*. In: Frankel, S.J.; Kliejunas, J.T.; Palmieri, K.M., tech. coords. Proceedings of the sudden oak death third science symposium. Gen. Tech. Rep. PSW-GTR-214. Albany, CA: U.S. Department of Agriculture, Forest Service, Pacific Southwest Research Station: 481–482.

Webber, J. 2004. *Phytophthora ramorum* and *Phytophthora taxon* C. Annual summary of research, 1 April 2003–31 March 2004. Farnham, UK: Forest Research. http://www.forestresearch.gov.uk/forestry/INFD-5zjhvl. (April 2010).

Webber, J.F.; Rose, J. 2008. Dissemination of aerial and root infecting *Phytophthoras* by human vectors. In: Frankel, S.J.; Kliejunas, J.T.; Palmieri, K.M., tech. coords. Proceedings of the sudden oak death third science symposium. Gen. Tech. Rep. PSW-GTR-214. Albany, CA: U.S. Department of Agriculture, Forest Service, Pacific Southwest Research Station: 195–198.

Werres, S.; Kaminski, K. 2005. Characterisation of European and North American *Phytophthora ramorum* isolates due to their morphology and mating behaviour in vitro with heterothallic *Phytophthora* species. Mycological Research. 109: 860–871.

Werres, S.; Marwitz, R. 1997. Triebsterben an *Rhododendron*—Unbekannte *Phytophthora*. Deutscher Gartenbau. 21: 1166–1168.

Werres, S.; Marwitz, R.; Man in't Veld, W.A.; De Cock, A.W.A.M.; Bonants, P.J.M.; De Weerdt, M.; Themann, K.; Ilieva, E.; Baayen, R.P. 2001. *Phytophthora ramorum* sp. nov., a new pathogen on *Rhododendron* and *Viburnum*. Mycological Research. 105: 1155–1165.

Werres, S.; Wagner, S.; Brand, T.; Kaminski, K.; Seipp, D. 2007. Infectivity and survival of *Phytophthora ramorum* in recirculation water. Plant Disease. 91: 1034–1044.

Werres, S.; Zielke, B. 2003. First studies on the pairing of *Phytophthora ramorum*. Zietschrift für Plfanzenkrankheiten und Plfanzenschutz. 110(2): 120–130.

Whetzel, H.H. 1929. The terminology of phytopathology. International Congress Plant Science Proceedings. 2: 1204–1215.

Wickland, A.C.; Jensen, C.E.; Rizzo, D.M. 2008. Geographic distribution, disease symptoms, and pathogenicity of *Phytophthora nemorosa* and *Phytophthora pseudosyringae* in California, USA. Forest Pathology. 38: 288–298.

Widmer, T. 2008. Investigating the potential of biological control against *Phytophthora ramorum*. Proceedings, sudden oak death third science symposium. In: Frankel, S.J.; Kliejunas, J.T.; Palmieri, K.M., tech. coords. Proceedings of the sudden oak death third science symposium. Gen. Tech. Rep. PSW-GTR-214. Albany, CA: U.S. Department of Agriculture, Forest Service, Pacific Southwest Research Station. 491.

Winton, L.M.; Hansen, E.M. 2001. Molecular diagnosis of *Phytophthora lateralis* in trees, water, and foliage baits using multiplex polymerase chain reaction. Forest Pathology. 31: 275–283.

Yakabe, L.E.; Blomquist, C.L.; Thomas, S.L.; MacDonald, J.D. 2009. Identification and frequency of *Phytophthora* species associated with foliar diseases in California ornamental nurseries. Plant Disease. 93: 883–890.

Yakabe, L.E.; MacDonald J. 2005. The effects of a surfactant on *Phytophthora ramorum*. Phytopathology. 95: S115.

Yakabe, L,E.; Macdonald, J.D. 2008. Soil treatments for the elimination of *Phytophthora ramorum* from nursery beds: current knowledge from the laboratory and the field. In: Frankel, S.J.; Kliejunas, J.T.; Palmieri, K.M., tech. coords. Proceedings of the sudden oak death third science symposium. Gen. Tech. Rep. PSW-GTR-214. Albany, CA: U.S. Department of Agriculture, Forest Service, Pacific Southwest Research Station: 113–114.

Zepeda, G. 2001. Personal communication. District ranger, Chetco Ranger District, Rogue River-Siskiyou National Forest, 539 Chetco Ave, Brookings, Oregon 97415.

Zobel, D.B.; Roth, L.F.; Hawk, G.M. 1985. Ecology, pathology, and management of Port-Orford-cedar (*Chamaecyparis lawsoniana*). Gen. Tech. Rep. PNW-184. Portland, OR: U.S. Department of Agriculture, Forest Service, Pacific Northwest Forest and Range Experiment Station. 161 p.

Made in the USA
Columbia, SC
05 December 2024